Goddess S'arada (Sharada) of Kasmira (Kashmir) –Adi Shankaracharya—Buddhism –S'arada Civilisation Connect –Facts And Myths

Goddess S'arada (Sharada) of Kasmira (Kashmir) –Adi Shankaracharya—Buddhism –S'arada Civilisation Connect –Facts And Myths

Brigadier Rattan Kaul

Edited by
Leena Gaur
Aparna Kaul

GYAN

ISBN: 978-81-212-9654-0

First Published, 2023

Published by

Gyan Publishing House
C-30, Satyawati Nagar,
Delhi – 110052
Ph.: 011-47034999, 9811692060
www.kalpazpublications.com
E-mail: kalpaz@hotmail.com

Printed at: Gyan Press, Delhi.

To
Our Three Gems
Praharshita, Nirbhay and Trishay
Blessings of Our Life

Acknowledgements

Millions of followers and devotees of **Adi Shankaracharya**, the great Saint and Philosopher and **S**'arada Shrine (s) /Temple (s), which spurred me to unravel the truth in the form of this Book.

Ms Leena Gaur MA (English), B Ed (Canada/India) for taking pains in Editing this Book on Priority, in spite her other commitments and rearrangement of contents, chapters and their sequence.

British Editor (UK) and **Ms Aparna Kaul (UK)** for their advice on the flow and language.

Ms Shobana Ravi Chennai. Writer in her own right, very well conversant with various facets of Religion in South India and Institutions of Adi Shankaracharya.

Unknown friend of Gilgit Baltistan, who managed to send me Photograph of the Monument in 2003. First time in India after gap of over 65 years.

Dr Rukshana Khan, who opted for **S**'arada as her subject for her Doctorate thesis. A forerunner to unravel the history of Kishanganga/Neelam Valley, **S**'arada and excavation activities like an expert Archaeologist.

Khawaja Abdul Ghani, an adventurer and writer from Shardi. Main source of latest Inputs, Photographs, which to large extent shaped my fresh revelations and assessment.

Suresh Pandita (Kaloosa) and S N Bhat (Jammu) for inputs Sardibal (Bandipora-Kashmir)

Muhammad Shafi, Senior Geologist Consultant US

Embassy Pakistan by giving me some important Geological Details etc of Kishanganga Valley.

Dr Saleem Beg, Member National Monuments Authority, Ministry of Culture, Government of India. A casual exchange which led to exchange of views about Gilgit Manuscripts and **S**'arada University.

And not for so good reasons, fringe groups playing S'arada Card with motives best known to them, creating new stories to exploit beliefs. Wish they had instead delved seriously about **S**'arada as a Goddess, S'arada Shrine (s), their antiquity and interpreted old chronicles diligently.

Brigadier Rattan Kaul

Preface

"Truth is one; sages call it by various names. – Rig Veda"

The Verse from Rig Veda impelled me to try to unravel the truth and facts around S'arada Tirath's (Shrine's-Temple's) of Kasmira, Her manifestation as Goddess and Adi Shankaracharya. The S'arada Shrine/Temple Kishanganga Valley in focus is across the line of Control in POK (Pakistan Occupied Kashmir).

(The reference in this Book as Kishanganga, Kishanganga and S'arada Shrine Kishanganga Valley etc is on the current status of this shrine).

Over the last two centuries S'arada Shrine Kishanganga Valley has been in focus for more than one reason, which for last few decades has been termed as forgotten monument. One cannot deny or change the existing standing of Kishanganga Valley S'arada Shrine achieved during last few centuries in Jammu and Kasmira (India), and Azad Kashmir (Pakistan), more so in recent times. Six decades back the Shrine, which is in ruins, was seldom mentioned. There was resurgence in the mention of this S'arada Shrine, with new write ups, not only in Kasmira but in South India when its photograph was shared in 2003 AD.

Its historical background was strictly as per general impressions and interpretations from various chronicles and travelogues. Inquisitiveness and available interpretations led me deeper and that is where truth and facts stared at my face.

Many questions and doubts rose and needed cross checking. I banked on Jenab Khawaja Abdul Ghani, from the ground zero-Sharada, a writer, adventurer resident of Khawaja Seri (S'arada Tehsil Neelam Valley), who apart knew the area like palm of his hand and my main conduit to provide latest information and photographs. His knowledge of the shrine and area has helped to bring out certain unknown facts, names and topography of the area.

Nilamata Purana (Sixth Century AD) gives details of ancient rivers, places of worship and monuments with pointed references of Kasmira Valley. Rajatarangini by Kalhan (English translation) with casual mention's in Tarikh I Hind by Al Biruni and Aine-e-Akbari by Abu Fazl added to the information bank. Auriel Stein's Rajatarangini translation version with his detailed amplification notes etc gave additional inputs. It is humanly impossible to cross check details of each and every verse of Rajatarangini and Stein's interpretation thereof (Even at many places he has shown his inability too). Mool (root) source for S'arada Shrine study is Rajatarangini with brief mentions figures in the Chronicles of Al Biruni and Abu Fazl combination had created a different and differing canvas about S'arada Shrine's and rivers.

I discounted subsequent mentions etc by various other scholars, who solely interpreted the above, in their own way.

Simultaneous study of Life, Teachings and Institutions of Adi Shankaracharya (Eighth/Ninth Century) was coincidental, as some way or the other Kasmira, Kings of Kasmira, noted Philosophers and of course S'arada Tirath (Shrine-Temple) were connected with his accounts and biographies. These accounts of Adi Shankaracharya, Seven Centuries after his Samadhi from 14th Century onwards were not chronicled truthfully. The truthful events had also taken flight with his and his disciple's departure from this mortal world. Instead imaginative and fictional events, miracles, debates etc were apportioned in his accounts. Most of these accounts, chronicles penned by religious heads, learned scholars were taken as gospel truths. To a common devotee it did not matter, except that he continued unhindered with his Nityakriya's (Daily rituals), unaware as to how Adi Shankaracharya and S'arada Shrine (s) were projected.

From medieval centuries, ranging from 1000 BC the area of Kishanganga/Neelam Valley was part of Drava Country, which remained isolated; barricaded in South by mountain Range Shamasabhari. The area in terms of ancient civilisation could at best be termed as part of development of later Neolithic Period, mainly due to inhospitable terrain, absence of trade routes and harsh cold climate. It had a special place in the history of Kasmira but seldom part of it, due to the area remaining under War Lords (Damras), who beleaguered by split tribal loyalties, had to do a tight rope walking between Drava (Dardistan) rulers and Kasmira Kings.

In Nilamata Purana (Sixth Century AD) S'arada does not find any mention but reading of connected verses in Nilamata led me to certain revelations. Is S'arada Shrine of Kishanganga Valley the oldest and first such tirtha of the Goddess? Is the venerated dry Kund at the Shrine real S'arada Kund? Have various rivers, places mentioned in S'arada Mahatamaya, been metamorphosed or redactioned to be fitted with 'a shrine'? My vacillating inferences developed into revelations, which even I had not thought of. My interpretations of certain verses, extracts etc may be at variance with earlier interpretations and established view. I concluded that these had not been cross-checked and connected with contents of other chronicles, which I could not overlook and the new facts stared at me. What more can one ask for!

Adi Shankaracharya blessed India with his preaching's, sainthood, godly sanyasi life, his works, life events and institutions. Stories around Adi Shankaracharya were woven including experience in sexology in the palace of non-existent King Amaru of Kasmira and other events connected sexology in Amaru's harem and palace. Debates with religious philosophers, mostly connected to Kasmira created, when they were not even born. Conversely Adi Shankaracharya exclusive philosophy and connected institutions, were apportioned to create a different Adi Shankaracharya of his time. Have they succeeded? In most of the cases yes; so far. Only few bold, mostly in Southern parts of our Country, have so far called a spade a spade. My concern: why have these remained uncontested so far?

This book is a blessing in disguise as I have been able to find and confirm facts with new revelations. The oldest S'arada Temple/Shrine in Kasmira and mystery of S'arada Kund at Shardi has been solved. The Buddhist connection with S'arada Shrine is just a myth. The facts about institutions of Adi Shankaracharya, his actual place of Samadhi and that he never came anywhere Kasmira and so also the myth of his disappearance vaguely put at Dattatreya Caves, Badri and Kasmira. Mr Suresh Pandita of Kaloosa (on the banks of actual river Madhumati (Bandipur-Kasmira) (provided certain valuable information, which can be termed as revealing

I am not a staunch religionist, but I carry certain ethos, values and culture of my birth place-Kasmira. I may not have adopted the tenets of a particular religion, but I still revere certain beliefs, associated with S'arada (Sharada), Saradaamba and Adi Shankaracharya. The outcome is this book, with all my sincerity, honesty and utmost care to bring out historical facts.

Unravelling of truth is always bitter to many, who just would not like to see even light of a candle and may call it just a glow worm. So be it. It is meant for many, who are not aware of the true facts.

August 2022 **Brigadier Rattan Kaul**

Contents

Explanatory Notes and Abbreviated Forms

Place Names, Institutions etc, in Chronicles, Books, Treatises etc perused and referred are by different names, designations etc. To bring uniformity in the text of the Book, most of these have been referred to by combined names, acronyms as under.

1. **Kasmira-**For Kashmir (Kasmira is the ancient name of Kashmir)
2. **Sharada-**For Goddess S'arada (Sāradā developed out of late Brāhmī prevalent in the Kashmir region. *Sāradā* can also be found on ancient inscriptions written in Sanskrit, Prakrit or Dravidian languages.
3. **Muth-For Mutt, Maths-**Hindu religious institution and presided over by a person with succession.
4. **Temple-**A Hindu temple is a symbolic house, seat and body of divinity. Structure designed to bring human beings and gods together, using symbolism to express beliefs of Hinduism
5. **Shrine-**Place where the deities or the holy relics are installed for worship after sanctifying the area with special mantras and holy water.
6. **Peeth-**For Peetham, Peetha, Pitham. Means a seat of an Idol, Pontiff or Religious institute
7. **Adi Shankaracharya-**Refers to Sankara $8^{th}/9^{th}$ Century AD. Adi Shankaracharya for Hinduism.
8. **Adi Shankaracharya (BC Era)** -Muths/Peeths still take

Adi Shankaracharya's date of birth in BC Era as per Puranic Calendar.

9. **Abhinav Sankara-**None other than Adi Shankaracharya, but Muths sticking to Adi Shankaracharya of BC era, recognise Adi Shankaracharya as a philosopher, but restrict themselves from not recognising him as Adi Shankaracharya. They call him Abhinav (New) Sankara (His birth name).
10. **Bharatvarsh-**Erstwhile India, Hindustan.
11. **Saraswati-**In chronicles, verses Goddess Saraswati has mostly been spelled as Sarasvati.

1

Book Contours and Title

Open Mind. For a writer it is not difficult to 'create' history for formulating his own lines of expression, overlooking or not considering facts. It is easy in the case of history of a religious place (s), persons, religions and personalities closely associated with these. Present day electronic media and availability of digitalised copies of chronicles and manuscripts, enables recheck and authentication. However, this facility does not help in cases of created accounts, laced with myths, lore's and authors own creations. There are numerous instances where true accounts, antiquity and facts have either been moulded or unconnected ones fitted in. The result being it getting a different hue, which may be acceptable in short run but at one time or the other truth finally stares.

The phenomenon of creating fictitious accounts is more common, where no written or authentic *Shruti (*voice heard) and *Smriti* (remembered) has not been honestly and truthfully reproduced. An opinionated writer takes liberty to pen down his own version, which get further distorted and with passage of centuries radically changes the *mool* (root) contents. Over the past centuries different such versions of treatises, chronicles and biographies have appeared in one form or the other. Had they been written or put into some form, closer to the era when the facts were fresh, possibly these would have been factual to a large extent. When such works are deeply analysed one would ask: is it true! These deviations are not uniform and depends upon the part of the country, demography and community, while writer knowingly hopes that these will be accepted without any reservations. These are not like our Vedas, which have come to us in pure form, may be some verses were missed out.

Deviation Dilemma and Intellectual Honesty. With accessibility to various other inputs like traces of ruins, old accounts and chronicles in translated, print form etc, such deviations and falsifications are noticed sooner or later. These also make it easier for compilation, collation of true facts and accounts. Well-reasoned write ups, facts quoting sources with an honest analysis tinkered and conflicting ones fade away. Initially normal human hesitancy and doubts about the authenticity will arise, but with caution turns into inquisitiveness. It is the first phase of introspection when truth dawns that may be wrong facts have been fed so far. This is when phase of initial correction sets in, albeit steadily, and finally gets accepted.

For this book compilation, collation and authenticity assessment was a dilemma as well as challenge. With patience, cross checking, sequencing and formatting contents is best one could produce an honest effort with no holds barred to call a spade a spade. It is for readers to rate it, which may start process of self-convincing to over ride their doubts, inhibitions and reservations. Their acceptance is the best reward for a writer.

Crunch Objectives. Fourmain objectives have been kept in mind. **First**: Sanctity and truth of **S'arada (Sharada)** Shrine (s) (Tirath/Temple) of Kasmira. **Second**: Reverence of **Sharadaamba** in the form created in Eight/Ninth Century AD, at the confluence of Rivers Tunga-Bhadra (Karnataka). **Third**: Reverence and restoration of the factual legacy of

Adi Shankaracharya, the great Saint Philosopher of Bharatvarsh (India). **Fourth**: not to allow extraneous issues, imaginative lore's, myths, take away the basic true facts of historical and devotional value.

In popular accounts sacred figures offer a space, where astonishingly vibrant local myths and legends, incorporate influences from many different communities and traditions. The writer is revered as one of their own and that he was companion of God and the person concerned. In this case one cannot claim to be companion of either, but driven by avid aim in the dictum: "Truth Must Prevail"; guided by this verse:

There is no religion greater than truth and a truthful person knows no fear-Rig Veda

It is unjustified if we continue to allow myths, fiction and propagated theories to overtake the truth or allow such claims to gain credence.

The Book Title. Goddess S'arada (Sharada) of Kasmira Adi Shankaracharya and Buddhism-S'arada Civilisation Facts And My thesis the title of the Book**.** One may wonder as to how a goddess of extreme North, Goddess Sharada, a Sage and Philosopher of South, Adi Shankaracharya, get combined: geographically, ideologically and devotion wise. A different hue of absolutely unknown S'arada Civilisation claimcombined with Buddhism gets added, is apparently with Politico-Religio overtones.

S'arada of Kasmira. In Northern India **S'arada** is considered as the manifestation of Goddess of Saraswati (Goddess of Knowledge), especially in Kasmira. The description of the Goddess in S'arada Vandana (Praise) in Kasmira reads like this (Not in full); Kasmira Purvasini, Vidhya Dieyinam, Shawetambuj Viharinam, Chaturbuj Dharini..... Papanasheenam.. VitatRupenam... **Translated**; Residing in Kasmira from ancient times-Giver of knowledge-Seated on a White Bird (Swan) -Having Four Arms-Giver of moksha (liberation from the cycle of death and rebirth) and forgiver of sins-Just like grace of Vitasta (Jhelum River of Kasmira) -. This Vandana has undergone changes and addition of Moksha Vandana is recent.

Creation of Sharadaamba. Adi Shankaracharya, born in Kaladi, South India, gave a new life to Vedic religion in the Form of **Advaita Vedanta Philosophy**. He is founder of Advaita Philosophy, many philosophical works, created a form of Mother Goddess, based on certain actual incidents of his early association with disciple companion's wife Sarsawani: Sarada-Amba (**S**haradaamba-Devi **S**harada). This Goddess manifested in consonance with Advaita Philosophy, "is Guru Rupini; through the person of the Jagadguru, She dispenses Her Grace. She is the Goddess of Learning. She is the embodiment of all **three Shaktis**". He also describes "Goddess S'arada as Brahmavidya", identical to the incommensurable Brahman Itself and transcends to conception of Trimurti's, and corresponding Shaktis; Saraswati, Lakshmi and Ishwari.

In South India, **S**'arada of North India got addendum, affirmation of 'Kasmira Purvasini' (Residing in Kasmira) and morning of a devote's prayers are incomplete without oratory benediction, looking Northwards, of **S**'arada ('Kasmira Purvasini'). First thing in the morning he faces North and invokes: *Namaste* S'arada *Devi, Kasmira Puravasini, Twamaham Prarthate Nityam, Vidya Danancha Dehime* (O S'arada devi, resident of Kasmira, I pray to you every day, may you bless me with knowledge), definitely invoked as deity of knowledge. This is in comparison to Sharadaamba, which is embodiment of all three Goddesses (Trimurtis: Parvati, Laxmi and Saraswati).

Faith, Beliefs and Contradictions. In faith and beliefs, physical and geographical separation and distances don't matter and the two extremes of the Bharatvarsh got connected by devotion to Goddesses: **S'arada of Kasmira**, **Sharada**, **Sharadaamba of Adi Shankaracharya** and South India. It was inevitable that Adi Shankaracharya, who gave Goddess **S**harada-form as **Mother Goddess**, is equally revered all over the Country, as well as world. Certain amount of commonality between the two Goddesses will be evident as we go along.

Morning Veda Prayer, South India

S'arada (**S**harada) of Kasmira is purely a Hindu Goddess and her shrine (s) has to be a Hindu temple, however, unnecessary politico-religio assertion has been made as a **Buddhist Monument.** Reasoning: due to wide spread of Buddhism in then North-Western India, which it did not. A counter assertion; Shaivite Institution of learning for scholars existed at the **S**'arada Shrine. While former is driven by denying it as a Hindu Temple/Shrine, latter is primarily to connect Kasmiri Shaivism and Adi Shankaracharya legacy with Sharada. In few parts of North-Western India, a new civilisation is talked about; **S'arada Civilisation,** so different from known Civilisation of erstwhile ancient India.

Contours of the Book. Necessary to understand Bharatvarsh (Indian Sub-Continent) had a unique distinction of distinct ancient civilisations, spread from North most areas down to South and extending to East. Our past, settlements, demography, way of life adopted to changing environment adopted transformation to specific demographic requirements. This process started from evolution era and distinct demographic groups having common roots developed in different parts of the country. These then transited from select Civilisations to widely dispersed large demographic units, with overall commonalty and developing their own way of life, beliefs and even languages.

In outwardly unconnected mentions of: S'arada Tirath (Shrine) of Kasmira; Adi Shankaracharya; never heard Buddhism connection, S'arada Civilisation have been brought under one umbrella for study and analysis. As we progress it will be clear that though they seem to be intervined, there are also contradictions within.

Buddhism-S'arada and Adi Shankaracharya. S'arada Tirath (Shrine) of Kasmira) is purely dedicated to Goddess of Knowledge as S'arada (Manifestation of Goddess Saraswati). Nothing to do with Shaivism or Buddhism. It is in May/June 788 (Lunar Month Vaishaka, 26th year of the sixty years cycle) Sage Philosopher Advaita Founder Sankara (Adi Shankaracharya) was born, who came to revive Hinduism after great inroads had been made by Buddhism. From all accounts his teachings remained restricted to Southern India, where he laid the legacy of his philosophy. Revered even today, blessed the resurgent Hinduism with his teachings and philosophy during his 32 years on this earth. For six Centuries (9th to 14th), his life, times, preaching's, institutions did remain as they were during this period. There was one such effort to chronicle his effort in late

12th Century which nearly was truthful to a great extent. In 14th Century Adi Shankaracharya's life, achievements, teachings, institutions were chronicled, added with spice, fictional events, presenting the Sage absolutely differently. His life, works had not been timelychronicled, merely passed on as Shruti and Smriti andtaking advantage of this, his biographical accounts were given a different shade, which still overshadows the truth.

Buddhism after Ashokas reign wanned, but re-emerged in a different form through the efforts of Kushans, but restricted to Northern India beyond the frontiers of present-day India. In Kasmira, the Sarvastivada tradition of Buddhism was evolved. It is recent phenomenon, post 1947, to turn Goddess S'arada Temple Kishanganga Valley as **Buddhist monument** together with new Civilisation termed **S'arada Civilisation**.

Over Centuries, there are apt to be certain myths, lore's, sprinkled with fiction, which have to or have emerged. In this process, the origins and true evolution and manifestations of such religious monuments, accounts get blurred. Some of these (Myths, lore's and fiction), concerning Sharada-Adi Shankaracharya emerged; out of ignorance, creation of religious preachers-scholars, by those who wanted to leave their name to be counted, or their quest to be revered as of the same genre of; **Goddess Sharada-Adi Shankaracharya**. There is satisfaction that there is awakening to recount actual and factual life events of Adi Shankaracharya and many scholars have fearlessly come out with their views etc.

Truth is God. Denial of God we have known.
Denial of truth we have not known.
–Mahatma Gandhi

2

Bharatvarsh – Commonality of Religious Philosophies: Goddesses and Adi Shankaracharya

Ancient Bharatvarsh-North-South Commonality

Ancient Bharatvarsh (Erstwhile India). It is not possible for a reader to connect diverse but converging facts, myths or lore's, without adequate background and connections, as enumerated in Chapter I. Over the millenniums there has been North South connect between people, their religious philosophies, which continues even at present. The process of evolution of humans in different parts of our country was slow, steady and uniform, but finally all got connected as a single denomination; Bharatvarash. Once a single unit but geographically, demographically and culturally separated parts with differences, some significant though. There were also certain differences of physique, language, way of living, culture etc, from one demographic unit to another. These came about due to part of segmentation of areas, demographic limits, boundaries, development of separate languages and their adapted way of living. It was not a unique phenomenon with human beings, but common all over the world.

Not much evidence and details of Archaic Humans in Indian Sub-Continent are known, in-spite of all efforts and research. Indications are that Archaic Humans did exist, move in of modern humans into then the Sub-Continent was in an opportunistic manner. They avoided contact with archaic humans and possibly either outlived or even displaced them. They came in four migrations starting from Early Indians, including present day designated Dravidians and finally Aryans, in that order. Scientific studies have indicated that 'Early Indians' still constitutes 50-65 per cent of Ancestry of our Country. who generally moved into North-Western India and mixed with the Early Indians. This spread was added by the Harappan's, who also moved in and lasted from 2600 BC to 1900 BC.

Finally, immigrants from Central Asian Steppe, what we in broad terms call Aryans and others, was last major group between 2000 and 1000 BC. They were termed as **Vedic Aryans (Early Aryan's)** and **Later Aryans (Vedic Aryan's)** respectively. The latter group settled along Saraswati River and composed Vedas. **This is to segmentize Aryan's into two distinct groups**.

Finer details of the people, routes and stages of migration, nature of their early interactions and integration with existing populations in different regions of the Sub-Continent are yet to be fully established. Based on traces of excavated finds, Vedas, other scriptures etc, they can be listed as; **Dravidians, Dasa (Dasa), Dahe's and Aryan's; in that order**.

The map shows generally Indo-Aryan Migration into around 1750 BC and is representative routes of migration in general. Over the millenniums they got established as Kingdoms and Dynasties.

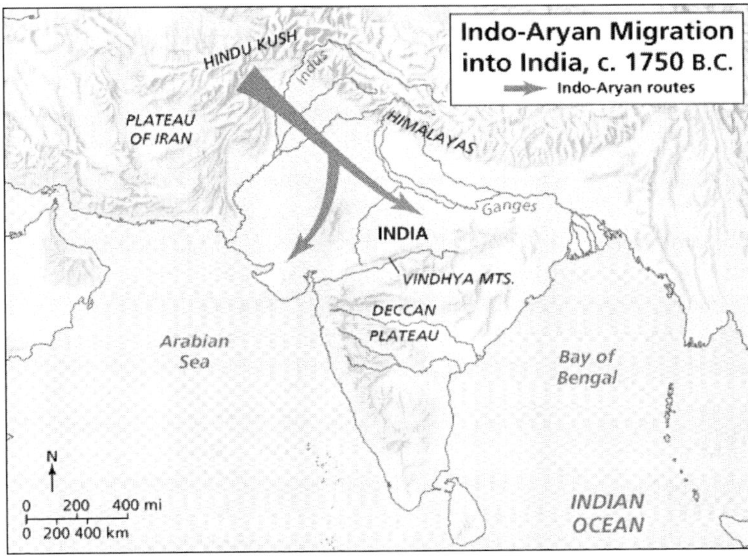

MisnomerAryan and Dravidian Races. Dravidian and Aryan as 'two separate races' is the product of an unscientific, culturally biased form of thinking that saw race in terms of colour. India's current population is mix of Early Indians and other three **Major Migrations**, that happened during the historical period. There is no such specific race (s) termed as Dravidian or Aryan. Both are biologically related branches, only when closer to the equator certain biological changes occur.

Aryans never called themselves Aryans, it is in later centuries this distinctive term was used based on Izvesta, which defined word Arya. Similarly Proto-Dravidian ancient language, which transited to Dravidian, is the linguistic reconstruction of the common ancestor of the Dravidian languages, differentiated into Proto-North Dravidian, Proto-Central Dravidian, and Proto-South Dravidian, although the date of diversification is still debated. The origin of the Sanskrit word *draviḍa* is Tamil, which was also used to denote the geographical region of South India.

Aryan-Dravidian Commonality. Though Dravidian languages are based on a different model than Sanskrit, there are thirty to seventy percent Sanskrit words in South Indian languages, like Telugu and Tamil, which is much higher percentage than North Indian languages like Hindi apart from similar construction and phraseology. This has caused some linguists even to propose that Hindi was a Dravidian language. In fact, we find similar sounds between Vedic Sanskrit and Dravidian languages. This clears the assertion Dravidians were in the same region as the Vedic people, and part of the same culture, Dravidians do not have to feel that Vedic culture is any more foreign to them than it is to the people of North India.

Aryan -Dravidian racial idea holders have tried to make some Hindu Gods Dravidian and other Gods Aryan, even though there is no such division within Hindu culture. For example, based upon a superficial identification of deities by colour i.e., Krishna as black and therefore Dravidian. Krishna's traces his lineage through the Vedic line of the Yadus, a famous Aryan tribe of the North and West of India, and also Rig Veda seers whose names meant dark, like Krishna, Angiras or Shyava Atreya.

Indo Aryan's-Vedic Aryan's. Indo Aryan's-Vedic Aryan's settlements, initially mostly along River Saraswati banks (*Avesta* named it *Harahwati*); were regarded as most central group of**Indo Aryan's-Vedic Aryan's**. These settlements developed over centuries a new civilisation named Vedic Aryan settlements came up. It is over many more centuries that they developed a religion and a new word came into usage along these Ashrams/settlements of Saraswati River; Arya or Aryan. Definitely Dravidians are pre–Indo or Vedic Aryan's, evidence is that these groups**, pre moved in**.

Culture, Cultural Similarities Dravidians and Aryan's. Rig Veda depicts the cultural differences between the Aryan's and non-Aryan's of Indus valley: referring to cultural opposition drawn between Aryan's and the indigenous people. While cultural traits of the Indus Valley civilisation are likely to have been absorbed by the successor Indo-Aryan civilisation in Punjab and Sindh, the civilisation in the far South changed out of recognition. The present South Indian civilisation is product of both Indo-Aryan and Dravidian cultures and the language itself is completely mixed with both elements. One of the cultural traits in the Indus Valley is that they had the bull fight. Even today in the South bull fighting and bull chasing are very common sports, which connect the Dravidian South with the Indus Valley. Such traditions are also in Spain and in Portugal and the Iberian Peninsula, which indicates pre-historic connection between these very similar cultures.

According to reputed historians, South India was occupied by very cultured people, whose religion was perhaps different from Hinduism, as propagated then in Northern parts of the country. But it was basically based on the foundation of **Vedas**. It is inevitable that there would have been differences in the propagation and interpretation of Vedas. Over the millenniums, both, North and South, were bonded by what is called Vedic Religion, of which Vedas were the base. It is amazing that in the 21st Century Vedic Pathshala's (School's), Veda Teachers and Priests are predominantly in the Southern parts of our country, as compared to other areas.

However, with time both parts of India, got somewhat divided, in terms of Kingdoms, Smaller states and pockets. North and North-Western India and Southern Peninsula had different clear segments what may be called Kingdoms or Dynasties. These have been amplified hereunder.

North and North-Western India Kingdoms-BC Era. Sixteen Mahajana padas (Kingdoms- or oligarchic republics that existed in ancient India from the Sixth to Fourth Centuries BC) extending up to the Tarim Basin (Northern Edge of present Afghanistan) with Kamboj and Gandhara.

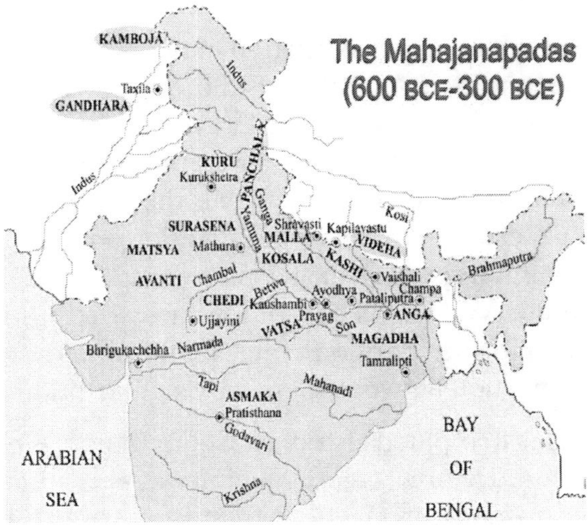

Maps Showing Mahajanpadas of North and North-Western India

Kasmira was one of the Janapada (Smaller Kingdom) as part of one of the Mahajanapada in the North, who like the Southern Kingdoms/Dynasties had vast ties with ancient countries of Central Asia and North-Western India

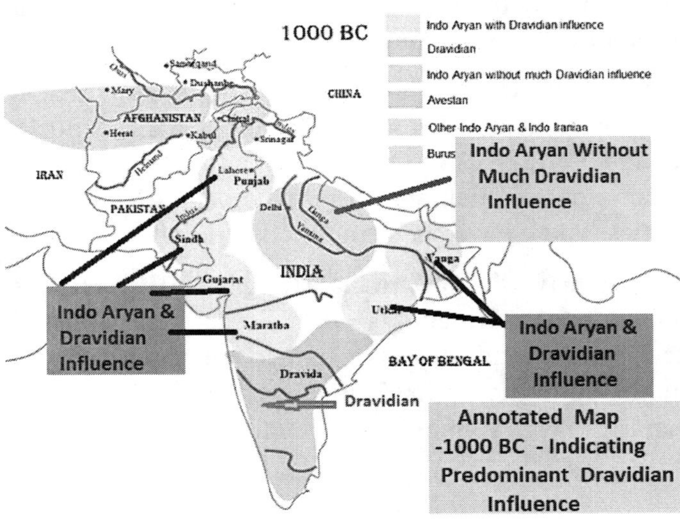

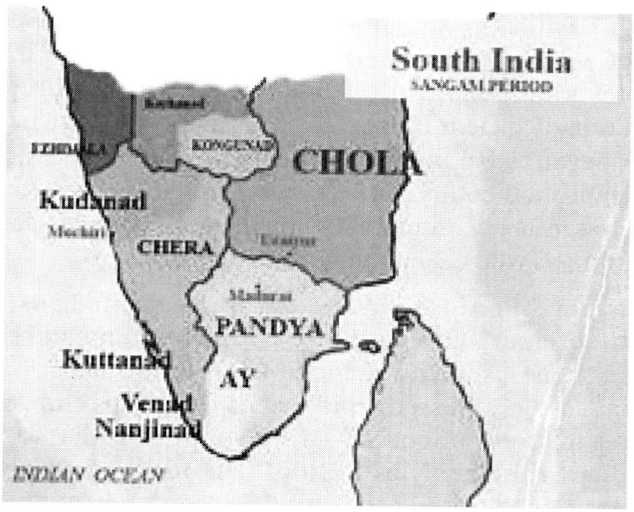

South India Kingdoms/Dynasties 600 BC

South India Kingdoms-Dynasties-BC Era. Similarly, Dynasties, more or less on the lines of Mahajanapada's came into existence in South India (See Maps above). Pandya's (One of the three ancient Tamil dynasties. Chola and Chera **being the other two), who ruled the Tamil country from pre-historic times,** alongside other dynasties such as Pallava's and early Pandya's, who were reduced to obscurity by the Kalabhra's, until their revival in the Sixth Century AD.

During their long existence as a recognisable people, the Pandya's (Sangam Period 600 BC) under Nedunj Cheliyan I, enjoyed diplomatic ties with the Roman **Republic and Empire (apparently dating as far back as 550 BC, when Rome was still an occupied** Etruscan **Kingdom),** the Greeks, the Chinese, the Ptolemy, Egyptians etc. The Pandyan Kingdom was also independent during the Mauryan **rule of Northern India, and had friendly ties with them.**

North-South Connection from Historic Days. Notwithstanding the different perceptions, there is no doubt that People of South India (**Fondly and respectfully called**

Dravidians) were the early inhabitants of Bharatvarsh along and the community spread 4, 000 years ago throughout the subcontinent; labelled as **Ancestral South Indian (ASI).** Thus, the Dravidian people and language family was born. The population of ancient Indian Sub-Continent, 5, 000 years ago, groups began to fan out, in much of what is present day India and established communities throughout the subcontinent. There was influx of immigrants called Dasa's, Dahye, Dasyu's and last one's who called themselves Aryan's.

Misconception of Dasa's. It is with pride that Indians living in North or South are humans, with almost common central roots and none is superior to another. It may be that one part or segment have progressed rapidly or have had ups and downs. There is misconception, mostly in Northern India, to term Dravidians, mistakenly as Dasa's. "The Rig Veda mentions sacrificer's or generous patrons, whose names do not appear to be Indo-Aryan, such as Śaṇḍa, Brbu, Araṭva Akṣa, and BalbūthaTarukṣa. Such names suggest a process that brough various peoples into Vedic culture by giving them access to the ritual tradition (Stephanie Jamison)".

The Dasa's were actually Turkic who today have been identified by several scholars as Dahae's. Hence, the Dahae, Dahu, Dahi become the Dasa of the Rig Veda, whom the Indian dynasties were in conflict with. Whereas the Sanskrit word 'dasa' means servant, the patronyms Dahae, Dahu, Dahi, have no relation to an origin as 'dasa' and are in no way as servitude in any Hindu scriptures. The common misconception by many writers, is that Dravidians, Dasa's were an 'aboriginal' group of India, while the Rig Vedic writers themselves were from outside of India. The fact that Dravidian's, Dasa's were a national demographic acronym and not a racial one and can be seen by Vedic seers writing of praying about them to become Arya. For example, Sage Bharadwaj prays that Dasa's become Arya. Hence, the possibility to become an Arya compatriot means that they were a cultural population. During their settlement Dravidians Dasa's built bonds with the

Arya communities (With early as well as later Aryan's (Vedic Aryan's), thereby becoming a part of Indian societies. Sage Vasishtha calls himself a "dasa" (**dasonamilhusekarani**) and says, "May I serve the god (Varuna) like a dasa, a lord." Being Arya was a social designation (Rig Veda X.49.3).

Kasmira Group. On the other hand, Kasmiri's are basically the early group of Later Aryan's, who, were serpent worshippers and were termed as Naga's and then Later Aryan's also migrated and settled alongside early group of Aryan's. There is no evidence that early humans existed in the Valley, except few (Unconfirmed) traces have been found on the mountainous fringes of the Valley. Most of the inhabitants of Kasmira were basically from River Saraswati and River Sindhu Basin's.

Reference to Vedas and Puranas. Initial Vedic Religion is concerned mainly with the worship of gods that are largely personifications of the powers of nature.The **Puranas** make the Dravidians descendants of the Vedic family of Turvasha, one of the older Vedic peoples. These ancient historians did not feel any need to limit the Vedic people to one linguistic group. The Vedas portray the large region of North India, which must have been then complex culturally as today. Puranic Hinduism began overshadowing Vedic Hinduism and indeed, one theory suggests that the Puranic traditions were consolidated in Southern India and even Agama (Doctrine-Agamas spiritual literature and practices) texts that describe temple rituals are clearly influenced by old Tamil veneration of hero-stones. Hero stones (**Virakallu** in Kannada, **Viragallu** in Telugu, **Naṭukal** in Tamil) are memorials commemorating the honourable death of a hero in battle, erected between the second half of the first millennium BC.

In the later Dharma Shastras (Religious Scriptures), it is in the entire Indian subcontinent, from North India to the Southern seas, the gradual shift of Vedic culture took place. Sangam literature (Sangam literature-earliest available Tamil literature). The Sangam age roughly extends between 300 BC and 300 AD. The word **'Sangam'** literally means association) reveals an awareness of the Himalayas and Kanyakumari, of Varuna, the God of Ocean, and Sagara. Each of the four Vedas were shared by the numerous schools, but revised, interpolated and adapted locally, during and after the Vedic period, giving rise to various recensions of the text.

Above was to bring the readers to a common grid of beliefs of Northern and Southern India and association with Vedas, during the last nearly four millenniums. This North -South connection thus is historical and even Pre Veda days.

S'arada of Kasmira, Saradaamba and Adi Shankaracharya

Religious Philosophies Commonality. From our past, settlements, religious philosophies we have many common Goddesses. There is a **unique umbilical** cord between **North and South: Goddess S'arada (Sharada) (of Kasmira), Goddess Sharadaamba and of course Adi Shankaracharya**. There seems to be misconception about the form, role of the Goddesses mentioned and how they came to be worshipped at respective places. Goddess S'arada in the North was not restricted to Kasmira only, but was associated with S'arada Language and Lipi (Script). However, later her worship got restricted as Goddess of Kasmira, whereas S'arada Lipi (Script) and language, spread beyond the borders of Kasmira, mostly North-Western India and did not touch even the fringes of Northern India and further down.

Southern Parts of our country are the torch bearers of Vedic tradition; rituals in places of worship are as per Vedas and temple architecture owes their origin to inferences from Vedas. Rivers, The Vedas over centuries gave occasion to saints and religious scholars to bring out the subtle nuances of the Vedic Hymns and rituals. Adi Shankaracharya's works were based on the hymns of Veda and his saintly interpretation.

Here is what is quoted about Vedic India in Eighth Century AD. "The masses had moved gradually towards abandoning the Vedic way of life, comprising of the various duties in accordance to the sacred tradition and the Ashrama -stages in life. There was a strong and urgent need for the revival of the Sanatana Dharma, lest it crumble to non-existence." "In the course of practice, the sacrifices and rituals were upheld as the ultimate goal and the true Vedic dictums were forgotten. Spiritual insight was conspicuous by its absence and at such a crucial juncture, **Adi Shankaracharya**, respected since across the world as the greatest philosopher and revered as an incarnation of Lord Sadashiva, walked the earth".

Misrepresentation of God's/Goddess's and Saint's. In popular worship, sacred figures offer a space where local groups, communities and traditions signal their places by creating Myths and Lores in the community, which then spreads. Such Myths, Legends are a figment of commonly held beliefs, that are mostly untrue and over the centuries have incorporated influences from many different communities, traditions but astonishingly oscillate and shake the truth. If the Goddesses and Saints are embroiled in fictitious Myths, Legends, Lores, Controversies, not only it changes the hue of truth but hurts the centuries old sentiments and spiritual connections with them.

Many scholars, to exhibit their knowledge of the subject and writing acumen, supress the actual history or facts. S'arada Temple of Kasmira, a Hindu Monument, is now talked about as Buddhist Creation and Monument. Sandalwood Sharadaamba idol of Adi Shankaracharya dislocated from its original place, Kudali, placed at Sringeri in a separate temple but in chronicles and biographies of Adi Shankaracharya, lore and legends the new assertion is taken as the truth. A pure saintly life of mixed with fiction, many imaginative events and incidents have been associated with him. Not really a new phenomenon, it started way back in Thirteenth/Fourteenth Century, when many religious heads wanted to apportion fictional created accounts and incidents associated with Saints and Sages. They were not ordinary people, most of them religious heads whom common devotee would not challenge. In present day we have more than 200 known Shankaracharya's, while there was only one Adi Shankaracharya (Sankara). Such deviations are direct violation of sacred ordains.

Even a Self-Styled Shankaracharya, who claimed to be Shankaracharya of S'arada Kasmira-meru is cooling his heels behind bars for terror activities. Many embroiled in moral turpitude, litigation, succession disputes and many in amassing wealth. Not to talk of another Muth head recently coming under limelight.

Adi Shankaracharya. Study of works, treatises and Philosophy of Adi Shankaracharya, which came down the centuries, after he had left this mortal world, Bharatvarsh (India) was blessed by his setting foot on this earth and our country. More than 1200 years back a new religious philosophy was propounded by Adi Shankaracharya, which even today stands on the highest pedestal amongst other religious philosophies. His attaining samadhi at just young age of 32 years, did not prevent his covering a vast canvas of his teachings. It is blasphemy to attribute incidents, actions which he never could even think of. Adi Shankaracharya was a mighty genius, a master of logic and a profound thinker. His sagely philosophy and works attributed to him, brought solace, peace and illumination to countless persons, soothed the sorrows and afflictions brought hope, perfection and calmness to many. No wonder his system of philosophy commands the admiration of the whole world, a Vedic scholar and teacher (acharya), whose works present a harmonizing reading of the *sastras*, with liberating knowledge of the self at its core and synthesizing the Advaita Vedanta teachings of his time.

Birth Date-Year of Adi Shankaracharya

Birth Year Controversy. As per various accounts of Muths Great Adi Shankaracharya (Also called Jagatguru, Great Adi

Shankaracharya), named Sankara (*San* means prosperity and *Kara* means the giver) was born 2500 years back at *Kaladi* (Kerala); son of Sivaguru and Aryambal. After him started the legend cum pontiff's seat called *Acharaya's.* His descendant lineage has the *Acharya's* of four established *Muths* that exist even today; Puri, Sringeri, Jyotir Muth (Badrinath) and Dwarka. The fifth one at Kamakoti (Kanchi) is considered as the original seat of Great Adi Shankaracharya, where he spent his last days and Kanchi was intended to be the nerve centre of all the other Muths.

Notwithstanding various records of all the *Muths*, extensive research indicates Adi-Shankaracharya was born in May/June 788 AD (Lunar month of *Vaishakha,* 26th year of the sixty-year cycle) and attained *samadhi* in the month of May/June 820 AD (*Vaishaakha*or *Pausha* of 58th year of the sixty-year cycle). The difference in number of years converted to Christian Era is; is around 1209 years: Great Adi Shankaracharya (409/414 – 516 BC) – Adi Shankaracharya 788 AD= 1200+-years.

Both dates in respective eras are correct. The problem with BC Era dates conversion is that the era pertains to a different calendar other than Christian Era, while AD era dates are of Christian Calendar. The fault lies as to how Muth's, still used the BC era dates to give antiquity to Adi Shankaracharya's birth and Samadhi. Earlier calendar in Bharatvarsh was with 60 cycles of 60 years each, 27 *Nakshatra's* and twelve months. Notices by the Greek historians *Pliny* and *Arrian* suggest that, during the Mauryan Dynasty (322 –185 BC), the calendar used in Bharatvarsh began in 6676 BC. Apparently, this was the basis of calendar on which Arya Bhatta worked on during Sixth/Seventh Century BC. Whether this was earlier '*Saptarishi*' calendar, with a beginning of 6676 BC, is difficult to prove.

Historians, Scholars, Edicts make it apparent that for calculating the era's, Arya Bhatta 'somehow missed' 1200 years (±), out of 60 years cycle, since he relied on earlier Puranas for these dates. Like Arya Bhatta calculates the years of King Brihardatha and Pryodata Dynasty from around 3150 BC (Brihardata) to Last King of PryodataNandivardhdhana (1994/2000 BC), based on Yavu and Matsya Purana.

In the case of Adi Shankaracharya, the era in vogue was based on Purana calendar, Yavu and Matsaya Purana amongst them. I can easily quote about similar era aberration by famous Chronicler Kalhan of Kasmira, who wrote famous Rajatarangini in mid-12th Century (1148-49 AD). We know for sure that King Ashoka (304 -232 BC) ruled from 273 – 232 BC. Kalhan's dates Ashoka's rule over thousand years before his real known date. Many scholars and researchers are of the view that Adi-Shankaracharya of Eighth/Ninth Century is actual Great Adi Shankaracharya. Government of India rightly celebrated 1200th anniversary of Adi-Shankaracharya's birth in 1988 indicating his birth in 788 AD.

S'arada Shrine/Temple Kasmira. There are few Goddess S'arada Shrines/Temples (Tiraths) in Kasmira amongst other Goddesses/Temples, most being indigenous manifestations. It is in later Centuries these Goddesses, mostly Gram Devi's (Village Deities), were associated with Goddess Spouses of the Trinty (Vishnu, Shiva and Brahma viz. Laxmi, Parvati and Saraswati). In this process, their role, as individual Goddesses got diluted, most getting associated with Parvati-Durga. This is not a phenomenon restricted to Kasmira but Hinduism in India. Apart from creation of plethora of forms of Goddesses to ther regional manifestations like Sharada, Saradaamba, Devi S'arada etc are the various names of Goddess S'arada in various parts of our country, their basic roles and importance differing from area to area, community to community.

A Photograph of Shri Sringeri Sharadaamba

Surprisingly the awareness of Goddess S'arada of Kasmira, was and is more in Southern parts of the country, than amongst the Kasmirai Aryan Saraswat Brahmins (In present day usually referred to Kasmirai Pandits). In recent decades, post partition, awareness of the Shrine/Tirath of S'arada (Kasmira) amongst them was bliss of ignorance. However, currently for last two decades, the monument/tirath, in ruins, has become an issue to be flouted.

Somehow certain stories legends, attributions, controversies around this S'arada temple of Kasmira and Adi Shankaracharya have been created over the centuries, more so after 13th Century AD, mostly emanating from Sringeri. These created legends and controversies, misinformation, beginning 14th Century were not honest but with creating a place for themselves and coming from a religious head, simple worshipper and devotees of Adi Shankaracharya took it as gospel truth. More legends, myths were added over the centuries fiction and created accounts kept truth at bay. The task was first to find out and know the truth to the extent possible.

My Own Association. As a young boy I used to hear folk tales from my paternal Granny, but what interested me was her narration of travelogue, experiences of our ancestors, passed on from one generation to another. One of the tales, casually, was visit to S'arada Shrine of Kasmira (Kishanganga Valley), where. one of my ancestors lost his life at the temple, while having a ritual bath in Kishanganga River. This incident is still held in the memory of locals where Shrine/Tirath is located. It was then casually mentioned, S'arada was a Roop (Form) of Goddess Saraswati (Goddess of Knowledge). But alas, unlike other places, which I could visit, I had to satisfy myself with imaginative details of places mentioned in her travelogue, including S'arada Shrine/Temple. One thing leads to another and I also somehow got connected with the life and times of Adi Shankaracharya. Further S'arada Temple (Kasmira) and Adi Shankaracharya got connected in my book; **History of Kasmira (Kasmira) (2013)**.

S'arada of Kasmira. In Kasmira, somewhat unknown, that there is a S'arada Shrine/Temple (Tirath) beyond the boundaries of Kasmira Kingdom. Sharada-Saraswati in Kasmira are worshipped as the goddesses of learning; former a manifested form of Saraswati goddess, who imparts and blesses with the essence of knowledge. In Her form of Saraswati, She is a manifestation of the Supreme Truth and spiritual wisdom. Depicted in pure white in colour, of exquisite beauty and is worshipped as seated on a lotus. Her four hands hold: a flute (Veena), book, rosary and one hand in blessing posture. There was no idol at S'arada Shrine Kishanganga Valley at any time and object of reverence was a Kund (Spring-since dried up and now covered with a thick stone slab) in the Centre of the Shrine/Temple Sanctum Santorum. (More of it in later Chapter).

In the Kasmira valley hand painted images of Goddess S'arada were made by Family Priests and presented to children on a particular day; Guru Tritya (Usually January/February). There are references in one odd scripture as to the shape of Goddess S'arada of Kasmira, perched on a Swan and carrying a pot of glittering gold (Nectar?). A myth has been created in Kasmira, even South India that a **Chandana (Sandalwood) S'arada Idol** existed at the S'arada Kasmira shrine and during purported visit of Adi Shankaracharya, it was taken away and installed it at Sringeri. Most people are not aware that there never was any idol at S'arada Kasmira Shrine. The fact is **Chandana (Sandalwood) S'arada Idol** was installed at Kudali in the beginning years of Adi Shankaracharya teachings and institutions. This idol was shifted to newly established Sringeri Muth in 14th Century and placed in a separate temple and not as idol of presiding deity.

Idol of Goddess S'arada (Sharada)
Attributed to Kasmira dating to Ninth Century AD
(The diol is in possession of Metropolitan Museum USA)

Roop (Images) of Goddess Sharada. Roop (Images) of Sharada, as Goddess of Knowledge and manifestation from Saraswati, vary in Kasmira as well as in the country. Above is a stone idol of Goddess S'arada attributed to Kasmira dating to Ninth Century AD. It is so different from the description given in Scriptures. A hallow around her Head and Diadem (Crown), Wings and Hands blessing two Young Children. Notably the idol indicates her role as Goddess of Knowledge in blessing Mudra (State). This idol, so different from other visualised images of Goddess, is true to her as the Goddess of Knowledge bestowing it to two young children. Her wings denote the heavenly blessings of the Goddess and the idol is the earliest depiction of Saraswati in her role as Sharada; giver of knowledge.

Images of Goddess S'arada (Sharada-Goddess of Knowledge) -A Form of Goddess Saraswati Peeth

Two Different Bronze Idols of Goddess Saraswati

Left :1150 AD Dancing_Saraswati
Hoysaleswara Temple Halebidu Karnataka
Right: Goddess Saraswati (Painting)

Goddess Saraswati-Sharada. In our Country there are many other Sharada, Saradaamba, Devi S'arada shrines/ temples, and each of them have a particular peculiar form, shape, representation, association and mode of worship. They run into thousands and I would like to list few of them and their role viz Goddess S'arada of Kasmira. **Goddess Saraswati** has typical depiction in mythology and pictorial references (See collages above). In countless sources she is denoted draped in white outfit/sari seated on a lotus flower and sometimes portrayed seated on the Swan bird. Symbolized as the **goddess of ultimate truth and knowledge,** with four arms conveying her Supreme Power and universal presence. Arms on front side symbolize presence in temporal world while those two arms on her back represent her presence in the spiritual realm of the world.

In totality they symbolize: **Manas (mind), Buddhi (intellect), Chitta (consciousness),** and **Ahanakara (ego).** Lotus flower Saraswati denotes the sense of **supreme reality or supreme knowledge, thus seated** means she is grounded in supreme reality symbolizing transcendental knowledge while her white sari is symbolic of the epitome of knowledge wrapped around Her. One of the hands holding **rosary** is symbol of attributes such as contemplation, meditation and concentration leading devotees to the **union with the divinity** known as *Samadhi.*

Sharadadevi-Kudali-Adi Shankaracharya. Notwithstanding the beliefs and make believe, Adi Shankaracharya established first Peeth at Kudali on the banks of Tunga River to be worshipped as Sharadadevi and installed Goddess S'arada as a Sri Yantra on a rock; later her sandalwood murti form was installed by him. Legend/lore, which is associated with this place, for Adi Shankaracharya to establish a Peeth has been covered separately.

Chandana Sharadaamba Idol -Now at Vidyashankara Temple

Gold Idol at Main Sringeri Muth

The most famous temple dedicated to Goddess S'arada is located at the Sringeri Muth, also known as S'arada Peeth. It is **claimed** that here Adi Shankaracharya installed Goddess S'arada as a Sri Yantra on a rock; and another, her murti form in a sandalwood as against that Adi Shankaracharya installed it at **Kudali**. This aspect is being covered separately. Here the stress is more on current S'arada Peeth at Sringeri, as the belief going around now is that this is the Peeth originally associated with Adi Shankaracharya. Is it so?

Sringeri Main Temple. The temple is that of Shiva (Siva), who's called Candramoulisvara and Goddess Saraswati who is called as Goddess Sharada. As per legend associated with this temple is that Mahaperiyavaa (Adi Shankaracharya) prayed here to Candramouliswara (Siva, Shiva) and Tripurasundari. There after he established Sri Saradambal (**Sharadaamba**) on Srichakra Peeth. Here Goddess S'arada is termed as embodiment of all three Shakti's and described; as Brahmavidya, which is identical to the incommensurable Brahman Itself, transcends the three qualified conceptions, known as **Trimurtis**, and their corresponding Saktis (Shakti) as Saraswati, Lakshmi and Ishwari and at Sringeri reigns as a single deity: Mother Sharada.

Goddesses S'arada Devi depiction as in idol: **seated** on the Sri Chakra Peeth, holding a **Japa Mala (Rosary), A parrot** perched on her upper right hand, lower right hand in **Chinmudra (Blessings),** upper left hand holding **Amrita Kalasa (Pot of Nectar)** and lower left hand has a **book**. Following the tradition claimed to be established by Adi Shankaracharya, the Sringeri Muth follows the philosophy of **Advaita Vedanta**. It is in-charge of the Black Yajurveda, which is prevalent in South India. At Maihar Devi Temple at Maihar (Madhya Pradesh), She is depicted as Goddess Shakti: as Sharda Devi preaching the philosophy of Advaita of Adi Shankaracharya.

Unfortunately, my efforts to find image of Chandana Sharadaamba Idol initially installed by Adi Shankaracharya at Kudali and shifted to a separate Vidyashankara Temple at Sringeri, without much accruements did not succeed. However, it is evident that there are subtle differences in Mudra and posture of hands of this idol, so different from that of Idol at Sringeri main Temple. This also indicates and validates that visualisation of Adi Shankaracharya of Sharadaamba was different as has been made centuries after him. The purpose off detailed description of the Goddesses, Sharada-Sharadaamba was to bring out the subtle differences between the S'arada of Kasmira and Sharadaamba/S'arada Devi etc as venerated in Southern Parts of the Country. They have different philosophy of their role too.

Advaita Vedanta and Adi Shankaracharya. The Maṇḍukya Ḳarika or the Gauḍapada Karika, also known as the Agama Śastra is the earliest available systematic treatise on Advaita Vedanta-(Eighth Century AD) by Gaudapada (also Gaudapadacharya-Seenth Century AD), born in Gauda Desha (Present-day Bengal) and later on moved to Aparanta (Present-day region around River Narmada in Gujarat and Madhya Pradesh). The central teaching of Advaita Vedanta is in his Maṇḍukya Karika or the Gauḍapada Karika. His Shishya (Disciple) Govind Bhagwatpada (Govinda), taught Adi Shankaracharya. This treatise, first one, on Advaita Vedanta was in verse form and is considered one of the shortest but most profound Upanishads or mystical Vedas. These 13 prose sentences bring out subtle meanings in Advaita mantras in four brief chapters, namely: Traditional Doctrine (Agama), Unreality (Vaitathya), Nonduality (Advaita) and 'The Peace of The Firebrand (Alatasanti).

It was Adi Shankaracharya who brought forth the final form of Advaita philosophy and gave perfection and finishing touch to it. Advaita teachings of Adi Shankaracharya can be summed up in half a verse: "**Brahma Satyam. Jagan Mithya. JivoBrahmaiva Na Aparah**." Translates roughly as: "**God alone is real, the world is unreal, the individual is none other than God.**" The quintessence of this philosophy and spiritually is interpreted as; 'Brahman (the Absolute) alone is real; this world is unreal; the Jiva or the individual soul is non-different from Brahman (the absolute)'. The word Brahman has deep connection with Vedas and used by Adi Shankaracharya which connotes: "If Atman is the lord of the body, Brahman is the Lord of the universe. He is the eternal, indestructible, all pervading, Supreme Self, and synonymous with the Vedas themselves. The Vedas contain the hidden power of Brahman in sound form as the indestructible knowledge (akshara)".

A Painting of Adi Shankaracharya With His Disciples on The Banks of Tunga -Bhadra River Confluence (Kudali?)

Atman. 'The Atman is self-evident (Svatah-siddha). Brahman is beyond the reach of the eyes (Adrishya), without Gunas or attributes (Nirguna). formless (Nirakara), without special characteristics (Nir-Visesha), immutable, eternal. Non a performer supreme being, who is not bound by the responsibility of performing any duty (Akarta) and is above all needs and desires. Brahman is non-dual, one without a second. The world is relatively real (Vyavaharika Satta), while Brahman is absolutely real (Paramarthika Satta)'. Atman is also inferred from Vedas as: "Atman means the breathing one, the individual soul. According to Vedic beliefs it is without form and without attributes, and usually referred as the Self".

Thus, it will be evident that Advaita Philosophy is as a result of deep understanding of the Vedas by Adi Shankaracharya.

Advaita philosophy of Adi Shankaracharya is considered lofty, sublime and unique. A bold philosophy and logical subtlety, highly interesting, inspiring and elevating. It is claimed that no other philosophy can stand before it in boldness, depth and subtle thinking and this philosophy is complete and perfect. The position of Brahma-Nirvana, as taught by Advaita Vedanta, is also a finer type of Deep Sleep (*Sushupti* in Sanskrit) and refers to one of the four states of consciousness in Hindu and yogic philosophy. A peep into state of consciousness that comes after "deep sleep" (Turya (तुरीय ा)) which enables such Believers of Vedas (Vedantis) to see the truth-consciousness-bliss (Sat, Chit, and Ananda). Gaudapadaand Adi Shankaracharya were, in fact, doctrine practitioners (Agamics) of Srividya, and were highly devoted to the mother-goddess. However, followers of Shaivism (Shaiva's) of the south, have carried their philosophy to a position closer to mythology.

Ramanujacharya (Born 1017 AD) propounded **Vishtadvaita** (Modified monism), wherein ultimate reality is Brahman, soul and matter are his qualities and even after merging with Brahman, the Atman remains distinct. He expounded the grace of God as more important than knowledge.

Madhvacharya (Vidyaranya-born. 1296 AD. Vidyaranya was the head of the Sringeri S'arada Peeth (Sringeri Muth) during 1377-1386 AD and attained siddhi 1391 AD. During his period as head of Sringeri Muth propounded the **Dvaita philosophy** (dualism); 'the world is not an illusion and there is a difference between the Atman (soul, self) and Brahman (ultimate reality).' I would not like to comment on his philosophy, which to a large extent is opposite to what was propounded by Adi Shankaracharya.

A further modified Dvaita philosophy (dualism) was propounded by **Acharya Nimbarka**, born in South India, who established Nimbarka sect, which flourished in East India in the 13th and 14th Century AD, emphasising on Radha Krishna worship. He, a critic of Adi Shankaracharya and Ramanujacharya, stressed that liberation is attainable only through the grace of God. He founded the Krishna Muth at Udupi and emphasised on Radha Krishna worship. Propounded Siva-Dvaita, that Shiva is the ultimate reality, thus propounded **Dvaitadvaita** (dualistic monism).

Another **Vallabhacharyae** propounded **Shuddha Advaita** (pure non-dualism), wherein he taught that there was no distinction between Brahmin and the individual soul and the latter could get rid of bondage by Bhakti, asked his followers to offer everything in the service of Krishna and his idol worship.

Monistic Shaivism of Kasmiraviz Advaita Vedanta

Kasmira Shaivism and **Advaita Vedanta.** Kasmira Shaivism, as it is available to us, was academically developed by two traditions of Brahman scholars, one of them consists of the indigenous Aryan Saraswat Brahmins, called **Bhatta's** and the other one was of such Brahman families, which having migrated to the valley around the time of the great Karkota Rulers of Kasmira (Seventh/Eighth Century), who had also practically become Kasmiran's in all essential respects.

Kasmira Shaivism is **non-dualistic or monistic,** as it unites all differences in a single entity: **Shiva**. It differs significantly from philosophy, according to which the Absolute and the Universe are two independent entities. It holds that there is complete unity in pure consciousness, its subjective consciousness and objective perception are like a mirror and the objects that are reflected on it. The monistic Kasmira Shaivism is also different from the philosophy of Adi Shankaracharya, according to which only the Absolute is real; everything else is mithya or illusion. The world as seen is perceived only in the vyavaharika or secondary State and not in absolute the paramarthika (non-dual absolute state). On the other hand, according to Kasmira Shaivism, both the Absolute and the manifested are real. However, as all the manifested exist in the Absolute like the objects reflected in a mirror, they do not have an independent existence. Abhinav Gupta in his **Bodhapanchadaśi** refers to this by saying that all the light and darkness reside in the supreme light of God-Consciousness. It is a monistic philosophy establishing the fact that there is only one eternally existent reality and that is the infinite, eternal and pure consciousness alone and nothing else.While Advaita Vedant Philosophy spread almost all-over South India, it did not make any dent in the Kasmira Shaivism. On the contrary, it gained a high place amongst religious philosophies. Even in Southern parts of our country, Kasmira Shaivism has made inroads and many rituals incorporate certain nuances of Kasmira Shaivism.

Both these philosophies have maintained their respective positions in the country for over 13 Centuries. In Kasmira it started with the worship of Shiva from around Fifth Century BC, but could not overtake the worship of Vishnu. The philosophy of present Monistic Shaivism became popular in Kasmira predominantly after the immigration of several important families around the Eighh Century AD. King Lalitaditya of Kasmira (724-761 AD) went to Kanyakubja, the capital of King Harsha (Sixth Century) where he met Atri Gupta, whom he induced to migrate to Kasmira. The famous Abhinav Gupta was a descendant of Atri Gupta.

Abhinav Gupta was born around 940 AD and might have lived even beyond 1015 AD, when he is believed to have entered Birwa caves in Kasmira, reciting *Bhairavastava.* The date of his entering Birwa (Magam-Kasmira) Caves, never to return, is not fully established. He, during his life and after, had been extolled as "*Mahamahesvara*" by Kasmiri scholars, which precisely means the "great devotee of Shiva", or the "Supreme -Self" in Shaivistic parlance. About the same time, around 800

AD, Sangam Aditya another Shaivite Scholar systematized the Pratyabhijna school of Shaivism and settled down in Kasmira. Sometime around last part of Eighth Century AD, the ancestors of Vasu Gupta, author of the Shiv Sutras also arrived in Kasmira.

Somananda (Eighth Century AD), fourth descendent of Sangam Aditya, extracted the principles of monistic Shaiva philosophy from the scriptures and incorporated them in his own work, ***Shivadrishti,*** which gives the origin and is first philosophical treatise on Kasmiri Shaivism. The other scholars were; Eraka Natha, Sumati Natha and Vasu Gupta. Around last part of Eighth Century, Vasu Gupta found seventy-seven terse sutras etched on stone near Mahadev Peak, as revealed to him in a dream, which he named the **Shiv *Sutras.*** These teachers (Somananda, Eraka Natha, Sumati Natha and Vasu Gupta) established four different schools named; ***Pratyabhijna* School, *Krama* School, *Kula* School and *Spanda* School** respectively. Over the centuries and with the influence of different Shaivite scholars, certain other deviations and *agams* (Doctrines) took place and shape Shiva worship in Kasmira, which includes the combined worship of Shiva and his consort called Shakti. The Shaivism of Kasmira is called the Trika Sasana or Trika Sastra or simply the Trika School of philosophy and is essentially not a single philosophical system but a compendium of the philosophies of all the four schools of Shaivism. Abhinav Gupta integrated the philosophies of these schools in his Tantraloka, thus giving a common philosophy; Kasmira Shaivism.The Absolute, in terms of the Siddhas, is also the 'supreme station' of the Sufis. **Sufism** is mystical Islamic belief and practice in which Muslims seek to find the truth of divine love and knowledge through direct personal experience of God, which consists of a variety of mystical paths to ascertain the nature of humanity and of God and to facilitate the experience of the presence of divine love and wisdom in the world. It also generally refers to holy and pious people. (Sourced from Dr. Geetha Ananda and Professor T.N. Ganapathy)

Differences Advaita and Kasmira Shaivism. There is a vast difference between the two philosophies; Advaita Vedanta and Kasmira Shaivism. The latter unlike Vedanta, traces out the root cause of all phenomena within the divine essence of the Brahman of Vedanta, known here as Paramashiva. The same has been the case with the aspirants belonging to the Ardha-Tryambaka school of Shaivism, which flourished at Jalandhara Peeth, the modern town of Kangra in Himachal Pradesh. The practitioners of Yoga (Yogins) of Kasmira saw the infinite and pure consciousness as being limitlessly blissful in nature and discovered it as the one complete whole of all divine powers. Advaita Vedantins discovered the monistic metaphysical reality as infinite and absolutely-tranquil pure consciousness alone, but the Shaiva's of Kasmira saw the blissful self-awareness as the essential character of such pure consciousness.

Inroads of Advaita. The tradition of the Advaita Vedanta of Adi Shankaracharya did not at all get itself established in Kasmira before the rule of the Dogra monarchs (19th Century). It is because of the Dogra King's patronised Giri Sect of Dasnami's, who in collaboration with Dharmarth Trust, established by Maharaja Gulab Singh, spread the Advaita through the shrines and temples (Most in the State) by the Trust. The result is that many agams have got mixed up. The results have been strange, the indigenous Goddesses are invoked as forms of either Parvati or Tri-Devi's. Goddess Raghnya of Tulla Mulya was always considered as ancient locally manifested Goddess, who also became Kul Devi of many families of the Valley. It owed its origin to an Agrahara of Brahmins in ancient times even before Seventh Century. The power of Brahmins was such that a curse by a Brahmin turned into reality when King Jayapira (764-95 AD) next day was grievously injured and died day later.

Till Dogra rule there was no idol, just an Estrada in the middle of a spring at Tulla Mullya. Dogra's under Dharmarth constructed a temple and installed an idol of the Goddess of black stone. Soon another idol resembling Shiv Ling was installed side by side. The idol was that of Buteshwara (Shiva). Bhuteshwara is also a Bhairav companion of Raghnya. Thus, the Goddess was converted into Mother Goddess, called Durga etc. Few decades back Justice Shiv Nath Katju, a Shaivite Scholar also, asked a world renowned Shaivite Scholar of Kasmira "that the idol of Goddess Raghnya is black in colour, does that mean Raghnya is form of Kali". The renowned scholar replied in affirmative. The aim of quoting this conversation of early sixties, was to indicate, how mixed changes have entered even the Shaivism of Kasmira.

"To follow the path, look to the master, follow the master, walk with the master, see through the master, become the master."
– Zen Proverb

3

Vedas and Bharatvarsh Connect

Only the person having firm conviction and iron volition can attain Strength and energy. At no stage Karma does he ever hesitate

-Rig Veda

Vedas and South-North India Connect

Till few centuries back, Veda Hymns, ceremonies remained at restricted level, mostly in certain parts of the Country and rituals connected or ordained in Vedas had undergone change. With spread of Buddhism and Jainism, followers of Vedas reduced and remained mostly in areas where Buddhism had not made inroads. The light of Vedas was there, in certain pockets of India, but someone had to spread this light. It is at this Stage Adi Shankaracharya blessed India and the revival of Hinduism began with his preaching's mostly based on the tenets of Vedas. It spread during the next few centuries and with-it revival of Vedas in the form of worship, rituals and ceremonies took place and Veda teachings got impetus amongst priests, temples and the young generation. But today the knowledge of Vedas and their contents are absolutely minimal.

Vedas and Scriptures. Vedas are the first and foremost oldest religious scriptures which formed the foundation of religion in the country and remain as the basic tenets of present-day religion. Irrespective of changes, additions, new customs, Gyatri Mantra, remains the mool (root) hymn for invocation even today. Over the centuries many interpretations of Veda Mantra's have been made, most based on later scriptures, in spite of it all these convey the true meanings. Hymns and Mantra's of Vedas are explanatory of how the Vedic Religion differs from today's Hinduism. Their teachings remained as the bed rock of fresh philosophies including manifestation of Gods and Goddesses.

During the last century plus interpretation of Vedas has given a fresh and new insight into these scriptures. Vedas were translated, so also other scriptures that followed Vedas. The credit goes to Indologists, Indian Scholars and many Western scholars, who with their devotion learned Sanskrit in which the Vedas were available, translated them and refrained from giving their interpretation of the Vedic Hymns. The value of Vedas and their contents were understood much earlier as regional scholars had translated them into various Indian languages much before English translations. The Vedic Hymns echoed in the prayers at home or temples, translations helped in passing on the Veda contents to a larger segment of our country and even the world. Most translators struck to the principle; **"Each Veda Mantra is itself the testimony of its authenticity and infallibility of the central idea and need not be upheld by other supporting proofs".**

Vedas Fountainhead of Vedic Religion. Vedas gave Vedic religion, which transited to Brahmanism and its prime branch; Hinduism. A study of these will reveal that the religion of today is a mix of the teachings of Vedas and changes over the period, which were incorporated with the appearance of *Upanishad's, Grantha's, Purana's* and other specific religious scriptures. Many such religious scriptures took form on area/ region basis and not only did they change some basic tenets and understanding of Vedic religion, additionally veered towards area based religious manifestations to give rise to plethora of God's, Goddesses, Kul Deva/Devi's and even forms of worship. Hinduism which developed over the millenniums, is a mix of the basics of Vedas and other scriptures like *Purana's, Upanishad's* and works of various Rishi's.

Later day scriptures are our heritage too but in no way change the basic concept and contents of the Vedas. To quote Manu (Translated); **"The Veda is the source of all *dharma* i.e., religion, morality and righteousness. For those aspiring for the correct knowledge of dharma, only the Vedas are the highest authority."**

Evolution of Vedas and Their Contents

Vedas. Word **'Veda'** evolved from the element **'Vid'** which means **'knowing'**, synonymous to the word knowledge. Basically, the meaning of the Veda is knowledge, also known as **'Shruti'**; word **'Shruti'** from **'Shru'**, meaning **'hearing'**. Four Vedas (Rig, Yajur, Sam and Atharv) are, repositories of knowledge, conveying first and initial thoughts and religious philosophy. They are exhaustive scriptures; each Veda contains several sections and thousands of Hymns. The principal Vedas were originally only three in number: Rig Veda, Yajur Veda and Sam Veda. Atharv Veda, the fourth, was added later on. The first three were called '*trayi vidya*', meaning threefold knowledge. The name 'Rig Veda' was derived from the root word ***'Rik'*** which means 'to worship'. The name Yajur Veda came from the root word '***Yaj'***, which also means the same. With time the Rig Vedic Hymns became popular as Hymns for chanting and recitation, while the Hymns of the Yajur Veda came to be associated more with the sacrificial ritualistic aspects of *yajna* worship.

Vedas and Religion. Vedas gave birth to Vedic religion and throw considerable light on the scope and nature of Vedic religion and the life of early Aryan's. Changes over the millenniums are as a result of later scriptures, amalgamation of religious philosophy of entire Bharatvarsh; Dravidians, Aryan's and others who inhabited Bharatvarsh. **The most important *mantra* of the Vedas, which is considered the 'root' or all Vedas, is the *Gayatri Mantra*. It is so called because it is in a triad comprising of 3 units of 8 letters each (The word '*Gayatri*' itself has spiritual connotation).**

Veda worship and recitation at one time was all over Bharatvarsh, but with the passage of time their recitation and following of rituals underwent a sea change. Advent of Buddhism reduced importance of Vedas and after Buddhism waned many changes in ritual worship took place and different shades of Vaishnavism followed. This period was followed by the Advaita Vedanta philosophy spread by Adi Shankaracharya (Eighth/Ninth Century) followed by monoistic shades of Shaivism, which also thrived in North India and Kasmira (Kashmir). Enforcement of class system, strict code laid down by some later scriptures, kept the Vedas in the domain of upper classes only. **Aryans had broad based class system, based on work** responsibility system and did not take them away from the Vedic religion; Aryan priests *Arthavan;* warriors *Ratheshwar*, workers and herders *Vastrayosh* and camp followers *Hatoksha*.

At one time Vedic Religion was predominant in North-Western Bharatvarsh, subsequently it took stronger roots south of Vindhya's. While its spread reduced in North-Western Bharatvarsh, itthrived in the South, which still boasts Veda worship in pure form. Today Veda teachings and institutions are predominantly located in the South, where the recitation and rituals of original Vedas are strictly followed and no deviation or interpretation made. *Homa's* (Offerings), invocation, oblations are made to Vedic Gods, Rivers, Rishi's as they are in the Vedas.

Origins-Orthodox Belief. The orthodox belief is that all the four Vedas were revealed by God, at the time of creation of universe, to four pious Rishi's Agni (Fire), Vayu (Air), Aditya (Sun) and Angiras. The belief of this orthodox group that since revelation of Vedas was at the time of creation of universe, they preclude interpretation of names in their literal sense. In their interpretation and translations these names are termed and given different meanings by different writers, persons etc. Most of these are of late 19th Century vintage, when the Vedas were translated.

Origins-Common and Popular Belief. Most common and rational belief is that Vedas were composed on the banks of mythical River Saraswati by Rishi's and their descendants. They were evolved in the form of inner subtle waves to Rishis (seers), when they were in deep meditation cum penance. These waves developed in the memory of Rishis, as if they were heard, hence they are called 'shruti' (heard). Seers wanted to share these waves of knowledge and started teaching them in the form of sentences (sound) to their disciples and the process from one generation of disciples to another. Thus, Vedas took the form of sound and the language used was called 'Geervaana' (language of gods), which is the presumed as ancient form of now existing Sanskrit language. This language form of Vedas was in the form 'smriti' (remembered) and finally came down the millenniums. I am unable to find details of this language of Gods (Geervaana), its origin and form. Somehow it had to be vocal language, evolved during that time.

Many Rishi's listed above have been mentioned in the Hymns of Vedas, like **Jamadagini and Angiras (Rig Veda).** The mention of various Rishi's goes beyond Rig Veda and are mentioned in other three Vedas also. The entire knowledge in Vedas was codified and divided by Sage Veda Vyasa into four types, called Rig Veda, Yajur Veda, Sam Veda and Atharv Veda. It is an ignorant assertion that the Vedas were written by later Aryans.

Rig Veda, most sacred of the four Vedas and religious scripture is considered oldest followed byYajur, Sam and Atharv. Additions and deletions seem to have continuously been made and passed on through generations of Rishi*'s* and Aryan bards (*Arthavan*). As the Nobel Laureate, Rabindranath Tagore expressed, **"The Hymns are a poetic testament of a people's collective reaction to the wonder and awe of existence.... people of vigorous and unsophisticated imagination awakened at the very dawn of civilisation to a sense of inexhaustible mystery that is implicit in life."**

Later Scriptures, Vedas were followed by various other scriptures, ***Brahmana's, Vedanga's and Upa-Vedas***; these give us idea about varied subject, which are valid even today Astronomy, Medicine, (Art of war) and Music etc. **Vedanta's**

and *Upanishad's* followed, which constitute the intellectual aspect of Hindu philosophy and are continuation and link of the Vedic philosophy. ***Purana's,*** considered of later Vedic period**,** are legends connected with epics and law books. These scriptures were followed by other *Grantha's*, *Greh Sutra's* and other scriptures.

Vedas, Composition and Compilation. **Rig Veda** is in form of beautifully composed incantations ***Sukti's* (Hymns),** which means **'beautiful statements'**. Rig Veda contains praises for the deities like Indra, Agni, Rudra, and many other Veda God's. Tapping the energies of the Nature is given high importance in Rig Veda.

Rig Veda Manuscript (MS2097) in Devnagri

Rig Veda poetic Hymns were used by the *hotri* (Priests who used to lead a body of Aryan's while on move on a mission), calling on the **Gods** by reciting the Hymns aloud. The Hymns vary in style and length and praise a pantheon of gods. Rig Veda talks of Saraswati River as the focal point and then in other verses moves Eastwards towards Doab and even talks of Kasmira's sacred river Vitasta.It is difficult to assess as to when the first mantra was invoked, spoken or composed but it is evident that the tabulation took place later.

Sam Veda. Most of the Hymns of the Sam Veda are derived from the Rig Veda, but acquire musical connotation. During the *yajna* or sacrificial worship, the priest would chant Hymns from all the three Vedas in a systematic manner. Priest would sit and sing the Hymns from Sam Veda addressed to Agni (fire), Indra (lord of gods) and Soma (moon) to the accompaniment of musical instrument, such as the flute or *vina*. There are many interpretations as to its being called Sam Veda' most plausible being that 'Sam Veda' came from the root word '*saman*' meaning music. There is no clue to the date of the compilation of Sam Veda Hymns, nor has the compiler's name been handed down to us.

Yajur Veda. Yajur Veda; 'Yajush' means rituals and this Veda contains different rituals and sacrifices to be conducted to pacify gods. When a mantra is recited and its power is felt, then to make the mantra useful, a certain type of offerings are to be made the concerned god. It is in Yajur Veda that explains about these offerings be made to gods through Agni (fire), a practice still in vogue. Yajur Veda is divided into 'Krishna (Dark) Yajur Veda' and 'Shukla (Bright) Yajur Veda'. Bright Yajur Veda contains mantras used in the rituals while explanations exist in a separate 'Brahamana' work. The Dark Yajur Veda incorporates such explanations in the work itself, often immediately following the mantras. My own research and reading do not agree to the above inference. The name Krishna is associated with dark lunar fortnight while Shukla is associated with bright lunar fortnight. Apparently, the sages had evolved these mantras that where to be used in respective lunar fortnights. Brighter fortnight being considered more auspicious. There are 101 branches for the Dark Yajur Veda and 17 for Bright Yajur Veda.

It was the main Veda used by the priests in ancient India, deities being. same as the Rig Veda. Its series of sacrifices culminate in the ***Atma (ego)*** *yajna* or wherein the ego is offered up to the Divine. While the lesser sacrifices win the lesser worlds, the Self-sacrifice wins all the worlds and gains the greatest gift of immortality.

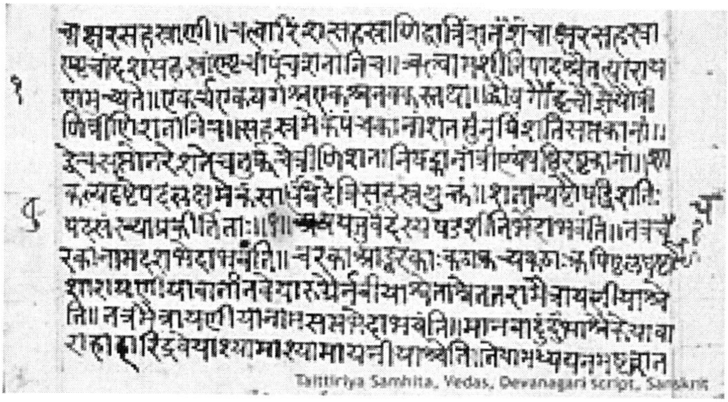

Taittiriya Samhita Yajurveda Manuscript Devanagari script

Yajur Veda was used by the *adhvaryu* priests (Priests who specialised in specific sacrificial *yajna's*) and contains offerings and specific sacrificial formulas, which are to be recited during that form of ceremony.

Atharv Veda. Atharv Veda was recognized as fourth Veda during the latter Vedic period and contains useful rituals to attain worldly happiness, containing description of diseases, their cure, sins, how to remove their effects and means of acquiring wealth. Atharv Veda, name is attributed to sage (Rishi) Atharvan and consists of number of Hymns and magical incantations composed by many other Rishi's and is the last of the Vedas. It has not always been accepted as a Veda, which are often spoken of as three but gives us a better idea of the life of common people in Vedic times. The deities of the Atharv Veda are also the same as the Rig Veda. Some scholars believe that this scripture may have originated with the pre-Aryan culture of indigenous people, as it deviated from the basics of other Vedas and was not at first readily accepted. Eventually it too was adopted as a ritual handbook by the Brahmans. To my mind, probably, after the composition of first three Vedas, Atharv Veda is the outcome of amalgamated ethos of Dravidians, Aryan's and Dasyu's and Atharv Rishi himself had imbibed the rituals of Dravidians.

Composition and Compilation. Rig Veda Hymns, the oldest of the four Vedas, must have started their manifestation after the Aryan's had developed mutual understandable language, composed in stages and not in the order they are at present. This process could have possibly started 3000 years BC ± and codified around 1200-800 BC±. As regards when Vedic Hymns were composed Max Muller opines: **"Whether the Vedic Hymns were composed 1000 or 1500 or 2000-or 3000-years BC, no power on earth will ever determine."**

Rig Veda was originally written in *Khartoshi* (*Khartoshi/ Kharoshti* script was from right to left and is attributed to Aryan's) prevalent in North-Western India. As Vedic language took roots amongst the Indo Aryan Race, *Kharoshti* (*Khartoshi*) became the script of the *Gandhari* (North-Western India) and developed into 'Vedic *Bholi*' (Sanskrit in its complex form) in the region, along with *Brahmi*. It also spread Northwards to Central Asia and Kasmira. The existence of *Kharoshti* (*Khartoshi*) numerals on Motif Tiles were found at Harvan Excavations (Outskirts of Srinagar (Kasmira)). The script ceased was in vogue in North-Western India, till around Fifth Century AD. Vedas were **'eventually' written in Sanskrit**, near the end of the third century BC, after the Sanskrit Grammar had been formulated by Panini.

Veda *Shakha's* (Schools/Versions). Vedas were written, progressively, in prevalent languages and scripts, in process many Hymns of these scriptures were either lost or fresh ones added over the centuries. On a fair estimate and as per Justice Shiva Nath Katju, a learned Scholar, there are 21 branches of Rig Veda, 109 of Yajur Veda, 50 of Atharv Veda and 1000 of Sam Vedas. Only two of the 1000 branches of Sam Veda are now extant in this world. Rig, Atharv and Yajur Vedas have similarly been depleted. There are numerous variants of Vedas in use in Bharatvarsh, based on areas, geographical locations and some of these are called by local names of Veda like *Paingi* Rig Veda; in parts of Tamil Nadu. Additions and alteration of wordings etc did occur over the millennium, basically most of them region-wise and as mode of worship of Gods and Goddesses emerged in the respective regions.

Veda Shakha's (Branches). There were approximately 200 *Shakha's* of Vedas at one time, including mixed *Shakha's*, which at one time had spread throughout South Asia. Some of these are:-

Shakala Rig Veda (Karnataka, Kerala, Tamil Nadu and to some extent in Uttar Pradesh); *Bashkala* Rig Veda; in Kerala; *Ashvalayana* Rig Veda: Manuscripts have been found in Kasmira and at many other places. *Paingi* Rig Veda; in parts of Tamil Nadu; *Shaunakiya* Atharv Veda: Gujarat, Karnataka, Coastal Andhra Pradesh; *Mauda* Atharv Veda, existed in Kasmira. Yajur Veda. *Madhyandina* Yajur Veda, *Kanva* Yajur Veda, *Charaka* Yajur Veda. *Charayaniya Katha* Yajur Veda; Existed in Kasmira. A text called '*Yajur Vedavriksha*' gives the geographical distribution of more than 100 *Shakha's* of Yajur Veda around Southern parts of the country there is a form of Black Yajur Veda. **Sam Veda.** *Kauthuma*, *Ranayaniya* Sam Veda and *Jaiminiya/Talavakara* Sam Veda. *Gautama* Sam Veda is said to have been prevalent in **Tamil Nadu** till 17th century AD. *Bhallavi* Sam Veda is said to have been prevalent **Karnataka** and parts of North India including **Kasmira.**

The aim of giving these *Shakha's* of Vedas is to bring home that variation in these scriptures exist from one region to another and one should not be surprised to find differing contents in Kasmira in comparison to Karnataka or for that matter even Tamil Nadu. These variations are not major and mainly incorporate local tradition, deities and requirements.

The earliest known surviving copies of any of the Vedas are copies of the Rig Veda and Atharv Veda that are currently held in the Bhandarkar Oriental Institute in Pune, Maharashtra, India.

Vedic Religion Gods and Goddesses. Initial Vedic Religion is concerned mainly with the worship of gods that are largely personifications of the powers of nature. The Hymns are mainly invocations of these gods, meant to accompany the oblation of *Soma* juice and Fire sacrifice of melted butter. It was thus essentially a **polytheistic (Multiple Gods)** religion, which assumes a pantheistic, worship of all Gods, colouring only in a few of its last Hymns. That they (Aryan's) were considered to have been originally mortal is implied in the statements that they acquired immortality by drinking *Soma* or by receiving it as a gift from **Agni (Fire)** and **Savitr** (Another God of Rig Veda). The gods were conceived as human in appearance, some appear equipped as warriors, especially **Indra** and others described as priests; especially **Agni (Fire)** and **Brhaspati (Guru; Jupiter).** The home of the gods is Heaven, where live a life of bliss. **Visnu** is just a god and not the supreme God as in current day Hinduism. The Vedic gods can most conveniently be classified as deities of Heaven, Air and Earth, according to the threefold division suggested by the Rig Veda contents.

Understanding of Vedic Religion. Some scholars have misunderstood Vedic Religion, which emanated from Vedas and later transited to Brahmanic period and during later centuries into various other schools of thoughts and Godhood. It is given to understand that present Hindu religion is in toto that of Vedas; **not so.** It is in the later centuries and when other religious scriptures appeared during Brahmanic period (*Upanishad's, Grantha's, Purana's* etc) that current day Hindu religion emerged with Gods, deities, ranging from the Trinty, Mahadevi's, to local deities Kul Devi/Deva's etc. Vedas and Aryan's had a major role in this development, factors which shaped religion and culture inhabited by various races, located in many parts and all these amalgamated over millenniums. Even today whole of Bharatvarsh does not claim to be Aryan's or Dravidian's alone. The religion, that took root starting from Vedic Period, with its rich pantheon of Gods and Goddesses, myths and legends, became the foundation of the Hindu religion, as the time passed and arguably became single most important common denominator of Bharatvarsh.

Gods and Goddesses of Vedas. The gods mainly stated in the Rig Veda; thirty-three in number, are divided into three groups of eleven each and distributed in Earth, Air, and Heaven; the three divisions of the Universe. This division of Gods in three groups has been suggested by contents of Rig Veda itself and there in no scope of dividing or terming them differently. There are celestial gods like **Varuna,** atmospheric gods **Vayu** (Air), and the **Water**. Certain rivers that are personified and invoked in the Rig Veda like Sindhu (Indus). The **principal divinity in Vedas** is **Indra,** the god of war and thunder. Initial portion of Rig Veda indicates and reflects confrontationist attitude and Indra mainly being used to destroy opposition. This can be attributed to Aryan efforts to settle down and spread across Bharatvarsh, in the initial centuries.

Vedic Goddesses play an insignificant part in the Rig Veda. The only one of importance is Usas (Usha; Dawn). Saraswati, celebrated in two whole Hymns as well as few others: Prthivi (Mother Earth); Ratri (Night); and Aranyani (Goddess of the Forest). The wives of the important Vedic gods are still more insignificant, mere names only mentioned.The second and smaller class of **abstract deities are** seven of them, comprising personifications of abstract nouns.

Importance of Some Vedic Gods. Interestingly except two books out of ten of Rig Veda start with invocation of **Agni**, indicating the importance given to Agni and rightfully so. Indra is invoked in nearly half of the Hymns of the Rig Veda, far more than addressed to any other deity; a favourite somewhat national god of the Vedic people, praised as the protector, helper, and friend of his worshippers. **Surya** is most concrete of the solar deities, always being present to the mind of the seers. **Varuna** also gets importance. There is also mention of **Prajapati**, more so in Yajur Veda and termed as overlord. This is not specific but used as a term as the holly one above them all; more of a salutation in recognition of certain super powers. In no way he is termed as Supreme to all other Vedic Gods.

In Atharv Veda Prajapati is mentioned many times in incantations but mostly as Lord of Creatures and mentioned likewise together with other Vedic Gods. **Visnu** occupies a subordinate position in the Rig Veda, being celebrated in only five or six Hymns. Thus, we see that Vedic Gods, except for the name of Visnu (Vishnu), are different from the Gods and Goddesses of Hinduism in later years/centuries. Visnu is also mentioned in **Sam Veda** and in similar fashion, in **Yajur Veda** where apart from some *homa's*, he is mentioned. The highest step of **Visnu** (Vishnu); in the Vedas, different from Vishnu of Hinduism, is just a god and not the supreme God.

It is with later scriptures Vishnu was given the title of the Trinty Head after ***Vishnu Purana*** was compiled and written (*Vishnu Purana*, covers five subjects namely primary creation, secondary creations, genealogies of gods and patriarchs). The importance of Vishnu of current Hinduism reduced once the

Shiv Purana and other scriptures were compiled. The example of this is though the Hinduism today revolves around the Trinty (Brahma, Vishnu and Mahesh) and their spouses (Mahadevi's; Saraswati, Lakshmi and Parvati), but in an overall count Shiva worship overtakes the worship of other Gods of the Trinty. So is with their spouses with Parvati having edged out the other two Mahadevi's and manifested in other forms as variously named Goddesses and Kul/Gram Devi's. It is not that only Vishnu is left out of Vedas, Shiva and Brahma do not find any mention in their present manifestation. In Vedas, Visnu's consort is Aditi (Not Lakshmi) and is mentioned together with other Vedic Gods.

In fact, except for Heaven, Fire (*Agni*), Air (*Yayu*) and Water, which are objects of veneration in current day Hinduism also, none of the Gods or Goddesses find their way in the worshipped pantheon of later day Hinduism. However, the rivers mentioned in the Vedas did get recognition of being holly; like **Ganga, Yamuna, Saraswati** etc, while others got revered on geographical lines like Vitasta, Kaveri etc.

Vedic Worship-Single God or Multiple God Worship. One has to transcend to the time of initial small group-wise settlements of Aryan's to understand their worship philosophy and even the religion they brought forward. These settlements were spread over vast areas of Bharatvarsh, closer to Rivers and where they could survive with the help of nature. The communication between these settlements would have been absent or rare even between close by settlements. Over the centuries they had observed ingredients of nature, on day-to-day basis, which formed necessary part of their lives; like Fire (Agni), Earth (Prithvi) which gave them food, Sun, Rain, Thunder, Night (Ratri), Water, Rivers etc. These were connected frequently, some on day-to-day basis, to their lives with something to contribute towards their survival. Naturally they became the objects of their initial veneration, which over the centuries graduated above the level of veneration; objects of worship. For their survival, for instance, there would have been fight even amongst the settlements or the original inhabitants for survival or supremacy. The thunder was all mighty and they called it Indra, a God; a warrior, an aggressive motivator to overcome opposition. Similar process evolved other Gods and over the centuries and even smaller essential elements became their objects of veneration. Necessarily all these did not manifest in one or few selected settlements, but manifested in vast number of settlements. This process, with improved physical communication and interaction, helped evolving a common vocabulary for these objects of veneration and their number increased and some, in this process, would have been discarded too. Thus, over the centuries a pantheon of Gods and Goddesses were evolved and slowly became the objects of worship through the medium of *Arthavan* or *Hotri*. Over the period Rishi's took over the onerous job of defining, minutely and in detail, attributes of these objects of veneration, which became the Vedic Gods and their praise or attributes found way as Hymns/Mantra's. Admittedly it was no different than what it is today; pantheon of Gods, Goddesses, Kul Deva/Devi's, Bhairava's etc. We do understand that there is someone above them all to whom these manifestations are attributed, but when it comes to day-to-day life and worship, it becomes specific to a God or Goddess. Grouping of Gods, eleven each, was culmination of well thought out role these gods were to perform.

Rig Veda begins with mantra/Hymn to God **Agni** designated as God **(Deva).** The reference to Agni as single God and reference thereafter to Gods is unambiguous. There appears to be no specific hierarchy amongst Vedic God's. In all the Vedas the word God (Deva) has been used very frequently and specifically pointing towards a particular God. Similarly, word Gods (Deva's/Devata's) has been used where a group of Vedic Gods were invoked.

An Old BW Photograph of a Man Reading Manuscript of a Veda

In the Vedas, more so in Rig Veda, each hymn is for a particular God and mantras in the hymn invoke him and, in many cases, together with his associate Vedic Gods.

Krishtinavichsharni! Patijargevrishkratu. (Praise him who, Matchless and Alone, was born the Lord of living men, Most active, with heroic soul) and **NOT** "O Man! Praise the ONE and only one Omniscient God, the lord of all beings." In such Hymns the particular God is quoted as *Sarva;* above others. It will be noticed that while Indra is the *Sarva* God in certain Hymns only.

Sacred Rivers of Vedas. Aryan settlements in Bharatvarsh, in the initial stages, were mostly South of Hindu Kush Mountain and Sindhu River. These settlements, in pockets, were spread in the North-Western Bharatvarsh including present day Northern portions of Gujarat, Rajasthan, undivided Punjab and at a later stage even Kasmira. As is with any human race, these settlements had come up around the sources of water, an essential ingredient to survive. The first major River in their daily life and which most of them would have seen or crossed by their ancestors was Sindhu. Sindhu River was revered. In Rig Veda Varuna is credited with cutting the path of Sindhu across Bharatvarsh and is invoked in Rig Veda. The mantra's concerning Sindhu (Now called Indus River, flowing all its course through present day Pakistan) talk about three rivers also; Sindhu's tributaries and **seven and seven refers to the seven rivers called Sapth Sindhu.** The most important and oftenest lauded river is, however, **River Saraswati** and frequently in all the four Vedas; "like a chariot, **Saraswati must be extolled by every sage**."

Aryan settlements also used River Saraswati as their defence and is termed as lady (Goddess). As the Aryan settlements spread Northwest and Eastwards, the came across other rivers who are praised thus; **"Favour ye this my lord, O Ganga, Yamuna, O Satudri (Satluj), Parusni and Saraswati: With Asikni, Vitasta (Jhelum, Wyeth), O Marudvrdha, O Arjikiya with Susoma hear my call (Rig Veda -10-75-5)."** The Rig Veda has special praise for Vipas (Beas) and Satudri (Sutlej) which apparently were flowing amidst Aryan settlements. The mention of the rivers would give a rough idea of the extent of Aryan settlements in Bharatvarsh, during the evolution of Vedas.In early Dharmashastras (Religious Scriptures), the homeland of Aryan's or Aryavarta is located in North India between Himalayas and Vindhya. There are many other Rivers mentioned in Rig Veda, many of whom cannot be recognised but find single mention in the Veda. Apparently, the Aryan's were conversant or their settlements were close to these rivers.

Vedic Rishi's. Saraswati, the mythical River was not only bountiful to the Aryan's but also Saraswati Bank Ashrams came up on its and banks of other rivers. The process was slow, steady and over a period of time. Aryan bards, singing Hymns, became priests called *Arthavan* and *hotri* (Priests who used to lead a body of Aryan's while on move on a mission) where the initial invokers of mantra's, more in the form of exaltation of the group of Aryan's they led. As the time passed, these *Arthavans/Hotri* took to teaching pupils, reciting and composition of new mantra's and where the beginners of *Guru-Shishya* custom. The exalted and excelled Gurus were the Rishi's, who in the Vedic Period composed the Vedas. This is the common as well as rational belief and is supported by the contents of Vedas, where many important Rishi's are mentioned by name. Analysis and deep study of Rig Veda reveals six of the ten books, two to seven, are homogeneous in character and Hymns contained in each of them appear composed or 'seen' by Rishi's or descendants **of the same Rishi family**, which handed them down. The tradition is borne out by the evidence of the Rishi's names mentioned in the Hymns, and by that of the refrains occurring in each of these books. The method of arrangement followed in these is uniform, for each of them is similarly divided into groups addressed to different gods. Books one, eight and ten (Rig Veda) do not appear to have been composed by a distinct Rishi or family of Rishi's and seem to have been composed by different Rishi's. Book nine is distinguished from the rest by all; its Hymns being addressed to one and the same deity, Soma, and by its groups being based not on identity of authorship, but of metre. Rig Veda talks of Saraswati River, banks of which Vedas have been composed by Rishi's. **Rig Veda--Saraswati;** "For thee, O Blest Saraswati, **Vasistha** hath here unbarred the doors of sacred Order. Wax, Bright One, and give strength to him who lauds thee. Preserve us evermore, ye Gods, with blessings." Rishi's **Jamadagni's**, Angiras are also mentioned. In Atharv Veda in one mantra other Rishi's: Viswamitra, Jamadagni, Vasistha, Bhardvaja, Gautama are invoked. In Yajur Veda there is specific mention of Rishi's thus: "May the gods take note of this (prayer) of mine; **may Indra together with the Rishis (take note of it**)!" Many more Rishi's are mentioned in the Vedas, while Atharv Veda is attributed to Rishi Atharvan.

The Sapth Rishi's (Seven Rishi's). In Brahmanical philosophy, Sapth Rishi's who are also attributed with the composition of Vedas or part thereof are; Bhrigu, Angiras,

Marichi, Atri, Paulaha, Pulastya and Vasistha, who founded the initial Brahaminical Gotra's. The fifth Rishi Paulaha brought forth demons (Rakshas); sixth Pulastya devils (Pisachas); while seventh Vasistha, died and appeared again as a descendant of Marichi. It will thus be seen that Angiras, who was amongst the first set of Rishi's could not become Gotra head as he could not properly represent as founders of families. Seven Rishi's heading Brahaminical Gotra's as enumerated in Satpatha Brahmana, a much later scripture, are different and are; Gautama, Bhardvaja, Jamadagni, Atri, Vasistha, Kasyapa and Visvamitra.

Relevance of Vedas. Vedas are treasure troves of knowledge of Aryans, their way of life and early worship. They are complete by themselves and do not need any support of later scriptures. Any effort to interpret them differently in the light of later scriptures will be counterproductive and take away the essence of their contents. Worship them as they are, as first scriptures of present-day Hinduism. In this 22st Century we must also respect the vast means of identification at our disposal, which was not so a century back. Healthy dissent is always welcome and that is what the Vedas have also taught.

Your mind is a powerful thing. When you filter it with positive thoughts, your life will start to change.
-Gautama Buddha.

4

S'arada Temple of Kasmira (Kashmir)

If you light a lamp for somebody,
it will also brighten your path.

–Gautama Buddha

(S'arada is the original written word in Sanskrit as well as S'arada Lipi. In common usage now it is generally referred to as Sharada. It is S'arada in Kalhan's Rajatarangini).

(The reference in this chapter as Kishanganga, Kishanganga/Neelam Valley and S'arada Shrine etc is on the current status of these places. Necessarily there are not all historically as they have been enumerated below).

S'arada Temple-Shardi (Kishanganga Valley)

Goddess S'arada of Kasmira. This temple in recent times has got lot of coverage in media, on both sides of the border and more you go into these, hazier becomes the actual history of this temple/shrine and the area. Three things of the shrine/temple get most prominence: Temple Structure and its construction; Veneration Spot (Kund) Sacredness and Goddess Sharada's Form and Role. Add to this claim of being a Buddhist Monument or its connection to Adi Shankaracharya!

Naturally in the maze of such claims, the actual history gets literally obliterated. The first time S'arada name is **chronicled** is in 12th Century by Kalhan in his Rajatarangini. A belief exists that there was a Spring/Pond (Kund-Known as S'arada Kund) in the centre of Sanctum Santorum, which centuries ago has dried up. This **Kund (Spring) of S'arada Shrine** is supposed to be the main object of veneration. It seems after the pilgrimage was resumed after a gap of nearly six centuries by Kasmiri's, after 1850's, the dried Kund was covered by six-inch-thick Stone slab becoming focal point of veneration, marked with vermillion, flower offerings and it is presumed a priest (s) (not many) would sit next to the slab to help with rituals. In normal case of temples, more priests would sit within the walled quadrangle to conduct individual religious ceremonies. Kund being main venerated spot one is unable to fathom the impression of a pilgrim, that there is no Kund but a stone slab inside the Sanctum or Santorum, in which legend says Goddess Saraswati disappeared. There was no idol in the past or confirmed record of any idol of Sharada, in her manifested role as Saraswati, inside the temple/shrine.

S'arada Form of Saraswati Worship. The deity, Sharada, was worshipped in Kasmira and even North-Western India, as Goddess of Knowledge. Simultaneously S'arada Language/ Lipi was also prevalent in North-Western India mid First Millennium onwards for many centuries. It remained as the Language and Script of Kasmira chronicles/scriptures and possibly connected with naming of the Shrine as Sharada. The S'arada Lipi/Language was synonymous with S'arada in her form of Goddess Saraswati a tripartite embodiment of the goddess **Shakti**: S'arada (goddess of learning), Saraswati (goddess of knowledge), and Vagdevi (goddess of speech, which articulates power). Shakti here does not represent a combined power of Tridevi's (Laxmi, Saraswati and Parvati). There is no earlier indication, chronicled proof whatsoever as to when; Shrine got the name Sharada, when did veneration of the tirath/shrine start and who constructed the temple around the Kund, in the centre of a fortified area. Is it a natural Kund or source is somewhere nearby? There are many more doubts which arise, like was the temple size tailored to the fitment of Kund or Kund size was dictated by the size of the temple Sanctum Santorum! From mid-19th Century to middle of 20th Century, pilgrimage to S'arada Tirath (Shrine) was termed as S'arada Tirath Yatra and not S'arada Mandir/Temple Tirath Yatra.

Glimpses of Sharada Shrine/Tirath/Temple

Temple With Backdrop of Kishanganga River

Sharada-Saraswati-Religious Philosophy. Sharada, as form of Goddess Saraswati, is celebrated in Kasmira on Guru Tritya (February) and another day on eighth day of rising moon in the month of September/October, as per lunar calendar. It was synonymous to use both S'arada and Saraswati, for it always meant the Goddess (s) of Knowledge and Learning.

With maze of accounts, folklore and myths; S'arada Temple seems to have become centre of Religious Philosophy, Chronicler's accounts, conflicting attributions, unknown events and debates. Most of these have been accepted, without any clue and also a different form of Goddesses S'arada (Saraswati) and Goddess Sharadaamba etc. The antiquity, attribution and *Mahima* (Sanctity) of the temple, deity, and changes, over the centuries, remained obscure, mostly hazy, or attributed to different sage's, scholar's etc. Frankly other than *Guru Tritya* ritual, one did not know anything more about S'arada or Saraswati. The word S'arada was not even heard, but reference was always to Goddess Saraswati. All that is heard is forgotten Tirath/Temple of Goddess Sharada.

Shrine or Temple-Rajatarangini. Word Shrine (Tirath), as it is the first known designation mentioned in earliest Chronicle; Rajatarangini by Kalhan. ***Rajatarangini*** (The River of Kings) is a metrical legendary and historical chronicle of the North-Western Indian subcontinent, particularly the Kings of Kasmira. It was written by historian Kalhan in 1149-1150 AD, in verse form, based on traditions, legends and inscriptions apart from older historical works of chroniclers before Kalhan. Rajatarangini provides the earliest source on Kasmira, that can be labelled as a "historical" text on this region. Although inaccurate in its chronology, the book provides is a valuable source of information about early Kasmira and its neighbours in the North-Western parts of the Indian subcontinent, and has been widely referenced by later historians and ethnographers. In Rajatarangini this temple, as shrine, (Tirath or Temple) gets mentioned in just four verses (Book 1 -V 37, Book 4-V 325 and Book 8-V 2557, 2706). The first time this Shrine is mentioned in any ancient scripture, specifically as ***S'arada*** only, no shrine no tirath), is by Kalhana in his Rajatarangini in 1148-1149 AD in Verse 325 Book IV, which in terms of time period is around (724-761 AD).

The ***Shrine*** word if analysed and as used by Kalhan at many places, has lot of inferences. The Shrine means a *Tiratha*, a place of pilgrimage. Tirtha (तीर्थ: Tīrtha) is a Sanskrit word that particularly refers to pilgrimage sites and holy places in Hinduism as well as Jainism.

Location S'arada Shrine. Situated in Kishanganga Valley (Now named Neelam Valley after Kishanganga River, for politico-religious feelings was renamed as Neelam River), few Kilometres from Line Of Control (LOC), in Pakistan Occupied Kasmira (POK), in a small village called Shardi; near the confluence of Kishanganga River. The original name of this River as given in Nilmata Purana is Krsna. The reason being the source of the river is Krishansar Lake on the Harmukh Mountain Range. Water from it drains out through a small stream into the adjacentVishansar Lake and gives rise to river Krsna (Short for Krishna). However, it appears that Krsna name was not much used, but locals claim **Parvati Ganga** is its oldest and some local legends and folk songs also indicate that it bore the name of **Parvati Ganga** in past. Not much more is known about its any other names, though Maha Sindhu, Sindhu Ganga, Parvati Ganga are also being talked about, though Sindhu Ganga is generally reference to Lower Sindh in the valley. The local records indicate that it is around 1850's during Dogra rule when trout fish was imported from France and were put in this river and the river officially christened as Kishan-Ganga River. Notable is that Kishan was substituted for Krishan (Possibly referring to Lord Krishna). Kankatori Stream is referred to as Saraswati and Madhumati Stream has been named in recent centuries as all along there is only one Madhumati River in Bandipora inside the valley. In fact the ancient names of various streams and places have been redacted to create landmarks for this shrine.

S'arada Shrine/Temple at its Highest Grandeur has been there for more than a Millennium at least. Though the area in which it is situated, had its importance as a belligerent strip of a valley, treatises, legends with woven stories have appeared in the recent past. Even now called **'a forgotten Monument'**: in ruins, physically protected by Pakistan Army as a Post, due to its proximity to dividing line of the divided Kasmira. Ironically for reasons unknown and unverified, Archaeological Survey of Pakistan has declared it as a **"Protected Buddhist Monument"**. This has added another dimension to the origin of the Monument and connected implications, which are more on the lines of **"Attribution of Monument to a different Religion"**.

Roop Bridge over Kishanganga River in Neelum Valley by Baden Henry Baden-Powell c. 1872

Mercifully, in spite of such claims, name of S'arada Temple (Tirath) and nearby village named Shardi remains, till this day. Though the demography of the area has changed, from original inhabitants Dards, the warrior tribe of ancient history, to a mixed population but some semblance in the Eastern and Northern parts of this valley, who retain a fair percentage of Dards.

Grandeur of the Temple. The temple is approached from West by an imposing stone staircase, from the direction of Sirhasila Castle/Fort, now nearly decayed and collapsed, which leads up in 63 steps 9/10 feet wide, between two flanking walls of massive row of parapet coping (Balustrade), now in ruins, to the main entrance of the quadrangular court enclosing the temple. The stairs rise rather steeply and one has a magnificent view of the valley down. The quadrangular court encloses the temple by a massive wall, six feet thick and eleven feet high, is an accurately oriented oblong; 142 feet long and 94 feet 6 inches wide. The later rises in pyramidal form, to a height of eight feet above the top of the wall, making it a **Fortress Wall**, which actually it was meant to be. There are number of inbuilt fighting bunkers, in the wall and remains of couple of watch towers. The thickness of walls 6 feet and 11 feet high, are unheard of in any Shrine, Temple in complete North-Western India. Such walls, without any design and unorganised construction have been seen in the North-Western India and also many places in the erstwhile Bharatvarsh, to wade off attacks by invaders. **Temple/Shrine in the Centre seems to be incidental**.

Entry Arch and Front Wall. The entrance to the central court is through a gate, with a double porch of *Kasmiri* design (When referred as *Kasmiri* design, it connotes design as found in other structures of later first millennium period in Kasmira). Remarkable points to note are: restricted entry space, unlike for important temples, recess in the entry gate walls apparently for sentries to be in position. Arch merged with the massive front wall and restricts any movement away from the narrow track and entry gate. The gate is in line with the porch, leading to the **sanctum sanctorum**. From outside, these walls around are massive, **more of a defensive wall with loop holes and shelters, similar to the fort walls**. It will also be wrong to assume that the walls were basically meant to be enclosure walls.

Two Views- Collapsed Temple Entry Arch (In Ruins)

Temple Walls. The stones used in constructing the walls are crude cuttings. The walls are irregular in height and uneven pattern, stones quarried from mountains close by and just cut in irregular shapes and sizes. The wall structure clearly and ubiquitously indicates that the walls were of Defensive role and it cannot be the defence of Shrine/Temple, as no invader worth his salt in the region would attack a Shrine/Temple. Definitely such walls are not constructed around planned temples. Outer walls of monuments in Kasmira definitely have a pattern; chiselled stone cutting done by artisans and laid according to a pattern. None of the temples have walls of such a thickness with loopholes or watch posts. Medieval Kasmira Temple enclosure walls are more part of the monument and merge aesthetically with the main structure. It may be quoted that there are walls around some important Temples in North-Western or Northern India and like Martand Sun Temple or Avantiswamy Temple at Avantipur (Kasmira). These two temples of Kasmira, had multi monuments within their precincts and space was meant for large gatherings including King's and entourage, which is not so in the case of S'arada Temple at Shardi. The walls of these monuments were well planned, not so thick or high, with proper measurements and quality and laying of stones.

The other three walls have blank archway, standing to height of about 20 feet from the base to the apex. In the centre of the Northern wall is a small recess 3 feet 3 inches square, reportedly containing two *lingas (Idols),* which opens by a Tera foil arched door towards the interior of the court (in earlier accounts there is no mention of existence of these idols).

Sharada Temple Walls- Mostly Collapsed- In Ruins
Massive Walls With Conspicuous Watch Towers

Left: Side of the Wall with Conspicuous Watch Structure
Right: Corner a Collapsed Watch Tower is Conspicuous

Side Wall with Recess

Walls With Watch Towers

Sharada Temple Walls- Mostly Collapsed- In Ruins
Massive Walls With Conspicuous Watch Towers

Left: Side of the Wall with Conspicuous Watch Structure
Right: Corner a Collapsed Watch Tower is Conspicuous

Side Wall with Recess

Walls With Watch Towers

Sanctum Sanctorum. In the centre of the quadrangle is the temple raised on a basement, perfectly plane square, of 24 feet by 5 feet 3 inches high. As per the Hindu Scriptures and Dictums; "a temple's specific alignments relate to the geography of the place and the presumed linkages of the deity and the patron. At the centre of the temple, typically below and sometimes above or next to the deity, is mere hollow space with no decoration, symbolically representing *Purusa*, the Supreme Principle, the sacred Universal, one without form. The temples face sunrise, and the entrance for the devotee is typically this east side. while west and south feature demons and demi-gods related to the underworld; has a superstructure with a dome called ***Shikhara*** in north India."

In this case, due to restraints of location, purpose of the walls etc, above norms of temple construction have not been applied. This is because the Shrine structure, it appears, has come up within a fortified area, where such dictums are not possible or feasible. It does not however reduce the sanctity of the Temple/Shrine.

First Time Coloured Photograph of the S'arada Shrine/Temple, Which I got in 2003.

This Photograph was shared by me in Various Periodicals, Articles, throughout India. It was First time in the Country the Latest Photograph (2003) was seen, shared and quoted).

Readers may find big stone block in the Sanctum Santorum in my photo of 2003. This is apparently was one of the collapsed stone block of the temple wall and not the thick slab covering the Kund. In later photographs of the temple Sanctum Santorum (Above), this stone block was apparently removed after 2003 photograph.

The entrance to inner temple is from the west side, which is approached by a flight of a few stairs, which now has just traces of collapsed flanking side walls, including the stairs. The cell of the main shrine/temple is 22 feet square. This can also state that it was on each side of the porch way are two square pillars about 16 feet high and two feet six inches apart. The 'capital' of both the pillars seems to have been hewn from a single stone. This aspect is very important, as similar evidence can be found in temples constructed in Kasmira between 9th and 13th Centuries AD and not earlier.

The interior of the inner temple is a square of 12 feet and 3 inches and it has no decoration of any kind; perfectly plane and scarcely has no traces of the usual pyramidal or Shikhar type dome type stone roof. From the absence of debris which when such roof when destroyed or collapsed, creates doubt as to whether a roof ever existed. In 19th Century the cella was covered by a low shingle roof (See Photos below). This too seems to have collapsed as no such roof existed when I got the latest photograph of the shrine/temple in 2003. The only conspicuous object inside reported by Sir Auriel Stein, as seen by him during his visit in 1892, was a **large slab**, which measured about 6 by 7 feet, nearly covering the half of the inner Sanctum Sanctorum, with a thickness of about six inches. This slab is **believed** to have covered ***kund*** or spring.

Glimpses of Sharada Shrine/Tirath/Temple

Temple With Backdrop of Kishanganga River

Front and Back View Right Photo: Shows Pakistan Army Structure/Sentry

Side Views and Sanctum Santorum

Mystery of Temple Kund -S'arada Kund

Sanctity of Kunds (Springs-Nags) In Kasmira. The sanctity of Kund's (Springs) also called Nag's, in Kasmira, so also elsewhere, are venerated even before the God's and Goddesses manifested. In fact, such venerated Kund's-Nag's were later associated or named after Goddesses (mostly) and most became places of pilgrimage-veneration. In the Kasmira valley there are many such sacred Nags-Kund's termed as Tirtha's, almost all of them venerated even now. Tulla Mullaya (popularly known as Tul Mul-Kheer Bhawani in the Country), was initially a small spring.

A Painting of Tulla Mullya Kund-Mid 19th Century which has been one of the most Venerated Shrine in the Kasmira Valley

Similarly, Kali Shree Spring (Spring Water outlet on the banks of River Vitasta (Wyeth-Jhelum) at Khanqah-e-Moulla (Srinagar), Maisuma Bhairav, Mattan, Vichar Nag, Sada Ganga, Kapal Mochan, Vyethvuttur (Source of River Vitasta-Jhelum) springs etc, which are venerated even now except the first one which is blocked inside a Kahnqah (Masjid). In many such places no temples had been constructed, but became pilgrimage places; Tirtha's (Shrines). Such natural Springs (Nags) are taken as gift of nature to the mankind, to be revered. At such places it was a ritual to look into the Nag (Spring), see own reflection, which was considered as a successful pilgrimage or sip water from these as Amrit (Holy Nectar). Subsequently temples came around such Kund's-Nag's over the Centuries.

This phenomenon is prevalent all over the country and the world.

Temple and S'arada Kund (Amarkund). Interestingly there is a small opening in the east side of the wall about three feet wide, which leads to a spring (S'arada Kund). A chance reading of amplification notes on Kalhan's Rajatarangini by Auriel Stein raised some doubts, wherein he perfunctorily mentions: "There is a small cella (Small room) on the east side of the enclosing wall, and about 5 feet to the South of it a square postern (Back door or gate), 3 feet broad. It gives access to the terraces on the hillside rising behind the temple, and to a spring called **Amarkunda**, somewhat higher up". It was surprising trail more so, when just a covered dry Kund in the Sanctum Santorum was venerated as the main spring. Apparently, for obvious reasons the actual Kund (S'arada Kund) was side lined and called Amara Kunda so that sanctity and importance remain with the temple Kund within the enclosed walls.

S'arada Kund and Temple Kund. A fresh input received from S'arada temple on 31 July 2022, unravels the mystery of **S'arada Kund, its Shrine connection**, which possibly changes the entire perception and history of the Shrine. Thanks to **Khawaja Abdul Ghani,** a Writer and Adventurer of Shardi, We are all made to aware that the Kund, in the centre of the Sanctum Santorum, had dried up centuries ago and was covered up by a thick slab, which also disappeared decades back, was venerated by Pilgrims, devotees as S'arada Kund. Lot of folk lore of treasure etc inside the dry Kund were floated in the area. In fact, many decades back, a clan head of a nearby area removed the slab and was disappointed that it turned out to be just a dried up Kund (Pit). The slab whereabouts are not known.

From around 12th Century till early 1800s the temple remained deserted due to disturbed conditions and Islamic rule. However, the main spring (S'arada Kund) continued to be revered by Chak's, Dard's and Muslim's of the area and even areas nearby. The reason for their reverence is understandable. From the time of their ancestors, passed on from one generation to another, remembered that a Kund around was a holly site. They too revered it but temple was taboo for them as their religion, Islam, did not allow entry to temples, more so that the Kund in the Sanctum Santorum was extension of main Kund. The Dards, though had converted to Islam but they carried with their ancient religious beliefs, which were more connected with Vedic Religion. To endorse the sanctity of the S'arada Kund, a legend of one S'arada Mai (Mother) added to the sanctity of the S'arada Kund. This legend and faith in S'arada Kund continues till today and has spread even to far off places.

Gilgit Baltistan had been under Muslim Rulers (*Khushwakhte* Dynasty) when Dogra's expedition to Gilgit Baltistan was launched in 1840 AD under General Zorawar Singh, who captured the area for Sikh Darbar/Dogra's. It became part of Jammu and Kashmir State in 1846 AD, when Gulab Singh acquired the Valley from British in 1846 AD but lost Gilgit Baltistan in 1852 AD. During the decade 1840-1850 there was hardly any pilgrim visiting this place. Gilgit -Baltistan was recaptured in 1876 AD during the reign of Maharaja Ranjit Singh. Of necessity for maintenance and control of Gilgit Baltistan, routes to Gilgit-Baltistan had to be secured. Dogra Army established staging points, small garrisons and posts in the area. A fortified post was established next to the temple. The pilgrimage must have started in 1870 ± and the first to visit where Brahmin priests from Gushi etc. Some even settled down in the nearby village, which got the name Shardi, after the Shrine. To my mind they must have found the ancient Kund outside the temple complex, which was apparently referred to as Sharadakund in scriptures, which they had known as S'arada Kund and thus restarted ancient worship. However, they must have found that an outlet or Kund had been created in the Sanctum Santorum, which was dried up. It seems that a slab was put in the centre for veneration and this is borne by the fact that it was marked with vermilion, flowers etc used to be offered on the slab. There being no idol to worship, two small idols must have been installed in the recess of the walls.

On 31 July, 2022, I got the photographs from my adventurer and writer Khawaja Abdul Ghani, who shared two photographs of the S'arada Kund: "This water pond has a special historic and religious significance..... This is the famous "**S'arada Kund.** water of this pond was carried to the main temple through a unique and amazing water supply scheme. Water supply pipes were made of compacted clay and were buried very deep to keep the running water safe. This pond is still considered auspicious among the local Muslims of the S'arada village. Much more legends and stories are associated with this pond. It is located some feet above the S'arada temple."

7th August, 2022. On my request Khawaja Abdul Ghani took a video clip of the S'arada Kund and then path towards the temple along a Narrow path, with shrubs and trees on either side. The temple top and temple walls are clearly visible from the path. It will not be possible to really fix the time line when this extension of Kund Water took place. One may guess that it may have been at the time of construction of the Temple and definitely as an add on. Could it be to facilitate the worship and water for the Damra (war Lord) living in nearby Sirhasila Castle?

S'arada Kund Facts. Certain details of this Kund have been covered in earlier part of this chapter. Underground deep dug in compact channels, brought water from the S'arada Kund to the centre of the Complex, which was inside a big thick-walled courtyard, built in later centuries. A look at the walls shows that there are recesses and openings to outside view, as is common in forts for defence purposes. The Kund (Spring) outside the complex seems to be the main object of reverence. It is evident that recess of about three feet in the Northern wall of the complex was kept so that the Pilgrims and devotees could also pay obeisance to the actual Kund, apart for bringing water to the complex.

S'arada (Sharada) Kund To Temple Kund

Underground Compact Earth Channel From S'arada Kund to Temple Sanctum Santorum

Photo's, Video Grabs Courtesy-Khawaja Abdul Ghani- August 2022

I fully understand that this new fact, may not be acceptable to many or even if accepted it will be with certain reservations. It is a fact that with passage of time, exchange of freshly discovered or recount of places, the history of a place is updated and slowly will be accepted, provided it has self-explanatory reasoning.

It could not have been called as S'arada Kund, ab-inito as S'arada word or Goddess was alien to the area. S'arada word trickled into the area, Kasmira much later, with the development of Sidhi-Matrika Lipi, name transited later to S'arada Lipi/Language around Sixth-Seventh Century AD in North-Western India.

Mahima (Grace) of Goddess Sharada. My Own Association. As a young boy I used to hear folk tales from my paternal Granny, but what interested me was her narration of travelogue, experiences of our ancestors, passed on from one generation to another. One of the tales, casually, was visit to S'arada Shrine of Kasmira, where. one of my ancestors lost his life at the temple, while having a ritual bath in Kishanganga River. This incident is still held in the memory of locals where S'arada Shrine/Tirath is located. Goddess Saraswati meant a lot to me, in my quest to do well in studies. It was then casually mentioned, S'arada was a Roop (Form) of Goddess Saraswati (Goddess of Knowledge). But alas, unlike other places, which I could visit, I had to satisfy myself with imaginative details of places mentioned in her travelogue, including S'arada Shrine/ Temple.

Time flew; in 1976, I was literally crawling on my fours to reach a mountain top in Kupwara District close to the dividing line called LOC (Line of Control between India-Pakistan in the erstwhile Jammu and Kashmir State), called as ***Raja Ram Di Lari*** (See Map). As I stood on top of over 14000 feet High Mountain; Hari Parvat, Nanga Parbat and K2 peaks (These are some of the highest mountain Peaks in the Occupied Kashmir, including Gilgit-Baltistan), all across LOC, formed the magnificent backdrop of the Northern skyline of Kishanganga Valley. The valley earlier was called Kishanganga Valley as Kishanganga River flowed through the area, but was renamed after a small town called Neelam, as Neelam Valley and Kishanganga River name changed to Neelam River, after 1947 when the area came under Pakistan's control. In the middle distance two peaks stood magnificently, known locally as Sharada-Narada Peaks. All this information was given to me by a local guide, who was conversant with the areas across the LOC. Prior to 1947, there used to be lot of to and fro movement of local inhabitants from both sides including some local Hindus, who dared to go on a pilgrimage. In fact, some of the priestly class, affiliated to the shrine, had created a nearby settlement along with locals and till this day is called Shardi village after the S'arada Shrine.

Along forward slopes of these twin-peaks I could not see the lake down below, but I could see, through binoculars, a structure in a thick-walled compound with a narrow-walled passage leading to it. Kishanganga River flowed few hundred feet below this structure, with many more rivulets, small and big, racing to merge with the river. It was S'arada Temple. Months later I was over the area in a helicopter and my pilot colleagues made it point to remain hovering over the area to enable me to have more look of the Shrine/Temple. The travelogue I had heard from my grandmother had got translated into close landmarks and did not remain just a fiction. Study of our history, religious places, translated scriptures, books, over the decades and inclination brought me to a stage that I could understand these accounts better.

Other S'arada Shrine/Tirath's in Kasmira. A series of S'arada Shrines/Tirath's came up within the valley. I would say, these were not established in isolation or any connect with Kishanganga Temple, but like other temples dedicated to different Gods and Goddesses. But it seems that **one**

at Kaloosa (Bandipur-Kashmir) is the ancient of them all, even before this Shrine, as it finds mention by Al Biruni (inference), also indirectly by Kalhan and Abu Fazal. This being important revelation, is being covered in full details in Chapter V. Somewhat strange that there were five S'arada Shrines in the Valley but Auriel Stein in Rajatarangini quotes only two but later mentions one at Rangvor (Gushi) which is on route to S'arada of Kishanganga Valley. An important landmark associated with S'arada Shrine is Madhumati. For unknown reasons the S'arada Shrine on real Madhumati was glossed over by him, taking readers to refer it to S'arada of Kishanganga Valley. Add to this; today the 5th September 2022 is S'arada Ashtami and supposed to be the day for pilgrimage to S'arada of Kishanganga Valley. Auriel Stein started for only visit to this shrine in September 1892. Ironically there were no pilgrims and he was accompanied by a Purohit of Sogam (Lolab) Sant Ram and next day was joined by Chandra Pandit another Purohit of Goethng. Does it ring a bell that pilgrimage in 1892 AD was not there, but he specifically wanted to find S'arada Shrine for his achievements, and for reasons unknown even though quotes Al Biruni, Abu Fazl's pointed reference does not visit S'arada Shrine at Kaloosa. Strange indeed!

Due to political conditions of Kasmira, Kishanganga Valley and suspension of pilgrimage coupled with natural difficulties of the route, series of substitutes for this Tirtha came up within the valley. The best known amongst these is the Nag (Spring-Kund) called **Saradakunda** at the village of Tsatsa close to Harvan, close to the city of Srinagar. No temple was constructed, only the Kund was revered and worshipped. This Saradakunda was visited exactly on the dates for the Sarada Shrine in Kishanganga Valley and large crowds used to visit the Kund on the designated day. Few other similar S'arada veneration places: Gushi, another Sarada is mentioned in near the village Kulyandi (Khuyhom) (North Kasmira). In all these places, one thing is common: a **S'arada Kund (Spring),** as also in **S'arada** in Kishanganga/Neelam Valley: a point of interest.

S'arada Mahatmaya and S'arada Kund. *Mahatmaya's*are scriptures pertaining to various pilgrimages. 51 *Mahatmaya's* existed or have been traced in Kasmira. Most of these have been extracted from *Purana's S*'arada *Mahatmaya*, is a similar scripture, narrates *tirtha* as seen by Muni Shandliya. Relevant extracts pertaining to S'arada Kund: "After reciting a hymn in praise of her triple form of *S*harada, *Narda or Saraswati* and *Vaghdevi*, goddess revealed herself to the Muni at the 'sacred spot.' a *kund* or spring, from which Goddess S'arada appeared to the Sage Shandliya. As per Mahatmaya thereafter "She disappears inside a spring *(Kund),* " invites him to Her residence at Sirhasila".

This *kund was to be* object of special veneration of the pilgrims. It is interesting to note that Nilmata Purana Verse 1278-79 (Sixth Century AD Scripture) "(by bathing in) the confluence of the Krsna and the Vitasta and gets the merit of performing Vahnistoma by seeing Cakresa (Shiva) erected by Shandliya on the bank of the Madhumati". Here in Kishanganga S'arada MuniShandliya is quoted. This is Definitely S'arada Mahatmaya is of later vintage. Can these two be same! In the Mahatmaya local names clearly betray a comparatively modern composition or given a hue of ancient names to give it antiquity. I would not like to mention, motive and why particular places nearly at the Northern edge of the Kasmira valley, nearer to a group of Brahmin villages have been used in the Mahatmaya. Definitely some of the place names did not exist earlier but have been created in this Mahatmaya. Sadly, most of these are back to their ancient local names. Stein himself admits: "S'arada Mahatmaya is 'claimed' to be from Bringhisamhita metamorphosed local names have been used clearly betrays a comparatively modern composition or at least redaction. Even in the comparative neighbourhood of ancient S'arada Shrine Kishanganga Valley and on the very route to it, a shrine had been created to adjoining the grove at Gusa (Gushi) known as Rangvor (Rangwar) with ancient and mentioned above a small walled enclosure in which few fragments of ancient appearance idols are kept and is considered is locally considered a shrine of Sharada". Another quote which gives insight into the facts of Mahatmaya's, Stein mentions about a Purohit who told him that a Mahatmaya was under preparation for a find of old lingas near Ganpatyar (locality of Srinagar). Few weeks later the Purohit brought a draft of the Mahatmaya and asked Stein's assistance to revise it. Stein found that the drafts were chiefly extracted from Nilamata and neighbouring tirthas within the city with laudatory verses culled from other texts. As per him the Mahatmaya was later circulated. My aim is to point out that as how Muni Shandliya was lifted from Nilamata in a similar way to fit in S'arada Mahatmaya and Mahatmaya's being quoted as old scriptures should be taken with a pinch of salt.

Inferences S'arada Kund and S'arada Mahatmaya. Inference from above two inputs are many, some of which may be different from beliefs, which exist even today. The main Shrine seems to be the S'arada Kund, outside the perimeter of the present Shrine/Temple complex. We are aware that the area was troubled area and as such Fort like perimeter walls surround the temple ruins. An underground channel seems to have been made to bring the water from the revered **holly Kund** to the centre of the complex and a little Kund in the centre became the place of veneration within a secure place. It also seems to be the source of water to the persons in the complex. This system seems to be operative till about 13th /14th Century AD. Troubled conditions and advent of Islam stopped any visits to the shrine. The period was long enough to block the "water supply pipes were made of compacted clay and were buried very deep to keep the running water safe" (It seems to be the channel more than pipes). The water channel ended in the small Kund, which apparently dried up due to blockade of the channel. Pilgrimage to the shrine were resumed only after 1850 AD during the Dogra rule and seems "The dried *kund* in the centre of the shrine was covered with stone slab, which was then venerated as the form of the Goddess." No need was felt for an idol as, in any case, during the medieval age, no firm shape was given to Gods and Goddess's and generally they were formless.

Saraswati Lake. Kalhan talks about River Saraswati, whose source is this lake, thus: "There when visiting the (Shrine of the Goddess) Sharada, one reaches at once the river Madhumati, and the (river of) Saraswati worshipped by poets." In fact, for the shrine as well as Kasmira were closely associated 'Land of Saraswati-Sarada'. **Could it be again reference to Kaloosa S'arada Shrine at Bandipur**? Here I must mention that details about Saraswati Lake in Kishanganga valley were provided by a close friend, with common interest Sharada-Kishanganga/Neelam Valley, Dr Rukshana Khan, who has been in fore front to unravel some of the archaeological finds in Kishanganga/Neelam Valley. I recall her account of visit to this lake, arduous, where her colleagues had given up, but she continued in her mission. It was during her exploration of the Saraswati Lake, she found proper Bathing Places, with well-placed stone slabs on the home banks of the Lake.

In the Vedas, more so in Rig Veda, each hymn is for a particular God and mantras in the hymn invoke him and, in many cases, together with his associate Vedic Gods.

Again, the name Saraswati Lake is alien to this area in ancient times. In ancient chronicles and memory the stream taking the water to the Kishanganga River is named **Kankatori. Madhumati stream is also a small stream and possibly required less attention than Madhumati River of Bandipur.**

Sharada-Narada Peaks and Sarswati Lake

Sharada- Narada Twin Peaks Above Saraswati Lake

Photos Courtesy: Dr Rukshana Khan- AJK University

The Peak names, various water bodies mentioned above are as per their connection with S'arada Shrine but are recent ones; three Peaks, with three lakes at their bases; highest Peak is named Katsil. However, they have been named Sharada, Narada and Vaghdevi. Actually, Narada was named Saraswati but also referred to as Narada. These lakes did not have any names earlier but seems to have been named around the visit to S'arada Shrine started. Now-a-days **Saraswati is called Chattian** lake, Sharda lake name remains and **Vagdevi is Nareel Sar (Lake)**; all adjacent to each other. The water streams from these lakes flows in different directions.

Saraswati River (Kankatori) Near S'arada Temple and joins Kishanganga River

Right-Satellite Map S'arada Valley

The Shrine was absolutely deserted before Sikh Durbar Invasion in the beginning of 19th Century when the Rajah (War Lord) of Karanav (Karanah-Titwal Sector) ruled practically as independent Chief of Kishanganga Valley. At the beginning of Dogra Rule, Goetheng Brahmins (Gushi Belt) were settled near to the Shrine for priestly ceremonies at a place close by which was named Shardi. The last head priest was appointed by the Dogra's in 1945, who now a nonagenarian has settled in an Ashram with lot of followers who are pursuing the cause of S'arada Shrine being made similar to Kartarpur Corridor.

Main Temple Construction. Overall, a careful study of the main temple cella, it has been built of a friable sandstone with blocks by no means remarkable for size or artisan dressing. The material used and solidity of construction, the shrine/ temple decidedly is inferior to the enclosing quadrangle. This also gives an indication that stress was more on the quadrangle walls than the temple. One cannot rule out that quadrangle was constructed earlier than the monument/Temple. The whole appearance as well as careful study, with the whole shape and appearance of the cella, peculiarities of its dimensions, the construction cannot be of any great antiquity. This is also the view of Sir Auriel Stein, when he visited the complex in 1892 AD. One of the most recent accounts of the visit to the Sharda is provided by A.R. Nazki in the book 'Cultural Heritage of Kashmiri Pandits'. Nazki visited the S'arada from Muzaffarabad in POK in 2007AD and in the chapter titled 'In search of Roots', he describes the treacherous yet tranquil terrain to Shardi made even more inaccessible after the earthquake of 2005. Mr. Nazki describes the state of ruin of the temple and details out all that has been able to bear the neglect of decades. He writes of the faint inscriptions in the Sharda script on the entry pillar of the temple and remnants of quarters where the Pujaris must have lived in the days gone by. Only the left half of the archway stands and the door and the roof of the temple are no longer there. The university which used (Sic reportedly) to thrive at Sharda has no remains and apparently there **used to be a pond with healing water** in the compound which has since dried up. Nazki writes, "The building presented a picture of ruin and is a victim of neglect, its academic and instructional importance appear to be only a dream". The words **"used to be a pond with healing water" definitely refers to S'arada Kund not the Temple Kund.**

Collapsed Stairs Leading to the Entrance to The Shrine/ Temple Complex and Late 18th Century Photograph, with Temporary Roof Structure.

(The Photograph of the stairs is latest-March 2022-Courtesy: Khawaja Abdul Ghani Neelam Valley)

Study of Collapsed Stairs. A careful study of the collapsed stairs, give clue and possibly how it existed before the stone slabs were laid as stairs. On the either side of the stairs, which seems to be path way to the Shrine Complex are typical gradients indicating that it was a narrow path approach to the complex. On the sides are relatively higher ground, which is normal way to create a path uphill. From 13th/14th Century the area remained disturbed with Chak, Dard, Bomba clans infighting and clashes. The place must have been used by the clans, War Lords to defend their territory also. In fact before Dogra rule and even preceding the Sikh Durbar invasion the Muslim Rajahs (War lord) of Karnah (Karnav) ruled as practically independent chiefs of the Kishanganga/Neelam Valley.

What does above indicate? First: it was Kund (Spring) just outside the Shrine Perimeter, from time immemorial and known as S'arada Kund in later centuries. The Kund was considered holly and became place of reverence. With the advent of S'arada Lipi/Language, which became predominant in Kasmira as well as North-Western India, somehow it got addendum Sharada. How the Kund got the name of S'arada Kund cannot be established with certainty. But it is evident that it came about after Sixth Century and before 12th Century. Former as Nilmat Puranam does not mention this name or Goddess and later as Kalhan mentions it in his Rajatarangini (12th Century). Rajatarangini Verse 325 Book IV, mentions "the visiting Sarada", however, in next Verse 326; "Seeing them eager to enter while King was away in a foreign country, the attendant priest closed the gate of the [temple of] Visnu Parihasa[kesava], which in terms of time period is around (724-761 AD). One cannot find reason of mentioning S'arada when the team of Gauda's reach temple of Parihasa (kesava) at Parihaspura (Paraspura). Surely two cannot be connected and gets more clarified in Verse 323, when the reason clearly indicates that Parihasakesava was made surety by the King Lalitaditya as surety of his guest. Apparently it was to reach Parihaspura to destroy Lalitaditya's favourite object of devotion: the Golden idol of Parihasakesava.

S'arada name seems for this particular shrine seems to have come up around 11th/12th Century, I am not even sure if any or anyone were even fully aware of the existence of the Temple in Drava country. Apparently for the Kishanganga Area War Lord (Damra) it was just a Fort with a Kund (Spring-S'arada Kund extension) in the centre of it and on which a Temple Structure was constructed. Even Jona Rajatarangini does not mention word S'arada Temple/Shrine (14/15th Century). On the other hand, Al Biruni had mentioned S'arada Shrine in 1031 AD in his Tarik I Hind.

(Photographs Courtesy Khawaja Abdul Ghani Neelam Valley-January 2022)

S'arada Script Inscriptions on Stones/Rocks Found in Kishanganga/Neelam Valley

Kalhan wrote Rajataranginiin Sanskrit writing in S'arada script. S'arada remained par excellence language and script of Kasmira as late as 19th Century, use of which was restricted to scriptures and Brahmin religious writings. It never lend its name to the valley, *S*'arada Deshand S'arada *Mandala,* owing it to deity S'arada but simply Kashir, Kasmira; seldom as Satisar. S'arada was evolved when the language of Kasmira was passing into Kasmiri, with its peculiar intonations, variations and sounds, as a result S'arada language, imprinted with vocal peculiarities, became unfit for Sanskrit but continued to be used for writing Sanskrit in Kasmira. A birch bark manuscript of *Munimata Manimala,* which is 'earliest known S'arada manuscript' discovered in Kasmira, belongs to this third stage i.e. 14th Century. *Kharoshti* belongs to the same period as Brahmi. Till 14th-15th Century AD, even tombstones of Muslims in Kasmira were inscribed in Sharada. S'arada was thus pushed under, however, older generation of priests continued with S'arada till fifties/sixties of 20th Century. I was sweetly surprised to see my horoscope, written in early sixties, in S'arada Script forcing me to learn S'arada alphabets.

S'arada Mahatmaya. The relevant extract from Mahatmaya have been enumerated in the beginning to connect S'arada Kund and Shrine/Temple. I recall around 20 years back I read S'arada Mahatmaya in detail and an article on S'arada Temple by Late PNK Bamzai, a noted scholar of Kasmira. I wanted to meet him, which I did, about S'arada Mahatmaya, apart from other topics. I specifically asked him; Antiquity of S'arada Mahatmaya; Could it also be Part of Bringhisamhita? Is it a later version by Priests of Gushi or Shardi, who have woven these details?

As explained few paragraphs earlier, my take is of its later Vintage. Notably most of the places mentioned in the Mahatmaya though under different names can be made out. She here is represented as *Mahadevi*-Consort of Shiva; Parvati or Uma, which she is not as S'arada of Kasmira.

Indicators from S'arada Mahatmaya. There are certain indications from *S'arada Mahatmaya;* it confirms that temple had not been constructed and it was the Kund (Spring-S'arada Kund) which was venerated. Peculiar names of places have been used; place names, features given in the account can even be identified today but many other names are more scholarly names.

Kalhan also refers to Sindhu Ganga and Madhumati, but these are different from Kishanganga and Madhumati of Sharada. Also, Kalhan's reference is to sacred river Madhumati (Near Bandipur) and not Madhumati of S'arada Shrine.

The custom of *shrada (Ceremonies for the Dead Ancestors), enshrined in the Mahatmaya* for this temple pilgrimage is not religiously connected with the Goddess of learning and fine arts; Sharada. Specific places for such rites for the dead have been designated in different Parts of the valley. Most probable reason for this could be that *Pitra Paksh* (Annual fortnight for *Shradha's* for dead ancestors) starts just seven days after the designated day of pilgrimage and by that time they, pilgrims, may not have returned to their homes and this ritual has been included in the Mahatmaya. To cover it up, *S'arada Vandana* (Hymn) in the Mahatmaya has been tailored as *Mokshadayini*and *Papnashneemam,* giving freedom to soul and forgives sins, another reason for including *tarpan (holy water in memory of dead)* rites as Part of the pilgrimage. Would not like to dwell on this further as this connection has been purposely been made, a closer place for Shrada ceremonies.

"Who but the Atman is capable of removing the bonds of ignorance, passion and self-interested action?"
–Adi Shankaracharya

5

S'arada Temple(s) Kasmira-S'arada Temple Kaloosa (Kalash) and Adi-Shankaracharya

A person can achieve everything by being simple and humble. – Rig Veda

Study of References. It is of utmost importance that references and sources are correctly interpreted and refrain from drawing own conclusions. Even if you do so, it must be cross checked with other sources and material. There are ample examples where such deviations completely change the base of account. S'arada Shrine/Temple of Kishanganga/Neelam Valley in spite of being quoted and covered extensively as an old monument, is not even mentioned directly in any chronicles of Kasmira of first millennium AD. Somewhat similar is the case with Adi Shankaracharya whose mention in chronicles started in 12th Century thereafter.

S'arada in Chronicles. This chapter is restricted to S'arada of Kasmira, where mention is made either directly or indirectly. Verses of Rajatarangini connected to **"Sharada"** have been reproduced in original, without amplifications and clarifications of Auriel Stein. He had used square brackets to distinguish words which **are not actually found in original** and round brackets **denoting additions having more the natures of glosses i.e., to render it plausible.** Study and comparison of Rajatarangini Verses bereft of brackets will make it clear that use of this code was unilateral and lead to a specific reference. By quoting some verses of Nilamata Purana, extracts from Al Biruni and Abu Fazl's chronicles, it should have been clear that these led to a particular area of and around Madhumati of Bandipora. But invariably he connected these to S'arada Shrine of Kishanganga Valley, whether it was Kishanganga River, Saraswati River, Madhumati River or idol of Durga. It will be wrong for me to attribute any wrong motive to this aspect by Auriel Stein, a noted writer ethnographer, known for his explorations and archaeological discoveries in Central Asia. However, I cannot refrain that if I could find the aberrations in his interpretations, possibly in the case of Sharada, that he was more focused to S'arada on account of his visit in 1892 AD. Did he take it as a new find and went all out to bring it into focus? May be!

Listed hereunder are the chronicles, in sequential order, which have references to S'arada or places connected with it. They are; River Madhumati, Saraswati, Sharada, Sārada Shrine/Temple, Durga. mostly separately, in of Nilamata Purana (Sixth Century AD), Tarikh-i-Hind by Al-Biruni (1031AD-English Edition 1888 AD), Rajatarangini by Kalhan (1048-1049 AD) (Translation Auriel Stein 1900 AD), Ain -I-Akbari by Abu-al-Fazal (1551-1602) (Henry Blochmann, Vol. I and II-1873 AD), The Valley of Kashmir (1895) (Sir W.R. Lawrence) and Auriel Steins explanatory notes on Rajatarangini.

Specific Mention in Above Chronicles

Nilamata Purana. Nilamata Purana (Vitasta *Mahatmaya*), an ancient text of Kasmira (scripture, chronicle), contains information on history, geography, religion, places of worship and lores of Kasmira. Nilmata Purana was one of the major sources of Kalhan's Rajatarangini, for style of living, religion, customs, festivals and topography. Mentions in (Nilamata Purana (नीलमतपुराण), Sixth Century AD) of: Goddess Saraswati twice, Saraswati River twice and **Madhumati River five times**. There is no mention of S'arada (Sharada) or Kishanganga River. Mention of Durga once as River (?), once as Goddess Durga and Once as Durgadvara (?). Temples of Durga has been mentioned three times, for specific worship giving indication that there were many Durga temples in Kasmira during the period (Sixth Century).

There is no ambiguity that there was and is only one sacred River Madhumati in Kasmira (called in later centuries as Bandapur Nallah). The source of this River is from two lakes on Harmukh Mountain Range, which though part of Shamasabhari Range is also called so. In this portion of narration in Nilamata Purana Purana the mention is connected with Rama son of Brigu (Rishi), who to avenged killing of his father's kills Kshatriyas. Who: "leaving Kasmira due to his fear, reached where there is the river Madhumati" and reach the hilly fort in Kasmira. After the killing Rama takes bath at the confluence of Suddha and the Saraswati. Climbing up the Grdhrakuta gets the merit of and goes to heaven (by bathing) in the confluence of the Vitasta and the Madhumati. Most important mention is this verse: "One gets the merit of one thousand cows the confluence of the Krsna and the Vitasta and gets the merit of performing Vahnistoma by seeing Cakresa (Shiva) erected by Sandilya (Muni Shandliya of S'arada Mahatmaya) on the bank of the Madhumati. One gets the fulfilment of one's cherished desire by seeing Durga (V 1278-79)." Note Cakresa, Sandilya (Shandliya), Madhumati, Vitasta and Durga in one these two combined verses. The word S'arada or Sharada, does not appear anywhere in the Nilamata Purana.

Al-Biruni-Tarikh-i-Hind-Sarada. The earliest and first mention of S'arada is in Al-Biruni's Tarikh-i-Hind (1031 AD). Al-Biruni (996-1031 AD) in his accounts describes Kasmira at many places regarding various aspects but in Chapter XI-About The Beginning of Idol Worship and Description of Individual Idols, he refers to Sharada. He never visited Kasmira valley but he had conduits amongst Brahmins of Kasmira as he had 'composed some publications for people in Kasmira'. In Chapter XXIX 'The idol of Hindus', Al Biruni lists S'arada one of the countries in the north-east (Aisana) (Though one odd name can be identified but a Country by name S'arada is unknown).

Al Biruni (996-1031 AD)

The relevant quote about Sharada: "In Inner Kashmir, about two-or three-days' journey from the capital (Pravarpura-Srinagar), in the **direction towards** the mountains of Bolor (Boloristan -Drava Country across Shamsabhari Range), there is a wooden idol called *Sharada*, which is much venerated and frequented by pilgrims". He talks of "**direction towards**" and two-three days and just mentions S'arada idol.

Al Biruni values coverage of distances in Firsakh at an average of eight miles per day. At best three days coverage would be about 30 miles, in the direction of Bolor (Towards Shamasabhari Range) and not counting the terrain difficulty factor. The distance takes us to general area are of Bandipur/Wular Lake. Route to S'arada (Kishanganga Valley), over the rugged terrain, would and took at least seven-eight days from Pravarpura-Srinagar and his reference cannot be that of S'arada (Kishanganga) across the mountain range. There is an ancient S'arada temple on the outskirts of Bandipore, Kaloosa, which is within two to three days journey from the capital Pravarpura (Srinagar). There is a shila of S'arada apart from various other idols, most dating to around Sixth-Seventh Century AD. This mention of S'arada is the first mention in any old chronicle of S'arada (1031-Translation 1888 AD). Though Tarikh-i-Hind does not go beyond this mention but in explanatory notes, Stein connects it with S'arada (Kishanganga) and also mentions the absence of wooden idol in the S'arada Kishanganga Valley Shrine. However, with the references and details given by Al Biruni about Wooden Idol seems possibly true. The reference seems to be authentic, as the details of the place etc. were conveyed to him by his Brahmin conduits of Kasmira (Also read above). Al Biruni's reference towards direction of Bolor is unambiguous with Bolor (Drava country) as a general reference. If one follows Ghazni's campaign in North-Western India, his thrust was through West Punjab and then he unsuccessfully tried Kasmira from the direction of South of Pir Panchal. Thus, Bolor was as alien to Al Biruni as to Ghazni and which during this period was under the rule of unknown dynasty of Muslim rulers. We also know that Kishanganga Valley was then under War Lord, inimical to Kasmira. Al Biruni joined Mahmud Ghazni in 1017 as court astrologer and accompanied Ghazni during his invasion of India just for few years (1017-1030). Samgramraja of Lohara Dynasty was the ruler of Kasmira from 1003-1028 AD and there is no mention of any activity Bolor, Drava or S'arada or anything connected with the Kishanganga Valley during his reign.

Rajataringini by Kalhan. Kalhan's Rajatarangini covers Kasmira covers the ancient history of Kasmira to the extent possible up to 1149 AD, with due mentions of Kings,

Monuments, Gods and Goddesses. Later Rajatarangini series covers Muslim rule till Moghul's took possession of Kasmira. S'arada (Sharada) finds mention just in few verses places (four) in Rajatarangini. For the first time S'arada is mentioned is in the introductory part of Rajatarangini, as praise of various Gods, defining various places etc.Verse 37 Book I "There when visiting goddess Sharada, one reaches at once the River Madhumati and Saraswati worshipped by Poets" (Verse is as in the original manuscript). It refers to Goddess S'arada on the river Madhumati and the last part of the verse refers to Saraswati as reverence by poets, who are supposed to be repositories of knowledge. There is no mention of a temple, no mention of any other river other than Madhumati and Saraswati. There is no mention of Drava country. Kalhan's reference without doubt is to sacred river Madhumati (Near Bandipore) and not Madhumati of Kishanganga S'arada Shrine.

On the other hand there are four places mentioned from) with specific connect to Madhumati in Nilamata Purana (Verse 1211-1229): "he reached near Grdhrakuta and Rajanirmala (V-1211), there is the river Madhumati (1214) and Rama son of Bhrgu 'reached near Grdhrakuta and after a bath at the place where the Suddha and the Sarasvati meet, the hands of Rama became purified' (Verses 1228-29)". While rivers Rajanirmala, Sudha cannot be identified, which seem to be tributaries of Madhumati. There is unambiguous reference to Saraswati reference in this area around Madhumati of Bandipur. Inference by Stein to refer both these to S'arada of Kishanganga must be seen that Kalhan had used Nilamata Purana for his references and could not have overlooked these Nilamata verses. In fact, there is no reason that Kalhan's verse should be inferred as such and Saraswati Goddess as well.

There is mention of S'arada (*Sharada)* at two other places, which I feel needs attention of the readers, more so of the period these two events took place. 'On the following day the son of Garga (Sasthacandra) arrived after visiting the *Sharada*, and added to the population of Indira's city by the fighters killed (Book VIII -v 2556) (Event is of 11th Century AD)'. 'At day then he pursued him with few with a few followers as far as the shrine of the goddess *Sharada*, but did not succeed in stopping him. (Book VIII-v 2706) (This pertains to the flight of Boja during Jayasimha's reign, when Kalhan himself was alive and writing Rajatarangini).

Ain -I-Akbari by Abu-al-Fazal. In Ain -I-Akbari by Abu-al-Fazal (1551-1602) (II), Fazal quotes Sharada: "At two days distance from Haehamun is the river named Padmati which flows from Dardu territory. Gold is also found in this river. On its banks is a stone temple called S'arada dedicated to Durga and regarded with veneration. On eight tithi of Shuklapacha it begins to shake and produces ". He pre-functionally mentions River Padmati flowing from Dardu (Dardistan) and a stone-temple on the banks of Padmati (Madhumati) dedicated to Durga and regarded with great veneration. This account by Abu Fazal is what he heard as he never visited the area across Shamasabhari Range. His assertion of Durga stone temple seems to be correct as it is also confirmed in Nilamata Purana: "Cakresa (Shiva Idol) erected by Sandilya (Muni Shandliya on the bank of the Madhumati. One gets the fulfilment of one's cherished desire by seeing Durga (Verse 1278-79). Reference to Padmati (River) is actually Madhumati, the sacred river of Kasmira. I tend to agree with his shaking of the temple or idol. The temple of stone being on the banks of Madhumati could have been affected by turbulent water of Madhumati. However, given a single date of a lunar month is imaginative. As far flowing from Dardu, is correct to certain extent as the origin of Madhumati can be traced back to the mouth of the Gangsar (Shalinisar and the Lolgulsar) high-altitude lake from Western slopes of the Harmukh mountain range and finally debouches into Vitasta/Wular Lake near Bandipore. Close to Grdhrakuta (Ancient name as quoted in Nilamata Purana (Dudhaaghata Fort called hilly fort in Kasmira -Dudkhut Pass). The Drava or Dardu country was controlled by Trakhan dynasty (1561-1821AD) lasted with a series of unknown local Muslim rulers until 1821AD. Dardu country (Gilgit-Baltistan) was ruled by many local rulers. One of the rulers of this era was Ali Sher Khan Anchan he had been dethroned and joined Moghul Army Actually, when Akbar conquered Kashmir, Ali Sher Khan Anchan was with him. Akbar gave him forces to reclaim his lost Kingdom, which he did. So as far as Akbar and Abu Fazl are concerned the area was under inimical ruler, and was not part of Kasmira. Even local Chak Tribe Chief Muzaffar Khan of Kishanganga Valley built a fort at Neelam to ward off Mughal armies of Akbar'.

Contents of the books refer to Sharada/Madhumati/ Saraswati/Durga, though reproduced correctly, were interpreted without differentiating interpretation, analysis as well as logical inferences. As the translated versions of above were published between 1888 and 1900 AD, it is fair to assume that inferences in various books, translations, reproduced chronicles would earliest be from 1900 and mostly around 1930's. The above is to confirm that what Abu Fazl referred was Madhumati was Madhumati of Bandipur. As far as idol of Durga is concerned read below.

During the reign of **Lalitaditya Muktapida (724-761 AD)** it is mentioned that a group from Gauda (Bengal) reportedly came to Ka'smira to avenge the death of their King by Lalitaditya Muktapida, 'under the pretext of visiting the *Sharada*, ' Instead they reached in a vigorous onslaught the silver Ramasawmin (located around present-day Jama Masjid (Srinagar) and mistaking it for Parihasa Idol at Parihaspora, they over tuned it and broke it.

Stein in his explanatory notes makes it as 'Affray at Parihaspura' and then takes this reference to S'arada of Kishanganaga valley. The explanation is that there was no shrine of Sarada around Srinagar and as such the reference is that of S'arada Kishanganga. The group of Gauda's had come to avenge the alleged death of their King with intention to destroy Lalitaditya's favourite idol of Parihasa (kesava).

Above connecting with S'arada Shrine/Temple is not borne by facts. Connect it with Al Biruni's account, we can come to a conclusion that the excuse of visiting S'arada Shrine route or alibi seems to be correct, but indicates that there was a **S'arada shrine nearby**. Kalhan would have included this Verse differently if even he thought that they were trying to go to S'arada (Kishanganga). Kalhan's chronicle is of 1148-1149 AD, prior to Al Biruni's (1031 AD).

Kalhan till the end of Rajatarangini calls S'arada of Kishanganga Valley Shrine and not temple, on the other hand he has been using word temple hundred times in his manuscript referring to temples which were either constructed or existed during his time. This is enough to give a hint that it was possibly after mid-12th Century (Rajatarangini 1148-49AD), the temple could have come up or was under construction then. Not being a great event, Kalhan did not think it fit it in his Rajatarangini. More so, it was beyond the Kasmira Kingdom of his time. It is significant that Sindhu River is quoted frequently, which is within the valley and taken Lower Sindh, as Ganga of Kasmira, in Nilamata Purana. Kishanganga is not mentioned anywhere in the chronicle. Krsna River has been mentioned both in Nilamata Purana as well as Rajatarngini. In former it is mentioned at the Confluence of Vitasta and in later mentioned at two places in the chronicle. There is mention of Madhumati at places closer to the confluence for crossing towards Hazara.

Similarly, invariably mention of Saraswati is taken as Saraswati River of Kishanganga Valley. What is termed as Saraswati of Kishanganga Valley is Kankotri stream a stream, from Sargun River. Even the Saraswati Lake is not the original name of the lake. Nilamata Purana refers to many Saraswati Temples and by reference any stream close by would invariably called Saraswati River and Stream. In any case Saraswati River of Kishanganga is not its actual name; the name is Kankatori. Ironically knowing it to be ancient name, Stein still sticks and tries to authenticate Saraswati reference by Kalhan to Saraswati River of Kishanganga Valley. At least I have no comment on this, though he knew Bheda Shrine and Saraswati Lake at Bheda Giri.

Leads to S'arada Shrine Within Valley

Ambiguity. The amplifications starting from Nilamata Purana verses is indicative enough that there has to be a Shrine/Temple of S'arada close to Madhumati. With indicators from Nilamata Purana, Tarikh-i-Hind, Rajatarangini and Aine e Akbari it is evident that the shrine referred to is closer to Madhumati. An intensive search and study the place is near today's Bandipore at a place called Kaloosa, which was recognised as S'arada Temple but lost in antiquity as the stress shifted to S'arada of Kishanganga Valley. To connect the above strings hereunder are the details of **S'arada Temple Complex even now known as Shardibal.**

Tirathsamgraha by Sahibram, which has been quoted by Stein, mentions S'arada shrines within the valley. Stein quotes four of them but conveniently does not mention S'arada Shrine at Kaloosa (Kalash). Possibly, mention of this would have brought his assessment in conflict with his assertion of S'arada Shrine Kishanganga Valley and Madhumati River. He in his amplification notes dismisses these mentions in Samgraha: "Otherwise vague note in, which connects one of the several S'arada Shrines by him (Sahibram) in Lolav (Lolab Pargana) adjoining the Kishanganga Valley from the South".

Oldest S'arada Temple at Kaloosa (Kalash)

Kaloosa Shrine. Without going into deep details, Nilamata Purana, Al Biruni, even Rajatarangini and Abu Fazl's accounts discussed above are clear indicators of River Madhumati, S'arada Shrine at 2-3 days journey from capital (Pravarpura-Srinagar) (Al Biruni). Team from Gauda to avenge death of their King reach Parihaspora under the alibi of S'arada Shrine (Rajatarangini by Kalhan). Abu Fazl's mention of Stone temple, Durga on the Banks of Madhumati. Verses in Book 13 and 15 Nilamata Purana give clear indication of location of Madhumati within the valley and its confluence. It also mentions about its sacredness. Most of all idol of Cakresa (Shiva) was erected by Muni Shandliya on the Bank of Madhumati and one gets the fulfilment of one's cherished desire by seeing Durga.

Few years back a young lady was recalling about S'arada Shrine at Kaloosa, a place of her maternal relatives. My mind then was fixed, like that of Stein, on S'arada Kishanganga Valley and vehemently told her that there was and is no S'arada Shrine at that place. Now while analysing the references, Kaloosa came to my mind for which I cheekily blame Auriel Stein. For Stein never mentioned about this shrine and seems to have side tracked the shrine. Now the dilemma was to do the available reference pertain to this very temple or not. Does any such temple exist on the banks of Madhumati? Thus, started my efforts to gather further information and indicators. These efforts succeeded as details trickled and video coverage together with Photographs from Ground Zero (Courtesy Mrs Suresh Pandita, Kaloosa). The shrine is called Shardibal and a with effort of denizens of Bandipur and Kaloosa, a temple complex, S'arada Temple (Shardibal) has come up in Jammu. I am not sure as to antiquity of the name Shardibal. Prefer to rely on photographic narration below with Brief explanatory notes, with reasons for this Shrine not being mentioned and being overawed by S'arada Kishanganga Valley.

Temple Complex Kaloosa. It is beyond doubt that the Temple Complex is ancient, Fifth to Sixth Century and with ancient name Kalash (I have not been able to find any mention of this name in any scripture or chronicle. Not abnormal). On the Banks of Madhumati at Kaloosa stand two Temples, both in proximity of each other, on the right bank of Madhumati, I would say literally on the Banks of Madhumati River. The smaller one is basically Shiva -Durga Temple and currently called Shivalaya. The temple Sanctum Santorum is around a very old Elm Tree (Brun in local language. Considered Holy) with many ancient Shila (Rock) idols. There are two Idols which require special mention. First one is that of Cakresa (Shiva) crafted from stone, which is not found in the valley. This idol installation is surely the same as referred in the Nilamata Purana Verse 1278-79 (Cakresa erected by Sandilya on the bank of the Madhumati One gets the fulfilment of one's cherished desire by seeing Durga). In this Verse both Shiva and Durga have been combined at one place: on the Banks of Madhumati. As far as I know there are only two idols of this type found in Kasmira, both attributed to Gupta Period Fifth and Sixth Century AD.

Oldest S'arada Temple of Kasmira- Kaloosa (Bandipur) 7-8th Century AD

S'arada Temple - Shivalaya Around Elm (Brun Tree) Ancient Shila (Rock) Idols Inside

Madhumati River At Kaloosa -Bandipora Aug 2022

Few years back a similar Idol was found in Harwan Reservoir. (See Photographs below). Size, shape, material and craftsmanship is similar. The only difference is that the one found inside the Harwan Reservior is more in preserved shape for obvious reason of being inside water, while the one in Shivalaya Kaloosa has certain wear and tear due to centuries in open and rituals of smearing the idol etc.

Ancient Idols at Śarada Temple of Kaloosa (Kalash) Bandipur (Kashmir)

Left: Idols of Cakresa (Shiva) installed on the Banks of Madhumati (Nilamata). The Idol is of Gupta Period (5th/6th Century AD) Right: Ancient Shila Idol of Goddes (Durga) (Both in Shivalaya Kaloosa (Kalash) Adjacent to Ancient Śarada Shrine)

5th/6th Century Gupta Period Shiva Idol Found Few Years Back Inside Harwan Reservoir

Close by are many more idols and the one which catches eye seems to be of Durga (?) (Locals call it Parvati idol). This idol is carved in a stone block of local rock and similarity of Shila rock idols of around Fourth/Fifth Century AD. There are few more Shila idols, which I am unable to identify correctly.

Next to the Shivalaya is the main S'arada Temple. The old temple constructed in 1925 AD on earlier depilated one has taken a new shape in recent years. There are many idols in this temple including a recent marble idol of Sharada. A stream passes through the complex now called Baudh Nala, which has confluence with Madhumati River. My take is that possibly it was called as Saraswati or Suddha Stream (Nilamata Purana Verse 1229). The reason is that complete verses in this block of Verses refers mainly to Madhumati and area around it, naturally these may have been there. Sharada temple had also a bring spring. There is a round Shila which is venerated as that of Sharada. The Shila is more symbolic than an identifiable idol, but the faith is there. There are many legends etc connected with this Shrine, Shila and one going around is just few centuries old. The mere fact that the area is mentioned in Nilamata Purana and Shiva idol found, I don't find need to either recount the legend nor believe in it.

I am wondering as to reasons why these two oldest shrines of Shiva and Sharada, well chronicled as references, were not considered in the valley. There seem to be many reasons and first and foremost is that worshippers around Bandipora themselves did not know and realise antiquity of these idols. The area during medieval and initial period of second millennium was part of Lahara (Lar) Pargana ruled by conglomerate of Damara's who most of the time were in conflict within and the rulers as well. During Muslim rule, it was targeted as the area was domain of Lahara (Lar) Warlords and Koteh Ren belonged to the place. Absence of a capable Brahmin Priest who could create even an readdicted Mahatmaya of this place. The area was at a limb and remained as a local worship place, with another S'arada Shrine at Kulyandhi village in Khuyhom.

Priests of Gushi/Lolab belt who lifted the Nilamata Verses and created a readdicted S'arada Mahatmaya. It was also wrong or intentional misinterpretation of Nilamata Purana, Rajatarangini, Al Biruni and Abu Fazl accounts by Auriel Stein and concentrate on S'arada of Kishanganga Valley. As he admits, that Kishanganga Valley shrine is mostly visited by locals of Kamraz, who apart had created another S'arada Shrine at Rangvor. The interest of Dogra Kings in the Kishanganga Area was part of their security of Gilgit and they tried to encourage visits to this area as best as they could; S'arada Kishanganga Valley being one of them.

S'arada of Kishanganga Shrine

Location S'arada of Kishanganga Valley. The Shrine/ Temple is not geographically located within Kasmira valley, which is enclosed within a ring high mountains ranges. Politically the temple area, for a century plus (1846-1947 AD), had been part of a combined State of Jammu and Kashmir; No longer. Part of the area North, beyond the valley across the mountain ranges, known as Drava Country (Daradistan), got split into two specific countries after 1947. One; part in Azad Kashmir (Pakistan Occupied Kashmir (POK)), though designated as a separate entity, but deeply part of Pakistan. Other; Gilgit Baltistan (GB), which was part of erstwhile state of Jammu and Kashmir, ceded on 15 August 1947 to Pakistan. In Kalhan's *Rajatarangini* people of the area are mentioned as Dardas, who frequently invaded Kasmira or were in intrigue with tribal factions within.

Assertions-Construction Attribution. Shrine (Temple) and its connection to vast area of erstwhile North-Western India has been made a ground for unconnected views, often contradictory and has been mired in controversies, misquotes, exploitation, conflicts, expeditions etc. Different versions have been created with imaginative and startling attributions, by Scholars, researchers of various hues, who want to create stories, to pad up their version. Of late leaders from Kasmira,

Azad Kasmira, Hindu/Muslim Scholars, Religious Heads of various Mutts want their version (s) stamped on the history of this Shrine/Temple. Some of these are:

"The Shrine/Temple is of pre-BC era, a Buddhist Monument, construction attribution ranging from Ashoka to Kushan period, meant to be a focal point for spread of Buddhism. Students from far off countries of the continent were studying Buddhism within the complex. Buddhist monuments existed in the area, which got destroyed without any trace, due to time gap of two millenniums and vagaries of weather". Archaeological Survey of Pakistan has notified it as 'Protected Ancient Buddhist Monument' called "S'arada Buddhist and Archaeological (Sharada)". This assertion by Pakistan ASI, is not based on finds but conjectures, with a tinge of religious denial bias. During Buddhism spread through North-Western India a large number of Buddhist monasteries, Stupas and specific Buddhist rock carvings doted the areas. None of such specific Buddhist ruins have been found in the area.

"Kishanganga Valley (Neelam Valley) was part of Prehistoric Greater S'arada Civilisation right from Neolithic/ Megalithic era, **unconnected** with other erstwhile Indian Civilisations". It is an argument to create different identity of the people away from erstwhile Indian Sub-Continent civilisations. However, saner elements accepting existence of late Neolithic era primitive stone slabs with markings etc, connect it to Parvati-Ganga-Sharada-Neelam Tahzeeb (Civilisation-Culture) (Parvati-Ganga is another ancient name to Kishanganga River).

"The area was on an ancient trade route (Silk Route), connecting the area to erstwhile Persia. Inhabitants of the area and beyond were a different race than Aryans". Ancient Silk trade route does not even touch the fringes of the area, in later centuries a subsidiary route from the main Silk Route was aligned through Gilgit-Baltistan-Tibet-China. Being different from Aryans, in a way is somewhat factual, as migrant groups settled in this Drava Country where from different tribes of East Murghab Valley of Central Asia.

Needless to say, all above assertions are religiously oriented assertions, to deny umbilical cord to Aryan's, Hinduism and Ancient Bharatvarsh. Opposite assertions oscillates from existence of Temple 'from time immemorial, which gave acronym of S'arada Desh to entire Kasmira and nearby Kingdoms'.

"The Temple construction attribution ranges from, Kushan's, Hindu Kings: pre as well as during Lalitaditya Muktapida (Eighth Century), Lalitaditya and Adi Shankaracharya (Eighth /Ninth Century)". Recently an Acharya of a Mutt (Calls himself Shankaracharya) in a video clip, claimed that the Shrine was built by Adi Shankaracharya.

"Adi Shankaracharya established the S'arada Peeth (Seat of a deity or pontiff) at the S'arada Shrine/Temple and ascended it, after debates with various scholars from all over, defeating many famous Scholars, mostly of Kasmira. A Sandalwood Idol of Goddess S'arada at the S'arada Shrine/ Temple Kasmira was installed by Adi Shankaracharya or already existed in the temple and was taken away by Adi Shankaracharya and installed at Sringeri Mutt (Karnataka). During his visit to Kasmira stayed at Gopadiri Temple) at Srinagar and the temple was named Shankaracharya Temple in his honour".

"Sultan Zain-ul-Abdin (15th Century) King (Sultan) of Kasmira went on pilgrimage to the Shrine/Temple place and on touching the Sandalwood idol its was shaking etc". This is quoted as chronicled by Jonaraja in Jona Rajatarangini. There is no mention whatsoever about S'arada Temple or Sultan's visit in the actual Jonaraja's chronicle.

"That pilgrimage to this Shrine/Temple has been from time immemorial and a residential University was established to teach Shaivism with convocation on Gauri Tritya (which falls in mid-February)". S'arada is not mentioned in any scripture or even Nilmata Purana (Sixth Century AD). The Shrine/Tirath came into prominence in later part of first millennium AD, when an expedition was launched to capture rebel nephew of King Jaisimha, Bhoja, who had been given shelter by War Lord (Damara) of Kishanganga Valley. About the convocation around mid-February, the area even today gets 6-10 feet of snow, temperature many degrees below minus degrees Celsius and locals do not venture out during the peak months of winter in the entire Kishanganga Valley (January-February). Madhumati

"Lakhs of religious books written on Birch leaf in the Shrine/Temple Library/University, were washed away during floods/rains or writing got erased due to weather". No such stocks or remains of Birch Leaf's manuscripts have been found in the area. Surprising Gilgit Buddhist Manuscripts were recovered in 1931 in Gilgit, which has much harsher cold climate. The shrine/temple area is at a higher ground, the argument of floods does not hold, rain intensity in the area is much less due to mountain barrier in its South. The heavy snow fall would have compelled the preservation in properly constructed storage cells, if at all these existed.

"A Sri Chakra (Tantric Symbol and diagram) was installed in the Shrine/Temple by Adi Shankaracharya and that he penned down various treatises like Saundarya Lahiri, Panchastavi, while sitting on the Sarvygna Peeth at S'arada Shrine/Temple". No sign of Sri Chakra has ever been found in and around the shrine/tirath. The only Sri Chakara installed in the entire valley region was in Seventh Century AD by King Pravarsena II (Mid-Seventh Century) on Sarika Parbat (Hari Parbat) hill named as Goddess Chakreshwari.

There are many more assertions, which apart from contradictions, not factual or chronicled and need not be seriously detailed.

Mention in Ancient Chronicles-Scriptures

Buddhist Scriptures. There is no mention of Sharada/ S'arada Tirath/Temple or Kishanganga Valley or sacred rivers in this valley in any of the Buddhist Scriptures or Travelogues by Buddhist Monks including famous Monks like Xuan Zang etc, who visited India in the beginning of Ist millennium onwards.

Subsequent Rajatarangini Series. After Kalhan, Rajatarangini series were continued and generally known as Jonaraaja Rajatarangini's, composed by Jonaraja, Srivara, Prajabhatta and Shuka (1127 AD to 1579 AD). Jonaraja's Dvitīyā Rājataraṅginī is a continuation of Kalhan's Rājataraṅginī and brings the chronicle of the Kings of Kasmira down to the time of the author's patron Zain-ul-Abidin (1418-1419 AD and 1420-1470 AD). Sharada-S'arada word or reference to it does not find any mention in Jonaraja's series.

It is interesting to note that 350 additional verses have been added to Jonaraja's Rajatarangini, none of these have been found to be genuine and do not exist even the MSŚs. The visit of Sultan Zain-ul-Abdin to S'arada Shrine in Kishanganga Valley and legends connected thus are not factual.

S'arada may have been mentioned in subsequent chronicles, however, explicitly the word Sharada, S'arada of Kasmira and the temple is mentioned in any chronicle for the first time in the Country outside Kasmira, is in Madhavacharya-Vidyaranya's (1296-1391 AD) **Sankara-dig-vijaya**, known Biography of Adi Shankaracharya. It is well known by now, as to how distorted account of this Shrine/Temple came about in the Biography (Discussed in later chapters).

A curious incident took place around 1890 AD. A Samkarasramasavmin Pontiff of Dwaraka Mutt paid a visit to Lahore and specially requested Sir Auriel Stein to give information as to **Saradatiratha** in Kasmira, to which he desired to make a pilgrimage. The pontiff subsequently abandoned his project, whether due to difficulties of the route or for other even more material reasons, Stein was unable to guess.

Prabhavaka-Carita Mention. In a quote, Hemacandra (1088-1172 AD) a Jain Scholar of Gujarat (Now Pakistan) in his Prabhavaka-Carita, claims that all his manuscripts had come from Temples of Saraswati (*Does not call it Sharada*). The author places the said temple of Saraswati at Pravarpura (Srinagar), where we know from the ample historical material, chronicles, accounts available then or now to us, that no such temple existed in Pravarpura (Srinagar), either during Hemacandra's time or ever thereafter. On examination of his work it has been proved that this account cum assertion came from other sources, not from Hemacandra, if reference is to S'arada (*Sharada)* Shrine or Saraswati (Prof Buhler in Hemachandra's life and Sir Auriel Stein).

S'arada and S'arada Desh-Mandala. Kasmira has **occasionally** been referred as S'arada Desh (Country of Goddess Sharada), but it remained just Kasmira Kingdom through the two millenniums. S'arada Desh acronym was seldom used in chronicles referring to Kasmira where S'arada Language and Lipi (Script) was in vogue around mid-first millennium AD. Kalhan refers Kasmira as **Aryadesa** 'The land of Aryans' and **not S'arada Desh.** Other microscopic view: 'S'arada Mandala' which means a political formations as federation of kingdoms or vassalized states, a misnomer emanated from some religious institutions of South India, which Kasmira was not.

Temple Construction-Era, Attribution

General Thought Process. Some facts still remain to be unravelled till this day, as far as S'arada Shrine/Temple Complex, including the main Shrine/Temple monument is concerned. The Shrine/Temple complex is located on a hill above the village named after it-Shardi and adjacent spurs are inhabited by locals. An impressive, now collapsed, stone stairway of 63 Steps 9/10 feet wide, leads up the hill past Pakistan Army post to the complex. Though only portions of the boundary wall, parts collapsed, remain, it is not difficult to note that enclosed quadrangular court are aligned with the cardinal points. Smack in the middle of the quadrangle stands the temple, built of locally quarried reddish sandstone. The Boundary Wall is thick with built in Bunkers with Loop Holes, covering likely approaches of 'any attacking enemy'.

Since there is no chronological mention of the construction of the Complex, all assumptions cum assertion theories, research works are being floated, most during last couple of centuries. These are vigorously propagated, most of them tainted politically, religious and sectarian motives. These are more of guess works and laced with half-baked facts.

Antiquity of Sharada. S'arada Complex is claimed to be many millenniums old related to Hinduism for the Worship of Goddess Saraswati in the form of Sharada; Goddess of Learning. Present day Hindu Religion is later denomination of Vedic Religion (around 1600 BC), based on Veda Verses evolved over Centuries within Aryan settlements in the Sindhu (Indus) Valley and Saraswati River Basin. The manifestation of Trinty in Bharatvarsh took place around 900 BC and few centuries later their spouses manifested after Puranas were composed. There is no Temple or Shrine of the era before 700 BC anywhere in Bharatvarsh, which has idols or connection with Trinty or their spouses or their other forms. The phenomenon of Temples/Shrines named after specific Gods came after manifestation of Trinty and their spouses, which were adopted to name such monuments and called a specific Temple. No way does this assertion, Millenniums Old S'arada Shrine/Temple, stand.

A Buddhist Monument. A Buddhist Monument over two millenniums old, which had lakhs of books and manuscripts for spread of Buddhism is a tall claim. The time line of this assertion ranged from reigns of Ashoka (Third Century BC) to Kanishka/Kushan's (First/Second Century AD). A new class of Religo-Politco, Writer's and Scholar's, propound theory that this particular area of Kishanganga Valley was pulsating with spread of Buddhism. If it was Buddhist Centre, a visit would have definitely be on the itinerary of famous Chinese Pilgrims and they would have mentioned in their travelogue. Faxian,

Xuanzang, and Yijing and many more were among hundreds of Chinese monks who made pilgrimages to India during the first millennium AD. This aspect has been covered separately in the book.

Peep into Buddhist Monuments of BC/AD Era. The absence of any ruins of normal Buddhist monuments of BC/ AD Era in the area also counters above claim. Buddhist monuments were of specific design and no other ruins can be taken as of Buddhism. Any university, that too residential, adjacent to the monument has to be significantly a big complex. Most of the rulers after Kushan's did not change the shape of any Buddhist monuments in their respective areas or convert them. Though unattended over centuries turned to ruins or left tell tales for posterity. There are many rulers in North-Western India who either patronised or built new Buddhist Vihara's or Monasteries. A peep to such Buddhist Monuments nearby.

Buddhist monuments of BC/AD era in the vicinity of Kishanganga Valley. Mankiyala round stupa located in District Rawalpindi (Pakistan) Third Century BC. Note the base stone craftsmanship and arrangements (Left). RightNimogram Stupa and Monastery (First-Fifth Century AD) in Swat Valley (Pakistan). Below is a composite Buddhist Monument, founded in First Century AD and was in continual use till Seventh Century AD; Takht-I-Bahi (Takht-I-Bahi. This Buddhist Monument gets its name as it is on a slope near village Takht-I-Bahi in district of Mardan (Khyber Pakhtunkhwa Province-Pakistan) and close to Kishanganga Valley/POK/Gilgit-Baltistan.

Takht-I-Bahi an Indo-Parthian Archaeological Site of an ancient Buddhist Monastery in Mardan (Khyber Pakhtunkhwa-Pakistan)

This site is the largest Buddhist remains in the ancient Kingdom of Gandhara which offers a glimpse of a Buddhist monastery monument of that particular era. It was first identified from the travelogue of Chinese monk-pilgrim Xuan Zang, in search of Buddhist texts. Few details of its construction, so as to enable readers to compare it with S'arada Shrine/Tirath/Temple as a Buddhist monument. The complex is composed of an assemblage of buildings and was a complete

Buddhist monastery. The buildings were constructed of stone in Gandhara patterns (diaper style) using local dressed and semi-dressed stone blocks, set in a lime and mud mortar (In case of S'arada it was constructed from locally quarried stones from Narada Peak). The ruins comprise a main stupa court, votive stupas court, a group of three stupas, the monastic quadrangle with meditation cells, conference hall, covered stepped passageways and other secular buildings.

In 1864 at the entrances of the site, broken pottery was found with inscriptions in Kharoshti, which was the script around then Buddhist period. Notable comparison is that only few rock carvings in S'arada Lipi have been found around Sharada. If S'arada was to be an important Buddhist monument with a university, then it would possibly have been on similar pattern.

Front View Martand Temple

Front View Sharda

Attribution to Lalitaditya Muktapida (724-761AD). A fellow of the Royal Geographical Society, who visited the S'arada complex in April 2018 writes. "The much humbler facade of the ruins of Sharada, one cannot but remark on the similarity of architecture (With Martand Temple). But adds a caveat; "Lalitaditya would have ordered this worship place as a sort of a **poor architectural** second to Martand for **local worshippers**". Possibly the visitor has not taken into his view, enormity of Martand Sun Temple, its Walls and Temple Design and that Lalitaditya was not ruling the area. It is futile to take this point seriously.

Sharda – Side and Back View

Front and Side View Martand Temple

Comparison of Shrine/Temple Walls with Ornamentally carved Walls of Martand Temple below.

Control of Kishanganga Valley by Lalitaditya. As part of the assertion that Lalitaditya constructed the monument, it is quoted, including in Rajatarangini, his campaigns towards the Dardistan and his control over it. The chronicled history which includes Chinese notices, has a different take. In 733 AD Lalitaditya sent his envoy to China, stating that if the Chinese

Sharda Outer walls Notice watch post

Temple Outer walls with Distinctive Doric style Pillars

Emperor were to send an army to Gilgit and also Baltistan, he would arrange food supply for two lakhs.In 736 AD, the Tibetans launched an attack on Baltistan and Gilgit and succeeded in reducing Baltistan and in 738 AD totally defeating Chinese army contingent stationed there, but Gilgit was saved by the Chinese. With Gilgit under their influence, the Tibetans were in control of whole area (744 to 747 AD), they had a firm hold from Ladakh to Gilgit.

Some writers think that Muktapida undertook his northern campaigns at the instance of and as the instrument of the Chinese. This happened 751 AD and after expedition to Baltistan and Gilgit, which gave him the control of the routes to Central Asia. However, the route taken by Lalitaditya was along Uttarpatha, the beaten track, which does not touch Kishanganga Valley or Lower Dardistan in the South.

Insight Into Temple Architecture. Below are three photographs to give an idea of construction of this Monument/ Temple. The gaps between main pillars and the main Sanctum Sanctorum portion filled with uneven stones, which at best can be called "unskilled". Sanctum Sanctorum wall construction is with bigger, different cut, size stones. It is simply unbelievable that it was got constructed by a King (Lalitaditya), known for his marvel constructions in Kasmira. Except the pillars, almost all construction does not appear at all by artisans, comparabale to other Shrines/Temples of Kasmira or Northern India.

Other Ancient Temples of Kasmira. Below is a collage cum comparison of S'arada Monument/Temple with other famous temples of Kasmira. It is futile to argue that the architecture and construction can be attributed to any King of Kasmira. There is no comparison of its plinth, platform, temple pillars, front arches, the intricate carvings on the temple walls of Kasmiri temples, except in the case of Sugandhdesha temple Pattan, where crude walls were built in later centuries.

Above is not to berate the importance of this temple and sanctity does not increase or decrease with design or architecture. It cannot be said Kasmiris made a shoddy monument for the veneration of Shrine/Tirath/Temple of Goddess S'arada (Saraswati).

Architectural Resemblance of Sharda Temple (Shardi) with Temples in Kas'mira Valley

***Martand Temple & Sharda Temple**
***Wangath Sugandhdesha (Pattan) Temple**
*** Two Views of Avantiswami Temple Avantipura.**
*** Backside Wall of Avantiswami Temple Avantipora and two sets of Sharda Temple Backside Wall**

Brigadier Rattan Kaul

Temple Connection with Dards/Dardistan. More than once the Dard rulers have invaded the Kashmir valley. Likewise, Kings of Kasmira have also marched into the Darda country, chastised its people and even converted some of them to their own culture and religion. Mihirakula (last Alchon Hun king of North-Western of the Indian subcontinent between 502 and 530 AD) is said to have re-established pious observances in this land which, overrun by the impure Daradas, Bhauttas and Mlechhas, had fallen off from the sacred law (Brahamanism) (Rajat: Book 1-Verses 312-16). Dardistan, the Drava or Dard Kingdom (known also as State of Gilgit) became a great independent power in the Seventh and Eighth Centuries as known from an inscriptions during the reign of Paramabhattaraka Maharajadhiraja Paramesvara Patoladeva Shahi, Sri Navasurendradityanandideva of Bhagadatta (Pragjyotisa or Assam) and also in a manuscript discovered in a stupa of the **Maha**, three miles to the north of Gilgit) (The Patola Shahis were great proponents of Buddhism). But their influence and control was beyond Kishanganga Valley, where Dards and Warlords held sway.

Dards who literally controlled the area, are mentioned during the reign of Shankar Varman (883 – 902 AD). Kalhan also names several Dard rulers and also refers to the invasions of Kasmira Valley by Darda's under Viddasiha, and also reprisals. Finally Damra (War Lord) Alamkaracakra took over as War Lord of the area and his Castle was Sirahasila.

Construction Attribution-Adi Shankaracharya (Eighth/ Ninth Century). A painful wild card assertion, that Adi Shankaracharya got the temple constructed and then occupied the Pontiffs Seat (Peeth of Omnisence). Established a university teaching Advaita with students from erstwhile Bharatvarsh and many foreign countries was established there. Adi Shankaracharya did not construct any temple nor did he create a Pontiffs seat for himself anywhere in Bharatvarsh. He just nominated four of his disciples to spread Advaita from four designated places and himself spent his last few years next to a temple at Kanchi. The basis of this is that Adi Shankaracharya visited Kasmira, defeated known and unknown scholars, constructed a temple, are imaginative creation by a religious head of a Mutt in 14th Century AD. This claimed visit of Adi Shankaracharya has resulted in many more stories being woven about his routes, stay and teachings, not only in Kasmira but at many places in India. In the South there still is lingering feeling that Adi Shankaracharya did visit Kasmira.

Constructed by a Damra (War Lord) of Kishanganga/ Drava. All places of worship of Kasmiri's are within the valley; enclosed within mountain ranges of Pir Panchal, Shamsabari and lower ranges of Great Himalayan Range. At best we have Gangabal, Amarkanth (Amarnath) and Bhedagiri on the inward periphery of these ranges, but none across the major mountain range. This must be viewed in the context of majority, nearly 98 percent, of then Kasmiri's were living within the valley. Construction era and person (King, Feudal Chief, Religious Head, Group etc) who may have been instrumental in construction of the temple remains unknown so far.

Kalhan talks of siege of Sirhasila (Sirhala) Castle (Rajatarangini), which took place in his own time (12th Century), but is silent on details of the shrine, even when using expressions of siege without giving reasons or any more details of the shrine. This siege took place in 12th Century, when Jai Simha (1128-55 AD) was the King; who repaired, restored many temples and shrines and laid numerous other pious foundations including at Naran Nag (Wangat). If it was constructed during his time, his name would have been mentioned. Sirhasila Castle siege indicates the area around S'arada Shrine to be part of Kingdom, under the fiefdom of a local revolting feudal chief, who had to be reigned-in. In Kasmiri chronicles only works of Kings and Scholars have been chronicled and many works/constructions undertaken by local warlords/feudal lords or chieftains remain obscure; this has also been so with our great Chronicler Kalhan also. It may be mentioned that there are mentions of Ministers, Queen's, Nobles etc. constructing religious monuments and Kalhan has been attributing them appropriately in his Rajatarangini. This area was outside the domain of King's of Kasmira and

Kalhan never thought of it even if it was constructed during his life period.

In all probability, nearing certainty, the temple of S'arada in the form described, was constructed in 11th or 12th Century during the reign Lohara II Dynasty, by a warlord of the **Kishanganga Valley**, who apparently was a strong devotee of Sharada. Though S'arada temple like Shankaracharya Temple (Gopadiri), *Chakreshwa*ri, *Jwala* temples is on a hill, its stairs, flanking walls, massive row of parapet coping indicates enormous effort to cater for vagaries of adverse weather and snow conditions and not really of great architecture design. This will also answer the question as to the simple but massive architecture of the temple walls, unlike temples, which had royal patronage; like Sun Temple at Martand, Shankar Varman's temples at Pattan and many others. The fort like walls indicate that the feudal lord was defending his domain, with a series of fort structures, most against the Kasmira Kingdom. Whether temple was constructed later than the walls, is any body's guess.

Entry of Adi Shankaracharya to S'arada Temple. Biography of Adi Shankaracharya by Madhavachraya (14th Century) hereunder is a brief, abridged account of purported visit to S'arada in the Biography which runs like this. "While Adi Shankaracharya with his disciples were at the Banks of Ganga (Kashi) someone brought him news that in Kashmir there is temple of Mother Sharada, with Four Gates dedicated to Goddess and inside is the Throne of Omniscence which only a Omniscient (All knowing) can occupy the throne". In the past three entrances were opened pertaining to three directions and was told that there has been no learned man from the South, qualified enough to get the Southern Entrance Opened.

The Temple/Shrine is small square plinth with a single-entry facing West/Northwest. Five steps lead to the **Single Entrance** and Sanctum Santorum. Four imaginary entrances have been created instead of single one and imaginatively

Fourth Entrance created in the South for convenience to show Adi Shankaracharya, who hailed from South, entering from Southern fourth gate. It is said, till now there has been no learned man from the South qualified enough to get the Southern Entrance opened". Incidentally in the South of the shrine, there is beginning of the hill slopes ending at a mountain top.

"On hearing this news, the Acharya, who hailed from the South, felt a prompting to get the entrance opened and efface the stigma on southerners that there never had been a scholar in the South competent to enter through the southern gate to the Throne of Omniscience. So, the Acharya started soon to that Temple of S'arada in Kashmiras". There were five S'arada Shrines in Kasmira including Kishanganga Shrine. It is not mentioned which one!! As Adi Shankaracharya approached the temple from the Southern Entrance, people hailed his advent began beating drums. When stopped was quizzed by a group of controversialists (What is meant here is religious scholars). On reaching the Southern gate; "a set of controversialists stopped him and said: Where are you going in great haste? First say what you want. A discussion follows and the Southern entrance is opened for him". The details of this entry event is as in Canto (Chapter) 16 of Sankara-Dig-Vijaya by Madhava-Vidyaranya will be covered in later chapters.

In the Biography by Madhavacharya (14th Century) in the Ninth and Tenth Sargas (Cantos), the Biographer mentions that when 'Sankara' was about to take his seat on the Sarvajna peetha, Goddess S'arada questioned him enumerate thus: "Holding the hand of Padmapada, he was· about to ascend that Throne of Omniscience, when he heard the disembodied voice of Saraswati (Not Sharada), the consort of Brahma and the presiding Deity of the temple, challenging him thus, That you are all-knowing is an already an indication Brahma, have become your disciple? To ascend this Throne, one should not only all-knowing but be. Absolutely be pure in life. Do not commit the grave impropriety of ascending this Throne, without reflecting whether you have been absolutely pure in life". In reply to her, the great Samyamindra. traversed all the sexologies, met her in all the arguments and triumphed".

In a twist to show Kasmira religious philosophers in poor light the write up brings in Bhatta Bhaskara who challenges doctrine of non-Dualism. Incidentally Bhatta Bhaskara was not even born by then. The Biography takes him not only to S'arada but also to Bahlika to humble Jains and Madhyamika (Buddhists). By his powerful dialectics he is shown victorious over (the followers of) Guru Prabhakara (the founder of the Mimamsa school), Bhatta (the follower of another Mimamsa school), Udayana (a leader of the Nyaya school), Khandanakara (the famous dialectician, Harsha) and others. Then he is shifted to Kamarupa where he wins victories over Navagupta, a leading thinker of the Sakta school and a commentator on the Vyasa Sutras from the point of view of that school. The reference is to Abhinav Gupta, who is also shown as sorcerer. "By Abhichara (a form of black magic) this evil one produced in the body of the Acharya a rectal fistula of an incurable nature". Really unfortunate to have gone to such a level to call a world famous Shaivite Scholar Abhinav Gupta **evil one**.The detailed analysis of Biographies of Adi Shankaracharya and particular connected chapters has been covered separately, which gives an idea as to how far imaginative accounts have been created.

Mind Set on Adi Shankaracharya's S'arada Temple Entry. Nearly a decade back a scholar (Doctorate and a Professor) from South (Bangalore) had seen the S'arada Temple Photograph I had shared in the country for the first time and my article on S'arada Temple on the internet. She was an ardent devotee of a Holy man (Possibly one of the Acharya (Calling himself Shankaracharya), wrote to me that she had been asked to write a booklet on Adi Shankaracharya for the organisation Acharya was heading. She was in a bit of doubt seeing the image of the S'arada temple, to confirm about Adi-Shankara having ascended the *Sarvajna Pitha*. She had a genuine doubt about the whole story of four doors etc. She understood that there was a single open entry and the temple was too small for even more than five people at a time. I also gave her the dimensions of the temple and that there was only one entry from the North. While she drafted the booklet, which covered other aspects of Adi Shankaracharya's life, she was hesitant. In her hesitant mind she had a conversation with Swami Ji. Well, a month later she sent me the write up which had the Temple Image as background shadow (She had earlier sought my permission to use it, as I held the copyright, which I had gladly gave. The write up was back to old story of four doors and triumphant entry from Fourth door by Adi Shankaracharya. When I wrote to her again about it, she apologetically replied, that Swami Ji had told her to write what was going around about the story of the entry by Adi Shankaracharya. She admitted that she being an ardent devotee of Swami Ji, though convinced, had to write what Swami Ji wanted. That is what she did. Of course, such fictitious accounts continue, though awareness of the size of the Temple, fictitious stories of his visit to Kasmira and non-existent Kasmira King's Harem go on and on.

The tongue like a sharp knife ...
Kills without drawing blood.
–Gautama Buddha

6

Adi Shankaracharya, Sārada Peeth Kudali –Kasmira and S'arada Temple

When there is harmony between the mind, heart, and resolution, then nothing is impossible. –Rig Veda

Adi Shankaracharya, Sārada Peeth Kudali

Search for Truth. Actual Life, Events and Works of Adi Shankaracharya came to us after he had attained samadhi. These works, in Sanskrit, were preserved and formed the basis of his teachings by his disciples, passed on in one form or the other from one generation to another. Over 300 texts are attributed to his name, including commentaries (*Bhāṣya*), original philosophical expositions (*Prakaraṇagrantha*) and poetry (*Stotra*). However, many are likely to be by his admirers or scholars who also named themselves Shankaracharya. A sincere effort was made by one scholar in 11th century but his account was overwhelmed by accounts by influential scholars, writers with imaginative, superhuman write ups; most starting from 14th Century.The writers of these write ups were those, who idolised Adi Shankaracharya, but added fictitious stories to add to the glory of Adi Shankaracharya. In most cases the scholars, pontiffs resorted to these crutches of fictional accounts for their own ambitions. This process was also adopted by pseudo scholars with creation of religious literature etc in the name or as original work of Adi Shankaracharya.

A revelation for the devotees of Adi Shankaracharya **(Eighth/Ninth Century)**, people in the country, more so in Kasmira and South India was needed. For past six centuries many devotees, scholars in Southern States have written to bring home the actual and truthful life of Adi Shankaracharya, resulting in some understanding of his actual life and times. However, simultaneously Adi Shankaracharya's legacy has been exploited for enhancing self-prestige and importance of their own religious institutions. In such a scenario of religious exploitation, name Shankaracharya has reached abysmal low level.

Genesis Exalted Adi Shankaracharya. The name of the great saint, given at the time of his birth at Kaladi by his father, Sivaguru, was Sankara, to indicate that he is the bestower (kara) of happiness (san). Name was also to commemorate that he was born out of Sankara's (Siva's) grace as a result of long observance of austerity and prayers by his parents. During his growing years, he was referred to as Sankara and once he grew, even his Guru referred to him as Sankara. His further life and teachings made him to be called Acharya (Preacher, Teacher) by his disciples: Sankara Acharya. After his Samadhi his disciples and successors respectfully referred to him as Sankara Acharya. The disciples looking after a particular institution were ordained as Acharya's. Thus, started the unwritten dictum that heads of institutions established by Sankara Acharya, will just be called Acharya's and the seats they occupied at designated place called Peeth (Pontiffs Seat), well chronicled and continued till about end of 13th Century AD.

Kudali Muth to Sringeri Muth. The saintly life and teachings of Sankara started at Kudali (Near the confluence of Tunga-Bhadra River (Karnataka). After his samadhi at Kanchi, he was succeeded by his main disciple Sureshwara at Kudali, as ordained by Sankara Acharya himself. Kudali, over the centuries, developed into small but sacred place (Muth) with proper succession of the religious head. Swami Vidyashankara was the last Acharya of Kudali Muth till 1310 AD when Bharati Tirtha, one of his disciples, became the officiating new Acharya in 1328 AD and shifted Kudali Muth heritage to Sringeri. Sringeri Muth claiming to be original Sankara Acharya Muth, started the list of Sringeri S'arada Peeth Acharya's list starting from Sri Sankara Bhagvatpada, none other than Sankara Acharya with Bhagvatpada suffix. Subsequent names continued with Sri Sureshwara Acharya (820-834 AD), the only successor with Acharya added to his name. Bharti who shifted the Muth from Kudali added Tirtha to his name as suffix, carefully selected as per *Skanda Purana* Tirtha (Jangam) refers to a rishi or guru. Probably he wanted to be recognised as such.

Travails of Kanchi Muth. With establishment of Sringeri Muth, Kanchi Muth claimed to be a fifth Muth of Sankara Acharya, as he spent his last years at Kanchi and attained Samadhi there. However, the Muth stuck to the dates of BC Era and the list started with Adi Sankara Bhagavatpada (482 BC–477 BC). They could not overlook the actual Sankara and listed him as 38th as Abhinava Sankarendra Saraswati (788–840 AD). They took great pains to predate Sankara Acharya to pre-BC Era and was called Adi (Adi-First or principal). In dilemma in naming and accepting actual Sankara Acharya, they called him Abhinava (New); Abhinava Sankara. Both BC era dates as well as AD era dates of Adi Shankaracharya are correct in their respective calculations; former era (BC) is based on Puranic calendar while the latter (AD) is of Gregorian calendar. Puranic calendar calculation predates by around 1200 years. This aberration has been seen in many chronicle dates like Rajatarangini.

For distorted history of life and events of Shankara Acharya and based on disputed last place of Samadhi, Kanchi Muth claim as fifth Muth has been vehemently opposed, with various fictitious stories of last days of Sankara Acharya. This was more like a political manipulation of current era, to deny recognition to a rival. Bulldozed Kanchi Muth accepted their presiding Acharya to be referred to as Parmacharya, but Samadhi debate has raged again.

Shifted Muth of Sringeri. Once Kudali Muth was shifted to Sringeri, it was initially called Kudali-Sringeri Sarada Peeth, later Kudali prefix was dropped. On the advice of politically suave elder brother, Vidyaranya (Madhavcharya), Acharya Bharti Tirtha started being addressed as Shankaracharya. Bharti Tirtha was succeeded by his elder brother, Vidyaranya (Madhavcharya) who continued with also being called Shankaracharya but also maintained his Sanyasi dual name: Vidyaranya-Madhavcharya. It is for the first-time history of any of the Sankara Muth's, the pontiff seat was shared by brothers one after another.

It required suave sagacity on the part of then pontiffs not to detach connection with original place of Sankara Acharya's teachings; Kudali. The politically suave pontiff brothers termed Sringeri as the Mool (Root-Initial) Muth of Sankara Acharya and to give authenticity, the line of Acharya's was addressed as Shankaracharya's. The other institutions established during Sankara Acharya's time also adopted Shankaracharya as the designation of their pontiffs, a custom which continues till date. It is different that most of the Godmen in the country and even abroad like to be addressed as Shankaracharya's of so and so sect, group etc.

In the institutions of Shankaracharya, there was **only one Adi Shankaracharya of AD era**, all others were or are Acharya's; heads of Muth's. However, general bane is as to why **lose the exalted designation of** Shankaracharya, by the past and present occupants, each having carved out a domain of his own. This is one of the main aberration in the veneration of Adi Shankaracharya. Few years back a Haridwar-based Sadhu (fondly called Baba Jee), Achyutananda anointed himself as 3rd Shankaracharya of Dwarka Sharda Peeth, adding to over 50 such Shankaracharya's of various 'fancy named' Peeth's, including one Sadhvi Bhawanta Saraswati of Triveni Prayag, Sharda Peeth. Exact numbers of such Shankaracharya's are hard to come; due disputes, litigations, inheritance and self-proclamation as 'desperate' move to grab religious offices. Most of these being false or imaginary institutions and for unknown reasons names are strongly connected with Kasmira. A man, claiming to be Shankaracharya of *Sarvegni Kasmeru S'arada Peeth*, proudly added to the list of burgeoning number, got grand receptions and felicitations from various groups of Aryan Saraswat's Groups of Kasmira in Delhi. He is now cooling heels behind bars, for connection with terrorists, embezzlement activities and drowning few prominent personalities of the community, in the maze of collusion.

(Except where referred as BC era, Sankara of Eighth/ Ninth Century is referred to as Adi Shankaracharya).

Adi Shankaracharya's Religious Institutions. Factually there are only two Muth's which are closely connected with Adi Shankaracharya. **Kudali,** which means confluence of two rivers and **Kanchi (Kamakoti)** Muth (The other Muth's are Puri, Jyotirmath (Badrinath), Dwarka). The **Sringeri** Muth was established in 14th Century, after shifting of Idol etc from Kudali and calls itself as Mool Muth, which is not factual. Over the centuries they established themselves in such a way that today Sringeri is accepted generally as Mool Muth. Notwithstanding the claim, many religious scholars, prominent scholars have repeatedly come out with facts, but in this world of perceived beliefs, the fact is slowly but steadily sinking in.

Kudali (Also called Koodli-Kudli) Muth. Dakshinamnaya Sri Jagadguru Sharada Peeth (Also called **Sri S'arada Maha**

Peeth) and has list of nearly 90 Acharya's (List not complete). **Sringeri Muth** calls itself **Sringeri S'arada Peeth** has a lineage of 36 Acharya's and is dedicated to Goddess Sri Sharadaamba. **Kanchi Muth** calls itself **Kanchi Kamakoti Peeth,** named after Kamakshi, referred locally as Kamakoti, or Goddess Durga. They too have a list of 68 Acharya's. All lineages start with Adi Shankaracharya either of BC or AD era as the founder; Kanchi with BC Era, Kudali is blank while Sringeri Muth with Sankara Bhagvatpada (Referring to Sankara).

Sringeri Muth **claims** Goddess Sharadaamba idol was **installed at Sringeri by Sri Adi Shankaracharya**, as the presiding deity. This claim is unfounded as Sandalwood Idol of Goddess Sharadaamba, in standing position, was installed by Adi Shankaracharya at **Kudali** and the very site where he **created a Sri Chakra on a Rock.** It is in 14th Century the Sandalwood idol was shifted from Kudali to Sringeri and an idol of Gold of S'arada (Amba), in sitting position, was installed at Sringeri. The Sandalwood idol of the Goddess shifted from Kudali, was placed at newly constructed temple **Vidyashankara** Temple by Vidyaranya, within the Sringeri Temple complex.

An insight between the lineage of Muth's. There is a yawning gap of 1200 years between BC Era Adi Shankaracharya (509–477 BC) and AD Era (Eighth/Ninth Century) (788-832 AD) Adi Shankaracharya. South Indian Scholars have unravelled how these 1200 years were filled over the period. A lineage list of 56 successors with dates filled the gap of 700 plus years: "procured from the records of Sringeri" and published in *Journal of the Bombay Branch of the Royal Asiatic Society* and in *the Theosophist*, April 1893. Some of these names are peculiar names of Kings, Rulers, Scholars and even from Kasmira. The history of the two Muth's, Kudali and Kanchi, during that time distinct from each other, is obscure.

Kudali Muth. Adi Shankaracharya started his tryst with S'arada at Kudali. There is an interesting story, like a coup, as to how this Muth's heritage was shifted to Sringeri. In 13/14th Century Swami Vidyashankara head of the Muth Kudali, for 81 years (1229-1310 AD), left Muth in 1310 AD in order to escape from the wrath of the invader Malik Kafur; presumably for Kashi. As per legend he was nearing 100 years of age and did not return for many years. Bharati Tirtha, one of his disciples became the officiating new Acharya in 1328 AD. As long as Swami Vidyashankara was presumed to be alive (1330 AD), Sringeri, which was a just a small religious place, was considered as a branch of the Kudali Muth. As Swami Vidyashankara did not return till 1330 AD, a new Acharya was installed at Kudali, according to the tradition. The claim of Bharati Tirtha as the natural successor to Swami Vidyashankara for Kudali Muth was ignored.

In another twist, Bharti Tirtha shifted the Muth to Sringeri, with an excuse of safe place. It is no mystery but for the political leverage of his elder brother Vidyaranya (Madhavcharya), who was prime minister ofVijayanagara Empire (Sringeri was part of the Vijayanagara Empire). In 1333 AD Bharati Tirtha declared himself as the true successor of Swami Vidyashankara, in newly established Muth at Sringeri with the excuse that for three years (1330 to 1333 AD) Swami Vidyashankara was in Lambika Yoga (Buried underneath the ground) in Sringeri. This was basically to authenticate that he, Bharati Tirtha, was the real successor of Vidyashankara. When Bharati Tirtha took samadhi in 1380 AD, Vidyaranya ((Madhvacharya), his elder brother became the Acharya of the Sringeri Muth. It is apparent that situation thus created made way for Vidyaranya to be Acharya after the death of his younger brother. Due to royal patronage from the Vijayanagar empire, to their erstwhile Prime Minister Vidyaranya (Madhvacharya), Sringeri prospered and gained eminence. Vidyaranya (Madhvacharya) as the new Acharya ensured his place in the history of Muth's, by writing Biography of Adi Shankaracharya.

The claims of the Kudali, the original S'arada Peeth, is supported by the Kanchi Muth, naturally not accepted by Sringeri Muth. In spite of other four Muth's and Kudali Muth sticking to Adi Shankaracharya of BC Era, Vidyaranya (Madhvacharya) started the lineage from Adi Shankaracharya of Eighth/Ninth Century AD, which in a way are correct dates of Adi Shankaracharya. Kudali, the original Muth, thus became non-entity and was termed as one of the branch of the Sringeri Muth.

Since Vidyaranya (Madhvacharya) had to bring the Sringeri Muth as Mool (Root Muth) of Adi Shankaracharya, he created fictitious accounts. He overlooked the fact that it was his brother who installed Gold Idol of S'arada (Amba) at Sringeri. With fictitious and vague accounts, he took away the importance of rival Kanchi Muth as final place of Samadhi of Adi Shankaracharya. Cleverly changed the original verses contents for Kanchi to be read as Kashi even Kasmira. In persuit of his avid aim to deny Kanch its proper place, created disappearance of Adi Shankaracharya in Dattatreya Cave in Himalayas or left him in Kasmira. None were wiser that time nor even now.

Establishment of First Sharda Peeth at Kudali. Adi Shankaracharya (Sankara Acharya) himself established the footprints of Sharadaamba at Kudali. There are Legends cum lores associated with establishment of Kudali Muth, with some variations. The legend (may be even lore) is as how this S'arada Peeth was established religiously accepted for last 1300 years.

Sankara (Eighth/Ninth Century) reached **Kudali**, on the banks of Tunga-Bhadra River confluence, along with his disciple Mandala Misra (Another scholar) and his wife Sarsawani (Ubhayabharati). While they were walking, Sarsawani (wife of Misra) did not move and stood fixed in the sands of Tunga-Bhadra River. When Sankara turned back, he realised that Sarsawani did not want to proceed any further. In Sarsawani, Sankara had seen the image of Goddess. Sankara created a seat, **Peeth**, for her, for spreading his philosophy *Advaita,* through this seat of *Sharadaamba*, as he called it. He also etched a *Holly Sri Chakra Diagram*, on a nearby rock to signify the importance of this place. A make shift temple was created by his followers and Mandana Misra where Sankara stayed.

There is another legend, Sankara and Sarsawani had come to an understanding that she will continue to follow Sankara, but if he looks back, she will stop at that very spot. Legend says that Sarsawani was wearing ankle trinket's bells, somehow, she stopped and as Sankara could not hear the sound of the bells he looked back. This gave an indication to Sankara that this is the place for Sarsawani as Goddess *Sharadaamba,* few metres away from the confluence of the rivers Tunga and Bhadra. At that moment Sankara bonded her with Vanadurga (Vanadurga (goddess) verses and prayed her to settle down at the proposed Peeth. The legend bonding her with Vanadurga Verses, the role which is far from Sharada, form of Saraswati. Vanadurga is the fierce form of Goddess Durga (Shakthi (power) and considered as an incarnation of Devi who plays a key role in destroying evil forces and enemies. For the followers of Sankara (Adi Shankaracharya) the tradition and philosophy started by Adi Shankaracharya is; "S'arada is supreme, is *Guru Rupini;* she is of the form of the *guru.*"

Mandana Misra (Eighth Century AD) was a Hindu philosopher, disciple of Kumarila Bhaṭṭa and a contemporary of Adi Shankaracharya and is said to have become a disciple of Sankara Acharya. Maṇḍana Misra's wife was Sarsawani (Ubhayabharati) and he is often identified with Sureshwara, who succeeded Adi Shankaracharya. Mandana Misra and his wife Sarsawani are facts and so also his being a scholar. Maṇḍana's wife Sarsawani (Ubhayabharati) is considered to be an incarnation of the goddess Saraswati in the folklore of Mithila. The essence of all above legends is to establish original place of S'arada Peeth at Kudali and Sarsawani termed as the incarnation of Sharadaamba.

Left-Centre : Idols of Vandurga.

A Ninth Century Idol of Durga-Kasmira

Above are the photographs of idols Vandurga and Durga (Kasmira). Idols mostly based on the visualisation from one area to another, is indicative of their respective roles in the areas where they are worshipped. In many parts of the country, mainly South, Vandurga worship is common. After his chronicled visits Sankara returned to Kanchi Kamakoti to worship Goddess Kamakshi, where Adi Shankaracharya finally took Samadhi.

(In the above narration Adi Shankaracharya has been referred to as Sankara, as the designation of Shankaracharya came later)

Kudali (Koodli) Mutt Temple

Left: Tunga-Bhadra River's Confluence Right: Old Temple Structure Facing Main Temple with a Stone Slab With Sri Chakra (?) Engravings

Kudali S'arada Peeth. This Kudali Peeth (Seat) was called the S'arada Peeth or the Seat of ***S'arada*** (***Sharadaamba***)."

is said to have been selected the site as the place to stay by Adi Shankaracharya and teach his disciples. This first *Muth* installed by Adi Shankaracharya, with the direction that all the heads of the other *Muth's,* in the North at Jyotirmath, near Badrinath, East at Puri and West (at Dwaraka who were his main disciples, *which he created at* and ordained his three main disciples, as Muth heads (*Acharya's*) who will have a lineage of *Shishyas* (Disciples), while Kudali will remain as **S'arada Peeth** under his successor Sureshwara Acharya. For last Seven Centuries, Sringeri Muth claims to be the **S'arada Peeth** so also claims **Kudali** and **Kanchi Kamakoti.** Each of these Muth's have got followers and they are proportionate to their political and religious patronage; Kudali almost forgotten. Sringeri Muth claim Adi Shankaracharya founded the original Peeth at Sringeri for fostering the Vedas and the sacred traditions and should be discounted.

Kasmira and Adi Shankaracharya Connect

Adi Shankaracharya, Shankaracharya's and Kasmira. Amusing though, Shankaracharya's, past and present, are in more flavour with Saraswat Brahmins of Kasmira, than in their respective Muth's. Religious scholars go out of way to write, praise, proudly claim inheritance of various customs etc to the Shankaracharya's. Recently it has taken politico-religious hue, with dash to various Acharya's to get their blessings, for their mission, to get their affirmation. In this process, people of Kasmira seem to have forgotten their own indigenously manifested Gods and Goddesses, Scholars and Kasmira's religious ideology. In Kasmira, for unknown reasons, the Gods and Goddesses worshipped from ancient times, have given to new stories as if they have been imported from other parts of the country. A new flavour has been added with Adi Shankaracharya's visit etc, exploited to the hilt by the persons, who themselves hardly know about the institution of Goddess Sārada; Sharadaamba, works, philosophy and life events of Adi Shankaracharya. On the flip side there is hardly any awareness of Kasmiri Shaivism viz Advaita Vedanta in the country. Of late there are certain groups, trying to understand, interpret religion philosophies of Vedanta, Kasmira Shaivism, Krishna Sect etc, which cannot be called as significant and remain just a flavour only at restricted scale.

Shankaracharya's Associated with Kasmira. None of the chronicles, scriptures of Kasmira have chronicled any Shankaracharya either born or visited Kasmira. The trend of Kasmiri origins and visits definitely started centuries after Adi Shankaracharya attained Samadhi in 820 AD. Mostly it started in 14th Century with Biographies of Adi Shankaracharya and almost all going out of way to mention Kasmira Goddess; Sharada. Kanchi Kamakoti lineage has been taken as the base for this elucidation.

Kanchi Muth Lineage List of Acharya's. As per Kanchi (Kamakoti) records about Adi Shankaracharya and others, 10 of Acharya's are associated with Kasmira; by birth, visits, mentioned and Samadhi. Their brief details of Kasmira connect, as per records of Muth's, have been given against each in the list. Most of these claims either are false or are not corroborated.

Sixteenth Acharya Ujvala Sankara (329-367 AD) reportedly visited Kasmira in 367 AD and attained *mukhti (Samadhi)* at Kalapuri, place named after him "*Ujjvala Maha Yatipura*".**There was is no Yatipora in ancient Kasmira.** Seventeenth Acharya Sadasiva (Sadasviendra Saraswati (365-375 AD) termed as son of Deva Misra, a Brahmin minister of Kasmira, there is no clue of any minister Deva Misra in Kasmira. Twentieth Acharya Muka Sankara, Samadhi in 437 A.D (Pontiff 402-437AD). Muka Sankara, author of Muka Panchasati**, which is mistaken as Panchastavi of Kasmira.** Thirtyfirst Acharya Chidanandaghana (Brahmananda Ghanendra Saraswati (Samadhi 672 AD (Pontiff 668-672 AD-4 years). Fourtyseventh Acharya Chandrasekhara IV (Chandrasekhendara Saraswati) Samadhi 1166 AD (1129-1166 AD), otherwise known as Chandrachuda (pre-sanyasa-

Srikantha). Fourtyeighth Acharya Advaitanandaboodha (Advaitananda Bhodendra Saraswati) 1200 AD (1166-1200 Pontiffship), was also called as **Chidvilasa**. Author of Cidvilāsīya Shankaravijayam (of Chidvilasa **biography of Adi Shankaracharya).** However, Adi Shankaracharya too has been mentioned but by name of Abhinava Sankara.

Abhinava Sankara. Thirtyeighth in the list Abhinava Sankara 840 AD-30 years (810-840 AD). As per Muth records he has been taken as one of the greatest among the successors of Adi Shankaracharya (BC Era), great indeed that he and his deeds are often confused with those of the great **Bhagavatpada** (Adi Shankaracharya-BC Era).

As per biographers, his life story has been described in detail in a work titled the Sankara Vilasa by Vakpati Bhatta and that he defeated Vakpati Bhatta, a great scholar of that time in ***tarkam*** (determining oscillation constituent in a mental process leading to inference is called ***taraka*** or ***ūha***). Vakpati Bhatta is connected with Kasmira by his name Bhatta, which is mere fabrication (Read Below). Sanskrit literature Scholar K. Krishnamachari in his History of Sanskrit Literature has referred to Shankarendra (Sankara) Vilasa by Vakpati Bhatta, as a biography of Dhir-Shankarendra Saraswati, the 38th Acharya of Kanchi Kamakoti Peeth. In Kanchi Lineage the listing is: 38. Abhinava Sankarendra Saraswati (788–840), both referring to Adi Shankaracharya. He, Abhinava Sankara (810-840 AD), is claimed to have ascended the Sarvajna Peetha in Kasmira, which in no way connected with him. It is said that he entered the Dattatreya cave in the Atreya Mountains in the Himalayas and that it was the end of his mortal presence (Again some claim Badri, Kasmira, and actually as proved it is at Kanchi). **He is the actual Adi Shankaracharya, who was born in May/June 788 AD and attained Samadhi in May/June 820 AD**. What a travesty?

Next, as per the account, he "went to the holy temple of Kanchi, which, according to the wise, offers the best means for overcoming the travails of Samsara. There he worshipped Ekamresa (Siva) and His Sakti, Kamakshi, who has taken Her abode in the sacred precincts to wait on His needs, as it were." The sentence has a deep meaning and is the sort of approaching end of life where you ask for forgiveness and Moksha. It is a historical fact that Adi Shankaracharya attained Samadhi at Kanchi but off repeated "Adi Shankaracharya entered caves in Kailash never to come back".

Somewhat it seems incredible that Kasmira has been associated with so many Shankaracharya's. The two religious philosophies remained different and distinctly apart from each other and Kasmira religious scholars did not claim inroads into the Advaita Philosophy. Surprisingly none of the chronicles of Kasmira have ever mentioned any of the Shankaracharya's.

The details above are of various listed Acharyas of Kanchi Muth, to conclusion that none of the Acharya's listed above have connection with Kasmira except, possibly, 50th Acharya Chandrachuda (1297 AD) pontiffship (1250-1297AD) having Kasmira connection.

A Revelation

Khiljis in South India. During (13th) Century Islam had taken roots, in pockets, in South and Khilji Armies were active for vigorous conversion to Islam, which including killings, loot and religious persecution till about 1335 AD. In 1307 AD Malik Kafur extended Khilji empire right up to the extreme South of India, all the way till Madurai. Pandyan's, were dealt with a heavy blow and even the famous Meenakshi Amman temple in Madurai was damaged. Even the areas of Kanchi, Sringeri, present day Tamil Nadu right up to Rameshwaram were affected by the Muslim invasions. Many scholars, holly men of South could not continue their religious inclinations and moved Northwards in different directions. A study of Biography of Vidarayana (Madhvacharya) also reveals that he was away during his Sanyasi days in the North, possibly to avoid persecution by invading Muslim armies. There is no mention anywhere about him he too had stayed in Kasmira. His visit during to Kasmira is unlikely, due to disturbed conditions prevailing in Kasmira.

Sankaraswami of King Simhadeva Period (1286 -1301 AD). There is mention of one Sankaraswami (Shankaracharya or a devotee of Shankaracharya?) in Jonaraja's Rajatarangini during the reign of Simhadeva (1286-1301AD). There is strong possibility, with cross references in Jonaraja's Rajatarangini, that this Sankaraswami, apparently a religious head, visited Kasmira during this period, ostensibly to evade persecution by Khilji's. 50th Acharya Chandrachuda pontiffship (1247-1297 AD), as listed in Kanchi Kamakothi Peeth Lineage List, seems to be have visited Kasmira during the reign of Simhadeva, with indications in Jonaraja's Rajatarangini. During this period Sringeri Muth shows Swami Vidya Tirtha (Vidyashankara) as Pontiff (1225-1333 AD) and that was at Kudali.

Quotes Jonaraja's Rajatarangini. ".....Shri **Sankaraswami** was the religious preceptor of the King, and the King gave him, as his fee for his tuition, the lordship of eighteen mathas (The names have not been given). When the king rose from his bed he always chanted the following verse: -"I bow to **Sankara** the lord of Gauri, whose eyes are pure as fire, whose feet are worshipped by thee learned and who is bedecked with the crescent of the moon (Shiva)". Again: -"When Sangrama Chandara (Damra of Lahara (lar) attained Samadhi, Simhadeva, a lion among men, ruled the kingdom reduced in size, and **built a Matha** within the city".

Who was Sankaraswami, mentioned by Jonaraja, during the reign of Simhadeva, who was King Simhadeva religious preceptor, given lordship of 18 Mathas (as per Jonaraja) and that Simahadeva **built a Matha in the City**. The era fits in well during the Acharyaship of Chandrachuda I (1250-1297 AD), whose place of death and Samadhi is not known. My research possibly gives complete confirmation, in conformity with Jonaraja's mention in Rajatarangini, that it was Acharya Chandrachuda I (1250-1297 AD) who must have visited the Kasmira.

Facts-Fiction, Adi Shankaracharya's Connect with Kasmira

During the last few centuries many fictitious accounts, stories, lore's to a narrative, have been created on historical matters and religion. Kasmir and Adi Shankaracharya have not been spared and many new assertions have been made to connect these two, on one account or the other. By such methodology a community, sect, region or religion surrenders established ideology and past to the whims and fancies of others, who are mostly interested to create their own versions. The most painful are that Panchastavi of Kasmira has been composed by Adi Shankaracharya. To add to this and add approval seal of Adi Shankaracharya's visit to Kasmira that the Sage composed **Panchastavi of Kasmira and Saundarya Lahari** (Sanskrit: सौन्दर्य लहरी) **while staying at Shankaracharya Temple (Srinagar-Kasmira**. Another version; "after he sat on the holy stone slab at the temple [Sharda], it gave him vision to compose *Saundarya Lahari* in praise of Goddess Divine Mother [*Shakti*]; considered excellent piece of poetic devotion after *Panchastavi.*" It is sacrilegious to distort the history of composition of both scriptures; former of Kasmira and latter of Adi Shankaracharya. Both these theories have no truth and are briefly dwelled upon.

Panchastavi and Saundarya Lahari. Stories have created many grey areas about inspiration, authorship and dates of composition of *Panchastavi* and *Saundarya Lahari.* Some chronicles and accounts credit Adi-Shankaracharya with the authorship of both, some talk of South Indian origin of both and some attribute authorship of both to Kashmiri Scholars. The resemblance between the two is remarkable and may be responsible for creating such a dilemma, but scholars cannot remain in dilemma and they ought to have gone deep into the history of composition of both before making such assertions. While Panchastavi author remains anonymous, researchers who have analysed Adi-Shankaracharya's works, acknowledge his composition attribution of *Saundarya Lahari.* Yes, few have raised doubts to its authorship by Adi Shankaracharya.

Panchastavi. An oral tradition prevalent in Kasmira is that *Panchastavi* was composed by Abhinav Gupta (11th Century) on the occasion of his discussions on *Shaktism* with Adi Shankaracharya. *Vedantist* teacher Sivopadhyaya, an 18th Century author of Shaivism, refers to the meeting of the two in his *Srividya*, a small work aiming at reconciliation between *TantricShaivism* and *Upanishadic Vedanta.* This itself is false; the eras of Adi Shankaracharya (788-820 AD) and Abhinav Gupta (933-1015 AD) have a difference of over 100 years. Vidyaranya (Madhvacharya) in one of his works, *Srividyama Vatantra* referring to '*Maya Kundalini*' verse of Panchastavi writes that this theological doctrine had been indicated by *Dharma Acharya* in *Laghustava.* The author of *Maya Kundalini* was about one hundred years later from the time of Adi-Shankaracharya and there is no evidence to prove correctness of any such attribution and further adds to imaginative accounts.

Panchastavi is a collection of five hymns sung in the praise of Mother Goddess; personified absolute God head of the Lord and lays stress on the Mother's worship. *Panchastavi*and *Saundarya Lahari* resemble in technique, with similar objective in view; to bring awareness of Mother's eminence. Even if it is taken that *Panchastavi*is post *Saundarya Lahari*, it could not have been composed after 1030-1040 AD as *Saraswati Kanthabharana* of King Bhoja, which has references to *Panchastavi* verses, was composed between 1030 and 1040 AD, the time *Panchastavi* must have attained sufficient fame and credence for being included in *Saraswati Kanthabharana.* Thus, composition date band of *Panchastavi* can be narrowed down between 800 and 1050 AD; may be second half of Ninth Century. Contents of the scripture, which is found in Kasmira alone and recited even today, is based on monistic Shaivism founded and propagated in Kasmira. The hymns convey importance of *Kundalini Yoga*, again not popular in Kashmiri tradition, but highly popular in Tamilian and Canara (Kannad) (*Saundarya Lahari* describes *Kundalini Yoga* as the main mean of unity with the 'Absolute'). The only common element between the *Sadhana* of the *Trika* system and *Panchastavi* is the worship of *Tripura*; common factor of nearly all *Shaiva/ Sakta* theology systems and traditions and cannot lead to any specific conclusion. To highlight his intentions to remain anonymous, the last verse of the first canto of *Panchastavi* gives his intentions.

Saundarya Lahari. Soundarya Lahari meaning waves of beauty consists of two parts viz. Ananda Lahari meaning waves of happiness (first 41 stanzas) and Soundarya Lahari (the next 59/62 stanzas). It is believed that Sage Goudapada, who taught it to Adi Sankara is the author of the first 41 Stanza and Adi Shankaracharya wrote the other 59 (62) stanzas and completed it. To add to this *Raghunā thācārya, in (2002) in his book. Śankarācārya. "that ... Scholars believe that Sankara composed Soundarya Lahari in Kasmira"*; just a fallacy." **Saundarya Lahari** Verses 1 -41 describe the mystical experience of the union of Shiva and Shakti and related phenomena. In fact, it opens with the assertion that *Only when Shiva is united with Shakti does he have the power to create.* This part of the text is often referred to, quite appropriately, as the Ananda Lahari, the wave of bliss. Verses 42 to 100 are more straight forward; they describe the physical beauty of the Goddess and are sometimes referred to as the Saundarya Lahari itself. However, many scholars refer to the entire text with one common name, namely Saundarya Lahari.

Legend has it that while a pilgrimage to Kailasa in the Himalayas, Adi Shankaracharya once began inscribing this work on the rocks lying on the slopes of that mountain, as an offering to the Goddess. This legend is entirely apocryphal, finds mention in no existing text, and may be a local ploy to legitimise, for commercial purposes, the identification of a certain specific Himalayan mountain as being Kailasa, the celestial abode of Shiva and his consort. French archaeologists have recovered from Cambodia 700 to 800 Sanskrit inscriptions in stone. All the inscriptions are in beautiful Sanskrit. One of them: -"Yenaadheetanisaastraanibhagavat-sankaraahvayaat; Nisseshasoorimoordhaalimaalaleedhaanghripankajaat". This verse emphasises the greatness of Adi Shankaracharya and says that all the great seekers of truth (soori) in the country, without exception, acknowledged the greatness of Sri Sankara by bowing their heads at his lotus feet.

Message From Soundarya Lahari. There is no merit in doubting the authorship of Saundarya Lahari by Adi Shankaracharya; at least Verses 42 to 100. The specific expressions and verses are definitely from the great Saint. One would not ever know, as to when he composed the verses, the places, indicators are that soon after establishment of Peeths he composed these Verses and many more other treatises. One would not know as to how they came down the centuries, Shruti, Smriti by his disciples or in manuscript form from the hand of Adi Shankaracharya and later turned into manuscripts. Some selected verse from Saundarya Lahari.

(i) When Siva is enjoined with Sakti (Verse-1)

(ii) Oh Bhavani! Bestow on me your slave, (your) look endowed with compassion" (Verse 22)

(iii) The devotee worships Siva and Sakti in the Sricakra within in the body. (Verse 36)

(iv) **The last verse (100).** ***"Pradeepa jvaalaabhir-divasakaraneeraajanavidhih Sudhaa sootes-chandraopalajalalavair-arghyarachanaa; Swakeeyair-ambhobhihsalilanidhisauuhityakaran am Tvadeeyaabhir-vaagbhistavajananivaachaamstu tiriyam".***

Translated "Composing these verses in praise of You, O Mother, in words originating from You, is like worshipping the Sun by waving a light, offering arghya to the Moon with drops of water dripping from a moon-stone and bathing the ocean with its own water." This last verse in Soundarya Lahari Adi Shankaracharya brought home to us the truth that all virtues and skills we claim to possess are derived from the Supreme Mother through Her grace. The Soundarya Lahari is a composition, the beauty of which has not so far been surpassed. It is in praise of Ambika, Herself the embodiment and source of all beauty. The beautiful words in which **Soundarya Lahari is composed are also derived through the grace of Ambika (Aamba).**

Shankaracharya Temple of Kasmira-Adi Shankaracharya

Origins of the Temple. One may wonder as to what has a Temple in Srinagar City to do with Adi Shankaracharya and named Shankaracharya Temple. It is so in case of Temple located, on the outskirts of the city on top of a Hill, which is part of a mountain Range. The temple was named Gopadiri constructed by King Gopaditya as a shrine of Jyesthesvara (Shiva) on the Gopa Hill, claimed in Third Century BC. In Kasmira Jyesthesvara has been worshipped as Shiva from ancient times. Gopaditya ruled after Mihirkula, the white Hun King (Reign -515-540 AD) as per Rajatarangini and Gopaditya can be safely be dated around end of Sixth Century. However, normal belief remains around Third Century BC and from that time Temple continued to be called Gopadiri Temple, hill also continued to be called Gopadiri. There is also a wild assertion, Jaluka, the son of Emperor Ashoka, built Shankaracharya Temple around 200 BC.

There is no mention of Gopadiri in Jonaraja's Rajatarangini, though there is mention of one Sankaraswami (during reign of Simhadeva (1286-1301 AD), granting Shankaraswami; "the lordship of eighteen mathas (The names have not been given)".

I am not sure if Gopadiri was one of the Muth's (Muth) given to this particular Shankaraswami. From all accounts the name Gopadiri name continued during the remaining Hindu period. Interestingly there was a legend created by one Ratnagar (Era not known), before Kalhan, naming it as *Jeetlark* of King Sandhiman, "who was from 'the territories of the Western countries came flying on his throne to Kasmira and descended on *Jeetlark* Hill". The name did not strike, nor the facts, but it gave way to a new legend.

Gopadiri to Takht-e-Suleiman Under Muslim Rule. Sayyid Ali Hamadani and later his son Mir Mohammad Hamadani (1380-1404 Band), a 20-point mandate was issued by Sayyid Ali Hamadani in 1384 AD; "No new temples, no renovations, Temples will be open for Muslims to rest". This period also saw renaming of various temples of Kasmira to Muslim names. However, it seems that *Jeetlark* story was woven into another creative story around King Solomon, during this Muslim period. It seems that at this stage Gopadiri name was changed to Muslim name "Takht-e-Suleiman" (Throne of King Solomon). Solomon according to the Hebrew Bible and Christian Old Testament, wise monarch of the Israel, whose reign was around 970-931 BC. In the Quran, Solomon is considered to be a major Islamic prophet, and Muslims generally refer to him as *Sulaiman ibn Dawud.* While nobody can contest the beliefs as laid in Quran, name Suleiman became very common amongst Kashmiri Muslims. Memoirs of the Venetian traveller Manuzio (Niccolao Manucci (1638-1717) Venetian writer, doctor for 48 years in Moghul Court, who wrote a first-hand account of the Mughal Empire. Referring to the Gopadiri Temple; "The remains of an edifice, built upon a lofty mountain, is called to this day the throne of Solomon". Bernier (Physician of Moghul Court), in 'Travels in the Mughal Empire' also refers to this old tradition indicating Solomon's arrival in the Valley, built a small temple on the hill and credited with "delivering the people of Kasmira from inundation of a thousand years..... to clear the impediment in the flow of the river (Jhelum)". William Wakefield (1840-1898 AD) who travelled widely in India, in Book 'The Happy Valley" which refers to Kasmira: "Prophet Solomon is supposed by all good Mussulmans to have taken his stand during the progress of the desiccation of the Valley.....". All this gets connected to theories of Kasmiris being lost tribe of Jews and even death of Jesus in the valley (Srinagar), at a place called Rozabal. At best it can be assumed that a group of Central Asian tribes around BC/AD must had landed up in the valley and been basis of this story. But Jesus burial at Rozabal is a fallacy.

The name of this Gopadiri top thus seems to have transited, as part of Muslimisation of Kasmira names to Takht-e-Suleiman. Since then, the hill is known as Takht-e-Sulaiman (Solomon's Throne), the hill as Koh-i-Sulaiman (Solomon's Hill) and in Kashmiri Suleiman Teng. A slightly altered form, 'Koh-i-Sulaiman' by Abul Fazl, in Ain-i-Akbari (Teng is a Hill while Koh is a mountain: semantics). In all these accounts of foreigner travellers there is mention of an edifice or temple remains. Whether it had turned into ruins or demolished is not known, but surely certain parts of the temple existed.

The presence of the Muslim worship place alongside the temple has been recorded by the 16th Century chronicler, Syed Ali in his Tareekh-i-Kasmira. It is thus apparent a mosque too was constructed. Francois Bernier, Aurangzeb's physician accompanying him on his visit to Kasmira in 1665 AD, also mentions "a small Mosque with a garden" atop the hill, whose remains were seen by R C Kak, a Kasmiri archaeologist in 1930 AD. It seems that ancient temple was in ruins and Muslim rulers did not find it wise to build a Mosque on the ruins, though they did construct mosques after demolishing standing temples or converting them during Muslim rule.

The mosque or its remnants being in disuse for long, following the advent of the Sikh/Dogra rule in Kasmira, was pulled down possibly in a clean-up operation during Pratap Singh's reign, when the renovation of the temple and its electrification works were undertaken. Pratap Singh, through an official order, had also banned entry of Muslims into the temple premises. Shankaracharya as the name of the hill and the temple atop it is a development which does not go into the past beyond the mid-19th century.

Temple details. There is no doubt that the original temple was constructed during Gopaditya's time and that is the time the place was called Gopadiri. The name Gopadiri continued till about 15th Century, when during the Muslim rule it was named Takht-e-Suleiman. Since area of Gopadiri Agrahara at the foothills of the Hill, till today is called Gupkar, is indicative that Gopa designation continued.

British architectural historian James Fergusson (1808-86 AD) (For about ten years between 1834 and 1843 he visited India repeatedly, investigating Indian architecture) claims, the temple was built in the reign of Jahangir. He says that "the temple as it now stands was commenced by some nameless Hindus, in honour of Siva, during the tolerant reign of Jahangir; and that the building was stopped at the date engraved at the staircase, A.H. 1069 (A.D. 1659), the first year of the reign of the bigoted Aurangzeb. It was then unfinished, and has consequently remained a ruin ever since, which may give it an ancient look". There were two Persian inscriptions: one dated A.H. 1069 (1659 AD). Both inscriptions disappeared sometime in the last few decades.

Bernier, who accompanied Aurangzeb to Kasmira in 1665, writes of the existence of an "extremely ancient building, which bears evident marks of having been a temple for idols, although named Tact-Souliman, the Throne of Solomon." These statements show that as early as the beginning of the reign of Aurangzeb the origin and authorship of the temple were lost in the mists of antiquity. They also prove that the temple had already fallen into disuse and ruin.

Shankaracharya Temple Srinagar(Kas'mira)

Temple Photographs By John Burke – 1868 AD

Recent Photographs of Temple

The Temple. In the area in front of the temple are the ruins of two Muslim structures, probably the remains of the small mosque and garden mentioned by Bernier, and belonging perhaps to the reign of Shah Jahan, when the Persian and Arabic inscriptions in the temple were put up. Interestingly, before the Dogra rule in Kasmira there is no historical evidence to suggest that the hill or the temple atop it was known as Shankaracharya.

It is thus, apparent that the present temple location is the same and on the same plinth, the temple was reconstructed. Though Gulab Singh (1846-1857 AD) constructed the steps to the hill from Durga Naag temple side, it is clear that by 1868, when John Burke took the photographs, the construction of main temple seems to have been just completed. This must have been done under Ranbir Singh who succeeded Gulab Singh. This is the time Dharmarth Trust came into being. Interestingly it is during this time Dasnami Akhara-Giri was established by

Dogra King. Adi-Shankaracharya had founded the Dasanami order; namely Aranya, Ashrama, Bharati, Giri, Parvata, Puri, Saraswati, Sagara, Tirtha and Vana. With the establishment of Dasnami Akhara Giri, of Adi Shankaracharya, it is around this time the two were joined by Common root Shankaracharya. Dogra's had allowed Dasnami Akhara Sect in the State from 1857 AD. The Akhara had a branch established in later part of 19th Century at Srinagar and closely associated with Dharmarth Trust, which was controlled by the Dogra rulers, both in Jammu as well as Srinagar. When the Linga was consecrated in the renovated temple, the abhishek was done jointly by the Giri Mahant of Dasnami Akhara and Maharaja Partap Singh. The present Shankaracharya temple at Srinagar was given such a name in the time of Maharaja Pratap Singh when the present linga was installed in the ancient temple which had remained empty for centuries after the reign of Sikandar Butshikan. The probable date is given 1908 AD. Since Amarnath Yatra had started under the aegis of Dharmarth Trust and Giri Dasnami Akhara closely associated with the trust, the custom of Chari Mubarik starting from Dasnami Akhara started with flag off by the rulers, which continues till today.

However, even during the Dogra period Temple name remained as Takht-e-Suleiman even on official maps. The official maps of that period identify the hill as such, as is evidenced by the maps of Kasmira reproduced by Stein from Survey of 1856-60 published in March 1897 by the Survey of India Office, Calcutta (now Kolkata) or another published by Jhon Walker, Geographer to the Secretary of State for India in Council on August 15th 1867. European travellers and officers of the Dogra administration have also mentioned the hill as such in their travelogues and records. The State Civil & Military Gazette published as late as in 1935 too describes the hill as Takht-e-Suleiman. In 1961 Shankaracharya of Dwarka Peeth put the statue of Adi Shankaracharya in the temple. The reason of Dwaraka Peeth taking interest is that Giri Sect of Dasnami's are affiliated to Dwaraka Peeth.

Shankaracharya Temple and Adi Shankaracharya Connect. It is unfortunate that fictional events are being created regarding Adi Shankaracharya's visit to Kasmira. In Kasmira a trend has been created with what I term **Kasmiri Assertions**. "Adi Shankaracharya visited Kasmira with the intention of advancing Vedantic knowledge. That time Kasmiris were culturally and spiritually much advanced and believed strongly in the greatness of both Shiva and Shakti. Adi Shankaracharya was not aware of this philosophy of Shaivism of, at the time of his purported visit to Kasmira". "During his visit Adi Shankaracharya, with his party camped outside the city of Srinagar, without any boarding and lodging arrangements. The people who saw this, a virgin was sent to meet Adi Shankaracharya. The first glimpse of Shakti was exhibited to Adi Shankaracharya by this girl, Shastrarth (religious discourse) was arranged between Adi Shankaracharya and a Kashmiri woman (The story does not indicate if the woman is the same virgin). This discourse continued for 17 days. Shankaracharya yielded before the lady in discussion and accepted the predominance of Shakti cult (greatness of Devi)". "After accepting predominance of Shakti cult, Shankara wrote Saundarya Lahari, in praise of Shakti, at the top of the hill, known till then as Gopadiri Hill comparable to Panchastavi is Saundarya Lahari. After the visit of Adi Shankaracharya to Kasmira, he became staunch believer of Shakti-Shri Chakra -the symbol of Devi (Goddess) as mentioned in 'Shankara Digvijay'". "Adi Shankaracharya has stayed here (Shankaracharya Temple) when he visited Kasmira to revive Sanatan Dharma in the early part of the Ninth Century. This perhaps led to the renaming of the temple as Shankaracharya Temple. Shankaracharya was also instrumental in popularizing the worship of Lord Shiva in Jammu and Kasmira".

(The tradition of the Advaita Vedanta of Adi Shankaracharya did not at all get itself established in Kasmira. It was inclination of Dogra Rulers towards Giri

Sect that Dharmarth Trust which till today remains under the Chairmanship of Dogra Scion Dr Karan Singh).

Riposte. It is preposterous to address each of the above assertions, connected with Adi Shankaracharya (May/June 788 AD-Samadhi May/June 820). There is no reference of any visit by Adi Shankaracharya in any chronicle, scripture of Kasmira. Adi Shankaracharya' s so called visit to Kasmira would have been during 800-820 AD, at that time the Kasmira Kingdom was restricted to Vitasta (Jhelum) Bhasin only and this period falls under the last few Kings of Karkota dynasty last one being Ajitpira (813-850). With this state of the Kingdom how could Adi Shankaracharya Biographers like **Madhvacharya** (Vidyaranya) and some pseudo Kasmiri scholars think and propagate a visit of Kasmira including S'arada Shrine, which in any case was not part of the Kingdom. As regards Adi Shankaracharya staying outside Srinagar (In Ninth Century it was named Pravarpura), ridiculous. All visitors to Kasmira, irrespective of their religion like Buddhist monks etc were received royally. Like Xuanzang was accommodated at various Viharas. Similarly, if Adi Shankaracharya and his party had stayed (Possibly near Gopadiri) they would have been received and looked after by Brahmnas of Gopadiri Agrahara.

It is also preposterous to think of story connected with a virgin, discussion over 17 days and Adi Shankaracharya accepting Kasmira philosophy of Shaivisim. The creators of such imaginative stories would have done well if they had studied his life and times of Adi Shankaracharya, about Mother Goddess (Shakti), Advaita Vedanta, his inscribing Sri Chakra Yantra on a rock at Kudali. Sri Chakra yantra is not creation of Kasmira but has been there from ancient times and not exclusive to Kasmira. The only Sri Chakra Yantra installed was by King Pravarsena II at Chakreshwari (Sarika Temple)-Sarika Parvat (Hari Parbat).

As far as name of the Temple as Shankaracharya Temple, read above. Originally being Jyesthesvara (Shiva) on the Gopa hill (Gopadiri-a transited name of Gopa Giri-Gopa after the name of King Gopaditya and Giri (Hill). It is amusing that **Madhvacharya** (Vidyaranya) claims that.

When the Great Reality is not known the study of the scriptures is fruitless; when the Great Reality is known the study of the scriptures is also fruitless. –Adi Shankaracharya

7

Biographies Adi Shankaracharya

Do not be led by others, awaken your own mind,
amass your own experience,
and decide for yourself your own path.
–Atharva Veda

Biographies. Bharatvarsh (India) was blessed with a Saint, Sage whom we revere and address him as Adi Shankaracharya. It does not matter if you date his life to BC Era or AD Era (Eighth/Ninth Century), irrespective of respective beliefs, the sage and Saint remains the same. Government of India rightly celebrated his 1200th year of birth in 1988 AD. Sages, Saints devote their lives to religious discourses, visits to holy shrines, teachings and few pen down their words of wisdom on palm leaves or Birch bark. Their saintly life accounts, teachings are witnessed and heard by their disciples, who memorise them and pass on as part of their own preaching to their disciples and their congregations. There is no confirmation whether Adi Shankaracharya's life events were ever put into manuscript form, during his lifetime or immediately thereafter, as none have been found. Over the centuries his life accounts, teachings, events were passed on as Shruti and Smriti. Inevitably with passage of time additions would have been made to further exalt the standing of the Sage and may be some events may have passed to oblivion or forgotten. It is only in 12th Century AD an effort was made to write Biography of Adi Shankaracharya, contents of which mostly depended upon the sincerity, motive thought process and perception of the saint by the author.

Institutions and Accounts of Adi Shankaracharya. As a preamble, most of these treatises, works and biographies, most have candidly stated and established that Adi Shankaracharya established monastic institutions (Muth's) at many an important and sacred place that he visited, during his visits as part of spread of his teachings. There is no evidence that Adi Shankaracharya established any Muth, leave alone the Sringeri Muth. What he did was selected some places or nominated places as places for religious teachings and these were no classical Muth's. From all accounts wherever he stayed for longer period similar such arrangements were made or he stayed around existing temples.

Unknown number of biographies of the saint, in various languages have been written; many by reputed historians, distinguished scholars and researchers. The earliest, possibly first known, biography was by Anantanandagiri (1119-1199 AD) "Anandagirīya Shankaravijayam" (not extant). The last known one; "Bhagavatpada Bhyudayam" by Mahamahopadhyaya Lakshmana Suri (1917 AD).

All these biographies were composed centuries after Adi Shankaracharya, it is but natural that there would be differences and variations. Biographies composed from 14th Century onwards were mixed with fictional events, accounts, which rather catered for the writer's own imagination and to some extent exalt his own position. Over the centuries many fresh ones appeared from unknown authors, mostly adding exalted Shankaracharya to themselves. The first Biography of such genre came about in 14th Century from Madhvacharya as Sri Vidyaranya, the 12th Pontiff of Sringeri S'arada Peeth (1380 to 1386 died in 1391 AD). This was the beginning of projecting

Adi Shankaracharya in a different hue, mostly imaginative and fictitious. This Biography got a wide coverage around Vijayanagar Empire and spread to the other parts over the centuries. It never crossed the mind of devotees, followers of Adi Shankaracharya that some or most of his life events seem either imaginative or could not have been true. For the faith that Pontiff of Sringer Peeth has written it, was taken as gospel truth. These biographies written over the centuries, have been analysed by scores of South Indian Scholars, who found repetitive fabricated accounts, imaginative debates, pepped up myths and events to bolster image of Adi Shankaracharya. Now the true self of Adi Shankaracharya is coming out, which reveals his real role, life events as a religious philosopher par excellence, founder of **Advaita Vedanta.**

The chief sources of biographies are; **Sri Shankara Digvijayam** and more or less same under **Sankara Digvijaya**: **The Traditional Life Sri SankarAcharya** (by Madhvacharya-Vidyaranya). Though there are as many as 14 known biographies; Shankara Digvijayam, Sankara Digvijaya (Both by (Madhvacharya (Vidyaranya) and **Sankaravijayam** byAnandagiri are most cited. The main Shankara Vijayams are:

1. Madhavīya Shankara Vijayam (of Madhava, c. 14th Century)
2. Anandagirīya Shankara Vijayam (of Anandagiri, not extant)
3. Cidvilāsīya Shankara Vijayam (of Chidvilasa, c. between 15th and 17th Century)
4. Keralīya Shankara Vijayam (extant, 17th Century AD)
5. Anantanadagiri Shankara Vijayam (extant from 15th Century AD, but controversial in nature) Not to be mistaken with Anandagirīya Shankaravijayam by Anantanandagiri (1119-1199 AD)

Having studied most and critically analysed of these biographies including available excerpts of Anandagirīya Shankaravijayam basically, I found biographies by Madhvacharya being the most controversial, full of questionable. These biographies written many centuries to a thousand years after Adi Shankaracharya's Samadhi, in Sanskrit and non-Sanskrit languages. Most are filled with legends and fiction, often mutually contradictory, imaginative, lifted names etc from chronicles of interested areas. Some biographies are proved forgeries by those who sought to create a historical basis for their own rituals or theories. Adi Shankaracharya died in the thirty third year of his life, and reliable information on his actual life is scanty.

Observation on Adi Shankaracharya. Below are the observations in the introduction to the translated Biography "**Sankara Digvijaya**" of Adi Shankaracharya by Madhvacharya-Vidyaranya) by **Swami Tapasyananda** (1904-1991 AD). He, a senior monk of the Ramakrishna Mission, wrote plethora of Biographies, Translations which includes Srimad Bhagavata, Saundarya-Lahari, Sankara Digvijaya and Sivananda Lahari of Shankara.

In the Preface of this translated biography, Swami Tapasyananda, interestingly notes:-"When he (Meaning Adi Shankaracharya) was born; where he met his teacher; where he wrote his commentaries; what were the routes he took in his all-India journeys for preaching and teaching; who were all his opponents and where he met them; how and when he came across his disciples; what temples he visited or renovated; what Muth's he founded or whether he founded any Muth at all; where he passed away-all these **are matters on which conflicting or widely differing views are expressed** in the different traditional books concerned with him known as **Sankara-vijayas**".

Swami Tapasayananda

Superficial Additions: Swami Tapasyananda continues: "In contrast to these are the traditional biographical writings on Sankara called Sankara-vijayas. All of them without an exception, **mix the natural with the supernatural**; bring into the picture the deliberations held by super-human beings in the heavens; bring gods and dead sages into the affairs of men; report miraculous feats and occurrences; and come into conflict with one another in regard to many biographical details."

Mythological Elements Included in Biographies: "If we approach the Sankara-vijayas without forgetting that mythological elements have entered into them, they would enable us to get a much more vivid and flesh-and-blood picture of Sankara than these learned discussions on dates and on the credibility of various texts and some of the details contained in them".

Fake Biographies: "I (Swami Tapasyananda-Translator) happened to meet at Bapatla, Brahmasri Vemuri Narasimha Sastri, during my recent tour (1920's) in the Guntur District, in quest of manuscripts, mentioned casually to him my doubts regarding the authorship of Madhaviyasankara-vijaya. He revealed to me some startling facts. When he (Brahmasri Vemuri Narasimha Sastri) was at Madras some fifteen years ago (Around 1905 AD), he had the acquaintance of the late Bhattasri Narayana Sastri, who wrote the Sankara Vijaya **published in the name of Madhava i.e., Vidyaranya, and that four others helped him in this production.**"

Other Observations on Biographies

Shankara Hagiography. Scholars note that one of the most cited hagiographies mostly include stories and legends about historically different people, but all bearing the same name of Sri Shankaracharya or also referred to as Shankara, but likely meaning more ancient scholars with similar names such as Vidya-sankara, Sankara-misra and Sankara-nanda.

Biography by Madhvacharya-Vidyaranya. Author of Adi Shankaracharya's two biographies, both having similar contents. Contents of this biographical accounts of Adi Shankaracharya, were taken by many religious scholars as the base by creating similar accounts; with more spice to add, to establish their own image. Little did they realise that in bargain of their ambition, they have created a maze of contradictions, fictitious accounts and visits, which gullible have taken as gospel truth.

Madhvacharya ascended the Pontiffs seat at Sharda Peeth Sringeri in 1380 AD. Before that he worked in various capacities and Chief Minister of Vijaynagara Empire (1336-1380 AD). During his life before taking Sanyasa and Pontiffship Madhvacharya is reported to have gone on pilgrimage to various places. During the pilgrimage he got message from his younger brother, then pontiff of S'arada Peeth Sringeri, to return to Sringeri, which he complied with, reaching Sringeri via Hampi. After Bharati Krishna Tirtha, his younger brother and pontiff attained *videhamukti* (Death), Madhvacharya succeeded his younger brother and assumed charge of the Sringeri Muth and reigned as **Jagadguru** (as designated) for six years from 1380 to 1386. He died in 1391 AD.

A General View of Kudali Temple on Tunga-Bhadra River Confluence First S'arada Peeth Established by Adi Shankaracharya (Eighth Century)

It was during pontiffship of his younger brother Madhvacharya (Vidyaranya), Bharati Krishna Tirtha then Pontiff, when the idol of sandalwood, originally consecrated by Adi Shankaracharya at Kudali (Close to confluence of Tunga-Bhadra Rivers) was removed and shifted to Sringeri. Instead, a golden image was installed at the newly constructed Muth Temple. **Sandalwood Idol and various original manuscripts were removed from Kudali and placed in the newly constructed Vidhyashankara Temple,** named after last pontiff of Kudali.

The Photograph collage above is that of Kudali Temple and the Tunga-Bhadra River Confluence, the place First S'arada Peeth was established by Adi Shankaracharya.

View of Vidhyashankara Temple (Below), named after Pontiff Vidhyashankara (Bharti Tirtha), constructed by the duo brothers, Bharti Tirtha and elder Madhvacharya (Vidyaranya) at Sringeri.

Sankara Dig-Vijaya. The biography of Adi Shankaracharya -Sankara Dig-Vijaya–by Madhava-Vidyaranya; Translated by Swami Tapasyananda, has 16 Chapters (Cantos), out of which three Cantos (Chapters) are relevant for analysis in this chapter, which basically adds to what Swami Tapasyananda has written: "without an exception, mix the natural with the supernatural... report miraculous feats and occurrences". The chapters are: **Canto (Chapter) 8:** Controversy with Mandana; **Canto (Chapter) 10:** Acquirement of Knowledge of Sex-Love (By Adi Shankaracharya) and **Canto (Chapter) 16.** Accession to Sharadapitha. The other biographies of Adi

Shankaracharya, have more or less similar contents, which have created absolutely different life of Adi Shankaracharya.

(This Chapter is basically connected with S'arada Shrine/ Temple of Kasmira and restricted to contents connected with this Shrine/Temple. First **Mandana Misra**, Second King **Amaruka of Kasmira** and event connected with him and **Third S'arada Shrine/Temple** and aspects connected with it. (In the explanations only brief of that particular relevant portion of the Biography have been quoted)

Mandana Misra and Sarasawani (Canto (Chapter) 6). Mandana in all the biographies of Adi Shankaracharya, is a scholar, mentioned differently by different biographers, most of the accounts connect him with Adi Shankaracharya, as his close associate and disciple. If one analyses all accounts, the accounts and biographies after Madhav-Vidyaranya and Anandagiri are cut and paste, as suiting to their write up. In Shankara Dig-Vijayam Mandana is shown as a Scholar incarnation of **Brahma** (known in his early life as Viswarupa) his wife as **Bharati** (later known as **Ubhaya-Bharati**) as incarnation of **Saraswati (Brahma's wife** in mythology). The reason for this explanation, unbelievable though, is that Mandana is later shown in scholarly light, while Bharati (Ubhaya-Bharati) as a knowledgeable woman, blessed by Goddess of Knowledge (Sharada-A form of Saraswati). It is of interest that the incident connected with Mandana's wife, **Sarasawani** actual name, that Sara'da (S'arada Peeth) was established at **Kudali**. By all accounts She was born as Sarasawani (Sweet Voiced-Sarasa-Sweet; Wani–Voice), but in many biographies she is mentioned as Bharti (A name of Saraswati), ultimately Ubhaya (a category of knowledge (*jṣāna*) obtained by clairvoyance (*avadhi-jṣāna*). It is apparent that her name to fit it in a particular role, name(s) was ***doctored*** to indicate Saraswati; Goddess of Knowledge. Adi Shankaracharya while composing the ***S'arada Bhujanga Prayat Stotra*** mentions the principal antagonist as Mother. One might be surprised at the word Sharada. It is the original designation as outcome of Sara (First two alphabets of name **Sarasawani** and da means her (Sarasawani-***Sarada*** Peeth) established by Adi Shankaracharya.

Her, Bharati (Ubhaya-Bharati), conversation is the start of connection with Adi Shankaracharya, when he reached Varanasi she addresses him thus: "The great Acharya (meaning him) has defeated (In Debates): **Bhaskara, Abhinavagupta, Neelakantha, Mandana** (her husband), and the rest". Unbelievable assertion: surprisingly all these Scholars are post Adi Shankaracharya era: -Bhaskara (900AD), Abhinav Gupta Ninth/Tenth Century, Neelkantha Bhatta (10th/11th Century).

Roots Mandana Misra. Mandana (Maṇḍana Misra (Eighth Century AD), was student of scholar Kumarila Bhatta, who wrote on the Mimamsa and Advaita systems; *Brahma-siddhi.* Born to a humble family in **Mithila** (present day Bihar), lived in a village **Mahishmat**i (?) in Mithila. In Kashi this conversation is quoted in the Biography, mentioning Mandana's residence: "Sankara now left Prayaga; and ***travelling through the skies*** (Flies), reached the splendid city of Mahishmati, the residence of Mandana" In **Canto (Chapter)** 3, Mandana's paternal home is stated to be situated in the capital of **Kasmira**: "These people are coming from the capital city of the king of Kasmira. Think twice before giving them your word, so that we may not have to go back upon it afterwards." Quoted conversation of Sarasawani's mother to her husband, when Misra family has to meet them to ask for Sarasawani's hand in marriage to Mandana.

However, in scriptures, Maṇḍana Misra reportedly lived in the present day Mandleshwar (Maheshwar) and debated with Shankaracharya at the Gupteshwar Mahadev Temple, town deriving its name after Maṇḍana. It is also claimed that Mandleshwar (Maheshwar) ancient name was Mahishmati (Pali-Mahissti). Mandana Misra connected with Adi Shankaracharya is known by several names: Oomveka, Viswarupa, besides as **Sureshwara,** after he became a Sanyasi. A well-known Vedantic text by name *Brahmasiddhi,* is attributed to Mandana Misra. Whether this Mandana is the same as the ritualistic philosopher, whom Sankara had to confront, is a matter of controversy. Because the views of the author of *Brahmasiddhi* are mostly Vedantic and not of the ritualistic philosophy. But the greater possibility is that the ritualist Mandana Misra who became Sureshwara, under Adi Shankaracharya's influence, is a different person. Apparently, the Biographer lifted the name from the chronicle *Brahmasiddhi.* Other contradictions connected with Mandana Misra, is place where he lived!

Chidvilasa in Cidvilāsīya Shankaravijayam also records Mandana as a resident of Kasmira. According to Anantanandagiri (AnandagirīyaShankaravijayam), he (Mandana) lived in Bijlabindu near Hastinapura. Mahishmati (Ancient Name no Mandleshwsar) is actually situated on the Narmada, as. quoted: 'the banks of the Narmada-all these places divided by vast distances claim to have been the residence of Mandana'.

"Mandana was given the name of Sureshwara -a name that came to be -favoured by the guardian (Adi Shankaracharya)". The Biographies of Sureshwara Acharya, the second Acharya who succeeded Adi Shankaracharya, was none other than Mandana, reportedly born in Kasmira as per Muth records and attained Samadhi at Kanchi and held pontiffship for 70 years. It seems that Sureshwara accompany Adi Shankaracharya to Kanchi and remained there till his Samadhi.

King Amaru, Adi Shankaracharya and Eroticism. One of the most unfortunate Part of this biography of Adi Shankaracharya is the description of Eroticism by Adi Shankaracharya, by entering the dead body of a King: Amaru a king of Kasmira. Ubhaya-Bharati (Sarasawani) challenges Adi Shankaracharya to discuss with her me the science and the art of love between the sexes (Kusumastra-sastram) and enumerate its forms and expressions. In this narration in Sankara-Dig-Vijaya Ubhaya Bharati, wife of Mandana Misra, challenges him with sexually coded questions. The questions are too absurd to be asked by a woman to a Saint about sex; its centres, variation in the sexes during the bright and dark fortnights and its manifestations in man and woman. One wonders as to how a Sanyasi pontiff could pen such expression, what to talk of indecency.

The biographer to build on above sexology experience makes Adi Shankaracharya and *his disciples travel though air by Yogic Power to enter the dead body of* the king of the Devas (King Amaruka) of Kasmira; "While the great Sankara began to rule the kingdom through the body of Amaruka" and thus live in his palace harem through his body to gain knowledge of sex-love, as asked by Sarasawani, to have direct study of the manifestation of love in women and their behaviour under its influence. This expression is just short of 'that a saint acquired knowledge of sex'. In this Amaru termed as King of Kasmira, use of erotic poems in the debate. Adi Shankaracharya is made to enter the dead body of Amaru to answer questions, enjoys his (Amaru's) harem for 100 days to learn about sexuality. Each day is denoted by one of poem, before returning to his own body. So each poem per day!!! Does a religious man, philosopher like Adi Shankaracharya has to be portrayed this way?

Biographer shows Adi Shankaracharya: "anxious to go to Mandana's home for finalising the debate. He, therefore, *travelled through air* to that house, where he found Mandana." to get the sexology experience approved by Mandana's wife Ubhaya-Bharati. Mandana: "Bhagavan Sankara now left **Prayaga**; and travelling through the skies, reached the splendid city of **Mahishmati** which had gained great reputation as the residence of **Mandana**" and after the debate with both Mandana and Sarasawani are left at **Mahishmati** (Chapter 8, 9). However, subsequently Madhvacharya (Vidyaranya) himself places the debate in Kasmira. This debate on sexology is chronicled in other biographies is at Kanchi.

There was no Amaru as King of Kasmira in the entire chronology of Kings of Kasmira nor was Mandana residing in Kasmira.

King Amaru-Who. One wonders as to why Madhvacharya brought in Amaru a poet of Erotic Verses and got Adi Shankaracharya connected with him. What was the motive behind it? All actions by the two brother Pontiffs of Sringeri during the period they developed Sringeri as an alternative to Kudali, smacks of blasphemed motives. The worst of it all is that his experience is finally asked in question form by Goddess Saraswati (as Sharada) at S'arada Temple Kasmira: even a Goddess was not spared.

The Amarushataka. Legend is that the Amaru was King of some place in Karnataka. It is opined by scholars that there was no such King Amaru, even in Karnataka, but fictious King Amaru created in a poetic composition **Amarushataka**, by a poet Amaru (Possibly poet Amaru wanted to remain anonymous and created nom-de-plume). But what are these poems called Amarushataka (Amaru's Hundred! It is a collection of 100 poems by the Seventh Century poet Amaru (nom-de-plume). A pre-Adi Shankaracharya poet has been created as King Amaru, to connect Kasmira, for sexual inclination. The collection has been a classic in Indian literature at least since the aesthetician Anandavardhana (820-890 AD), in his **Dhvany Aloka** (Anandavardhana was poet during the reign of King Avantivarman of Kasmira), which deals with the art of **suggestion** in poetry, praised his poetry: "a single verse can provide a taste of love equal to whole volumes."

There are at least four variant manuscripts of Amarushataka, some with up to 115 stanzas. Some stanzas are clearly the work of other poets, though the Indian tradition has always treated Amaru as a single person. The latest translation making round uses the 1420 AD version. Its subject is mostly ***Sringara*** (erotic love, romantic love), including aspects such as love, passion, estrangement, longing, rapprochement, joy and sorrow etc. Ámaru's sophisticated Seventh-Century AD "Hundred Poems" are as much about the social aspects of courting, betrayal, feminine indignance, and masculine self-pity as about sensuality. A sample: -

The sandal paste is rubbed
From your lifted breasts,
Your lip rouge is smeared,
The kohl's gone from your eyes.
Deceitful messenger,
Your soft skin's aroused
And you can't see your own sister's despair!
Tell me you went to the bathing tank
Not back to that scoundrel.

Prior to that, the major source of information on this sect was a chapter devoted to it in Vidyāraṇya's Sarvadarśana Saṅgraha. Thus, he used his collection, which is pre-Biography on Adi Shankaracharya by him, with what motive, none can expect it from a Pontiff of a Muth.

Amaru Experience. Scholar T. S. Narayana Sastry author "*The Age of Sankara*", deals with this major event mentioned in the Biographies; sexology experiences when he enters the body of King Amaru of Kasmira. Quote: "Sankara in the corporal case (After entering his dead body) of the King was gathering varied erotic experiences which, it is said, have come to posterity under the title *Amarusataka*".... "The amorous surroundings had for some time even made the great Sankara to forget the purpose for which he had taken so much pain of leaving his own body and living in an alien atmosphere". "No trace of this strange story can be found in any of the Sankara Vijayas. But Madhava in his biography of Sankara in the Ninth and Tenth Sargas (Chapters) has written this when Sankara was about to take his seat on the Sarvajna pitha (S'arada Shrine/Temple). Goddess Sarada had put him this question and answers ...... (See Verse's Box in Sanskrit below with commentaries in English)."

About the amorous conduct of Shankaracharya comments and verses. Quote: "After crossing many mountains and traversing through many countries, they reached at last the Kindgom of Amaruka. Throne of Omniscience" in Kashmir, (which some think is identical with Kanchi, as Govindanatha interprets it), and then went away to some place 'pleasing' to him *(ruciradesam).*" The narrative Part of the work abruptly ends with this, followed by three or four evocatory verses

[139] No trace of this strange story can be found in any of the Sankara Vijayas. But Madhava in his biography of Sankara in the 9th and 10th Sargas has written that when Sankara was about to take his seat on the Sarvajna pītha, Goddess Sarada had pu him this question' 'कला कियत्यो वद पुष्पधन्वनः किमात्मिका किंच पदं समाश्रिताः। पूर्वे च पक्षे कथमन्यथा स्थितिः कथं युवत्यां कथमेव पुरुषे ॥ In reply to her, the great Samyamīndra, traversed all the sexologies, met her in all the arguments and triumphed. 'वात्स्यायनप्रोदित सूत्र जातं तदीय भाष्यं च विलोक्य सम्यक्। स्वयं व्यधत्ताभिनवार्थगर्भं निबन्धमेकं नृपवेषधारी ॥' from this we learn, that the Teacher could have written some treatise on the erotic Seience and decidedly he could not be the author of the Amaru Sataka now extant. 'न तु अमरुशतक निर्माण सूचनमात्रमपि शंकरदिग्विजये समुपलभ्यते; न अपि अमरुशतके शारदा प्रश्नोत्तरानरूपं किमपि अस्ति तस्माद् एवं विधा निर्मूला जनश्रुतयः कथं प्रमाणत्वेन स्वीकर्तुमर्हाः?' (See introduction to Amaru Sataka by Narayana Rama Acharya Kavya Tirthâ). Sankara was a born rationalist; he would never have stooped down to perform this sort of miracle. Some inferior scribe, to give his imagination 'a local habitation and a name' might have woven this tissue of fancy and pure lie. Hence this strong romantic tale has to be dismissed as worthless and unfounded.

Kasmira Shaivism and Madhavacharya. Primarily either there has been misreading of original script, taking Kanchi as Kasmira or was it deliberate by Madhvacharya! It was deliberate as he was out and out to bring home, that Advaita Philosophy was supreme and Kasmiri Shaivism was more erotic and to proudly claim that Adi Shankaracharya's philosophy is supreme and Kasmiri Shaivism is mere hoax. The other reason was that while Adi Shankaracharya gave the philosophy of Advaita, Madhavacharya's works gave a further modification to Adi Shankaracharya's Philosophy. A deep study of the debate between Mandana and Adi Shankaracharya is indicative enough as to how in the garb of Adi Shankaracharya debate Madhvacharya propounded his own theory of **Dvaita philosophy** (dualism); "the world is not an illusion and there is a difference between the Atman (soul, self) and Brahman (ultimate reality)". To a large extent his Dvaita is opposite to what was propounded by Adi Shankaracharya (Read Chapter II). Since Kasmiri Shaivism is by indigenous Shaivite Philosophers, Madhvacharya was out and out to project Kasmiri Shaivism and Scholars as erotic. In pursuance of his intentions, many scholars of then Kasmira, or of Kasmira roots, have been quoted in this biography and berated. Most of them were either not born during Adi Shankaracharya's life period or just are unknown, as part of 'indiscriminate bringing together of writers of very different centuries, whom Sankara met and defeated. King Amaru, Mandana a resident of Kasmira, calling Abhinavgupta a sorcerer etc are few examples'.

Adi Shankaracharya's Biography and South Indian Scholars

South Indian Scholars. Kasmiri's day by day are adding narratives in praise of Adi Shankaracharya in connection with S'arada Shrine/Temple, in-spite of the fact that these myth and lore's were created based on fictional, imaginative accounts by certain Scholars. Learned Scholars and admirers of Adi Shankaracharya have critically studied and analysed the contents of various biographies, most were appalled the way his life events were chronicled; most found Madhavacharya's *Madhaviya -Sankcara-Vijaya* and the likes, most damaging to the great saint.

Noted South Indian Scholar **T.S. Narayana Sastri (1916)** asserts: "We know from very reliable sources that this *Madhaviya -Sankcara-Vijaya* was compiled by a well-known

Sanskrit scholar, who passed away from this world just about eight years ago (1908), under the pseudonym of 'Madhava'-a synonym for 'Narayana'-specially to extol the greatness of the Sringeri Muth, whose authority had been seriously questioned by the Kumbhakonam (Kanchi) Muth and the Acharya's of the latter Muth's. And has very strong reasons to believe that this *Sankara-digvijaya* ascribed to Madhavacharya, the *Sankara-vijaya-vilasa* ascribed to Chidvilasa, and the *Sankara-vijaya-sara* ascribed to Sadananda, had all been brought into existence by one or other of these three scholars, about this period, in answer to the *Sankaravijayas*.

Adi Shankaracharya Samadhi Controversy

Samadhi Controversy. For reasons of creating more imaginative events concerning Adi Shankaracharya, his place of Samadhi has been vacillating between Dattatreya Cave, Badri, Kasmira, Kashi etc, but not Kanchi where he actually attained Samadhi. Over the centuries it was dawning that Adi Shankaracharya did attain Samadhi at Kanchi and his most trusted disciple Sureshwara was with him at that time. He had been there for few years after return from his visit to Kashi. The complete Samadhi at Badri or nearby area was created subsequently.

Kanchi Kamakoti Peeth, also called the Kanchi Muth or the Kanchi monastery, is located in Kanchipuram, Tamil Nadu. The Kamakoti Peeth is named after Goddess Kamakshi, referred locally as Kamakoti, or Goddess Durga. Kancheepuram is referred to as Kanchi. It is located near a temple dedicated to Goddess Kamakshi (Durga, Kamakoti), along with a shrine for the Advaita Vedanta founder Adi Shankaracharya. Its founding is traditionally attributed to Adi Shankaracharya, who lived his final years here and attained Samadhi here. This is not accepted by the Muth's though a Samadhi of Adi Shankaracharya exists within the precincts of the Muth. Adi Shankaracharya established Four Muth's and the fifth one was the mool (root) institution: Kudali (Sringeri Muth did not exist till 13th Century AD).

According to the traditions relied on by Anantanandagiri (12th Century), Adi Shankaracharya came to Kanchi at the end of his spiritual mission and attained Samadhi there. As per chronicles he either founded a new Devi temple there, or renovated and reformed the existing one and helped the growth of the two blocks in that temple town; Siva Kanchi and Vishnu Kanchi. Texts like Siva-rahasya, mentions Kanchi as one of the centres he founded-in fact, as the Muth, where he finally settled down and passed away, thus giving Kanchi Muth special importance as one of the Muth's established by Adi Shankaracharya. Chidvilasa's Sankara-vijaya on the other hand texted only four excluding Kanchi. No wonder, as he too was the pontiff of Sringeri Muth.

The verse quoted below relates that, after travelling widely, Adi Shankaracharya reached Kanchi (Kanci) of his own accord, consecrated Kamaksi (Kamakshi dol) and attained final beatitude (Heavenly Happiness) at Kanchi itself. The verse reads thus:

"आगच्छन् स्वेच्छया काञ्चीं पर्यटन् पृथिवीतले।
तत्र संस्थाप्य कामाक्षीं जगाम परमं पदम्॥"

(Sanskrit Manuscripts in South India, by Dr.Hultzch, German scholar, (Published by the Government Press, Madras, in 1908).

There are plethora of chronicles, old manuscripts which clearly indicate Adi Shankaracharya's last days were at Kanchi. One finds it hard to believe that even the Samadhi or last days of a sage is put under dispute by the very religious institutes he established. It is absolutely clear that from around 14th Century AD with roots at Sringeri, this new theory of Samadhi at Badri, Kailsa, Dattatreya Cave and Kasmira was propounded more due to religious politics. It is a sentimental issue, now also in court and Kanchi Seer going all out to get the due of Kanchi

Muth. This brings me again to the point I mentioned that today the institution of Acharya's instead anointing themselves instead as Shankaracharya's, are more interested in rivalry, politics and activities unbecoming of religious heads. In view of the controversial nature of these respective assertions, instead of enumerating or quoting full details I restrict myself to just lead readers to understand that the Sage attained his Samadhi at Kanchi. A brief peep of the facts is, therefore, essential.

Etchings(Tamil)-Kanchi Kamakoti-Peethadhipathi- Jagatguru Shankaracharya
Adi Shankaracharya Samadhi at Kanchi ?

Samadhi of Adi Shankaracharya. It is revealing that a make shift Samadhi was made near Kamakshi Temple. Few centuries earlier, a Stone construction, improved later was made (Photo above). This was called Samadhi and was objected by religious scholars that a Samadhi Mandapam cannot be constructed within the precincts of the temple. When this was pointed out to Kanchi Muth, they fell in Line and the inscription was changed and renamed it the "Shankaracharya Samadhi". By jettisoning the "m" for a pair of "n", the Muth then turned a putative into a sanctum. The writings in Tamil are not readable completely but mention this: "Kanchi Kamakoti-Peethadipathi Jagatguru Shankaracharya." (Peethadipathi-Pontiff-Head). The argument about reported Samadhi somewhere around Badri and Kanchi claim was attributed as: 'Sages appear and take Samadhi anywhere and then return to other places'.

Brahat Sankara-vijaya written by Citsukhacarya, is the first and authentic one about the life of Adi Shankaracharya. This biography gives full details of Sankara's life, with dates. Although this rare text is not found in libraries, Scholar T. S. Narayana Sastry managed to obtain a manuscript of it, from which he brought out material in a book in 1916, "*The Age of Sankara*". The manuscript of the *Brhat Sankara-vijaya* used by Narayana Sastry seems to have disappeared, when he died in 1918 at age 48. His son writes in the preface to the 2nd Ed of *The Age of Sankara*, was published more than a Century ago (1916 AD). Mr Sastry has had insight into various other original manuscripts on the life and events of Adi Shankaracharya.

David Reigle, an American author and an independent scholar of the Sanskrit scriptures of India ***"The Original Sankaracharya"*** (Edmonton Theosophical Society, Vol. 5); "Far and away the most important of these (Biographies of Adi Shankaracharya) is the full *Brhat Sankara -vijaya* written by Citsukhacarya. Citsukhacarya was a lifelong companion of Sankara who says he "never departed from Sankara, from the time he left his native place until he attained his marvellous Brahmibhava (Samadhi-Death)". In other words, "he (Citsukhacarya) was an eyewitness of the life and doings of Sankara from start to finish, and one of his direct disciples."

According to Sankara-Dig-Vijaya Adi Shankaracharya went to Kedar via Badari after ascending the Throne of Omniscience in Kashmir and from there he entered into Kailasa, the realm of Siva, transfiguring himself into Siva's form. There is also a monument to Shankaracharya in that region to commemorate this event. But this version is questioned by other authorities. On this controversy, it is interesting to read the following statement issued by T. N. Ramachandran, Retired Joint Director-General of Archaeology of India: "At Kedarnath, on the way to Badrinath, there is a monument associated with the great Adi-Shankaracharya which His Holiness Sri Shankaracharya of Dwaraka Pith visited some time ago and expressed a desire to renovate (the memorial). His Holiness issued instructions to scholars of all parts of our country to ascertain the place of the Samadhi of the great Adi Shankaracharya. On this Dr Sampurnanand, Chief Minister of Uttar Pradesh, and myself (Ramachandran) bestowed some thought." Later "After having arrived at some conclusion on the point by mutual correspondence, we are of the opinion, that Kedarnath cannot be said to be the Samadhi-sthan (the final resting place) of the great Acharya. Yet it is a unique place connected with the life of the Acharya inasmuch as the great Adi-Sankara disappeared from amidst his followers while at Kedarnath. Traditions recorded in some works dealing with Adi-Shankaracharya point out to the fact that Sri Sankara went to Kailas from Kedarnath, brought the five Sphatika Linga's (Shivalinga's made of crystal) and a portion of the Soundarya Lahari Stotra, and repairing (Returning) to the South, attained Siddhi (final end) at Kanchi".

In his letter addressed to Ramachandran, Dr Sampurnanand wrote: (Naini Tal, letter dated July 6, 1958). "Dear Sri Ramachandra, Recently I had occasion to discuss the matter with the Shankaracharya of Dwaraka Pith (Peeth) also. In the first place the word 'Samadhi' is a misnomer in this connection.

There is nothing to prove that Sri Shankaracharya died at this spot. All that tradition says is that he came to Kedarnath and, in modern phraseology, disappeared thereafter. So, what is called Samadhi is really not a Samadhi but a Memorial. I myself do not treat it as Samadhi and such proposals as I am considering are based on this information. What I propose is that instead of the wretched structure that passes as a Samadhi, a new Memorial should be built in memory of the great Acharya. It should not occupy the place of the present construction which is in danger of being overwhelmed by an avalanche any day. It should be built at a safer place somewhere near the temple. I am getting a design prepared by our State Architect. The Shankaracharya of Dwaraka Pith (Peeth) has given me his support in the matter .... "

The tradition saying that Adi Shankaracharya disappeared from Kedara only to go to Sivaloka and return to the world of men with a number of Sivalinga's· to be established in several parts of India, and at last passed away at Kanchi. The "fact is that according to Markandeya Samhita and Sivarahasya, which are the authorities for this visit (exploit of Sankara), it was from Varanasi and not Kedara that he disappeared to bring the Sivalinga's. According one of these texts. Sankara did not go to Kailasa, but Lord Visweswara brought the Sivalinga's and gave them to Sankara at Varanasi".

The theory of four Muth's only seems to have originated from the fact that the Orders of Dasanami Sannyasins recognise and accept **affiliation with only four Muth's--with Sringeri, Jyotir, Dwaraka and Puri**. The Giri Sect is more powerful than others and exercised power on Sringeri and Jyotir Muth. In fact, the priests of Jyotir Muth are almost all Giri's. It is with connivance of Madhavacharya, the sect ensured that Kedar is shown as the final place where Adi Shankaracharya disappears.

I would not like to comment on the wisdom of Government of India unveiling of a 12 Foot Statue of Adi Shankaracharya at Kedar Nath in November 2021. Wise enough to call it a Statue rather than a Mausoleum, as the previous one destroyed by snow avalanche in 2013. This is what Dr Sampurnanand Chief Minister of Uttar Pradesh had suggested in 1958.

The pertinent lines below purport to state that Sankara (Adi Shankaracharya came to the earth in haste after obtaining the five sphatika Lingas-Yoga, Bhoga, Vara, Mukti and Moksa; vanquished Buddhist, Jain and other scholars and attained Siddhi (eternal bliss) at his own asrama at Kanci.

"संगृह्य लिङ्गानि जगाम वेगाद्भूमौ स बुद्धार्हतजैनमिश्रान्॥
तद्योगभोगवरमुक्तिमोक्षयोगलिङ्गार्चनप्राप्तजयः स्वकाश्रमे।
तान्वै विजित्य तरसाक्षतशास्त्रवादैर्मिश्रान् स काञ्च्यामथ
सिद्धिमाप॥" (ix-16-45,46)

[Verse above (ix-16-45, 46) is from a list of pontifical preceptors of the Bharati ascetic order of the Tungabhadra region].

It is difficult to understand how Kashmir can be Kanchi and even if Kashmir be Kanchi, it is sure that Adi Shankaracharya left Kasmira; according to *Sankara-vijaya* by Vyasachala (**Vyasachala Mahadevendra Saraswati** 54th Pontiff of the Kanchi Kamakoti Peeth from 1498 to 1507 AD). Among available Sankara-vijayas, only Anantanandagiri's gives clear support to this theory of Sankara attaining Siddhi at Kanchi. "This is the view of *Sankara-vijaya*of Govindanatha, also known, as *Acharya-charita.* Govindanatha, who claims his work to be based on Vyasachala *Sankara-vijaya*, which brings Sankara up to Kanchi at the end of his mission and makes him assume the **Throne of Omniscience** there **at Kanchi**, which he (Madhavacharya) settles to identify **strangely with Kashmir"**.

Compulsions of Sringeri Muth. The head of the Sringeri Muth, Madhavacharya who wrote this controversial biography, evidently did not like the idea that Adi Shankaracharya lived his last-days of life at Kanchi and that he established Sringeri Muth in connivance with his younger brother Bharti Tirtha, ascended the **Sarvajna Peeth** there, thinking that it will thereby enhance the value and importance of the Sringeri Muth. Madhavacharya wanted to omit that fact and started the theory that Adi Shankaracharya, after establishing the Sringeri Muth, went back to Kashmir and there after ascending the Sarvajna Peeth disappeared finally in Dattatreya Guha (Somewhere Himalayas. Exact location not given). However, in same Biography itself Adi Shankaracharya is shown having returned to Kanchi, giving full description of the city of Kanchi, construction of the three temples with the help of Rajasena, then King of Kanchi, and of the establishment of a Muth.

Here under are the three Stanza's and the spurious Stanza has been boxed in Blue. The contents, though in Sanskrit, clearly indicates the centre Verse stands out as a sore thumb. Omit the centre Verse you get Kanchi.

"सर्वज्ञः शिष्य संयुक्तः शङ्करो देशिकेश्वरः ।
भूमिं प्रदक्षणीकृत्य भूयः काञ्चीपुरं गतः ॥ १ ॥

जम्बूद्वीपस्य कुर्वाणे शोभां भारतमण्डले ।
शस्तं काश्मीरनामानं देशं विद्योतयन् भृशम् ॥ २ ॥

कामाक्ष्या नाम वाग्देव्याः स्थानं तत्पुर माप्तवान् ।
सर्वज्ञापीठमारोढु मियेष मुनिपुङ्गवः ॥ ३ ॥

Above Verse's, less boxed in blue, in Sanskrit as they appear in the original manuscripts used by Mr Sastry. First one mentions Kanchi, and third one Kamakshi named Goddess and SarvignaPeeth there. Where is Kanchi and where is Kashmir and how are they connected in the same mention? What has Kashmir to do with the city of the Goddess **Kamkashi?** One is entirely at a loss to understand why Bharata Mandala and Jambudvipa are introduced here. There is no further mention of Kashmir, and one cannot understand how Adi Shankaracharya went from the southern-most corner of India to the northern-most corner of the continent, if he really wanted to ascend the Sarvajna-Peeth at Kashmir. It is an ugly trick and an unsuccessful attempt to fabricate. A mere perusal of this portion will show how flat the verses are, and how absurd and incoherent they are.

Scholars Reportedly Defeated by Adi Shankaracharya

Targeting Kasmira Scholars. The biographies have not spared known and famous Kasmira Scholars like Bhaskara Bhatta (900 AD), Abhinava Gupta (Ninth/Tenth Century), Neelakantha (Neelkantha Bhatta) (10th/11th Century),

Mankha, Sri Harsha, Prabhakara, and many more (Chapter 6). **Unbelievable assertion, in that surprisingly almost all these Scholars are post Adi Shankaracharya era**. A modified Abhinav Gupta was created as a Navagupta of Kamrupa (Assam), alleged by Madhava as a sorcerer but unmistakeably to refer to Shaiva Scholar Abhinav Gupta of Kasmira. Question is as to why these Biographers, starting from Madhvacharya started this tirade against Religious Scholars of Kasmira, specifically by name and that too who were not born when Adi Shankaracharya was around.

Madhavacharaya's Motive. The whole debate and the defeat of Kashmiri Shaivite Scholars and even the Visit to S'arada Shrine of Kasmira was created with one purpose; to show that Advaita Philosophy was accepted in Kasmira and in debates with reputed Scholars of Kasmira made to demurringly accept defeat and Advaita Philosophy. The whole creations seems to add to his own Duvaita Philosophy, deviating from the one propounded by Adi Shankaracharya.

Sharadaamba, Sandalwood idol was shifted to Sringeri which was in Standing Position, change was made in the gold idol of Sharadaamba installed separately at Sringeri to sitting position giving reason that sitting position of the Goddess forgot that Sharadaamba, a form of Durga, is different from S'arada as Saraswati, with absolutely different positions in her form. Below is original Verse as Six Śāradāmbāstavanam (Sharadaamba Six Adorations (Nam) to amplify the Mahima of the Goddess Sharadaamba.

Śāradāmbāstavanam. "I visualize Sharada, who was worshipped by Śaṅkara and other supreme spiritual masters in the beginning. I visualize Sharada, who is served by the succession of kings of Mount Śṛṅga. (?) I visualize Sharada, who is right now worshipped by opulent persons, which are full of stable devotion, and Who is always popularized and enacted by the abode of knowledge and best among seers."

आदौ शङ्करदेशिकेन्द्रगुरुणा सम्पूजितां भावये
सेव्यां तस्य परम्परागतमहाशृङ्गाद्रिपीठाधिपैः ।
अद्यापि स्थिरभक्तिभावभरितैः श्रीमद्भिराराधिताम्
विद्यातीर्थयतीश्वरैरभिनवेत्याख्याति पूर्वैः सदा ॥३

Kanchi Muth-Kasmira as Rivals. The newly established Sringeri Muth was overshadowed by close by Kanchi Muth and there was awareness of various Shaivite scholars, specially of Kasmira, whose Kashmiri Shaivism philosophy had spread and making inroads in the South. The role of Goddess S'arada of Kasmira and Sharadaamba invoked by Adi Shankaracharya was known. It was known that Adi Shankaracharya spent his last days and attained Samadhi at Kanchi. The designation of the newly shifted Muth given by the brothers was "Sringeri S'arada Peeth". But S'arada of Kasmira was a hurdle and so also clout of the Kanchi Muth. Thus, all efforts were concentrated to get hold of S'arada of Kasmira and deny Kanchi any importance and veneration due to last days of Adi Shankaracharya at Kanchi. A mind, with such a vast political acumen cum machinations, deep knowledge of true story and events of Adi Shankara, laid down his priorities: Ascendance of S'arada Shrine Kasmira and disappearance of Adi Shankaracharya at place other than Kanchi. With such intentions Madhvacharya, however, forgot aspect of these being two separate Goddesses. Their special worship days are different; S'arada (Sharadaamba) of Sringeri during Navratra definitely indicated her role as Durga. S'arada (Sharadaamba) in South is worshipped specially during autumn Navratra's, while S'arada of Kasmira is worshipped on S'arada Ashtami falling in the month Bhadra (August) and on Guru Tritya (Margeshar Tritya Feburary).

Mission Kasmira. Madhavacharaya had three-fold objectives. Create a new **form** around Adi Shankaracharya's Advaita **Philosophy,** Shankaracharya sold his own **Duvaita**

philosophy as propounded by Adi Shankaracharya. This is amply proved by question answers between Mandana and Adi Shankaracharya at Mahismiti. The debate contents were created under the garb of discussion with clear pointers of stress on his **Dvaita philosophy** (dualism).

Since the Shaivite Philosophy of Kasmira was indigenous, Madhavacharya's target was to prove that Adi Shankaracharya's philosophy of Advaita, albeit his own, as having been adopted by people of Kasmira. In the process he targets Bhatta Bhaskara of Kasmira: "Here there is a great scholar named **Bhatta Bhaskara**. Find him out and inform him of our presence here." Further: "I came here to carry this information to you. In that commentary, he (Adi Shankaracharya) has refuted your unsound doctrines also. You may, therefore, abandon your false doctrines and **adopt the non-dualistic philosophy**". This supposed to be in Seventh/Eighth Century at S'arada Temple, when Bhaskara was not even born. Hilarious though, Shaivite Philosophy Kasmira had just started taking initial step and it was only in 10th Century AD it took shape. The proclaiming of victory of Vedanta Philosophy by the beat of kettle drums, all other doctrines claimed as dissolved and disappeared in front of Adi Shankaracharya's debate.

Creation of Kasmira visit by Adi Shankaracharya, albeit not physically but through the medium of this biography, was to indicate acceptance of Advaita by the Kasmiri scholars of Shaivism. It was known that the contents of the biography would be restricted to devotees of Adi Shankaracharya in the Southern belt and is un-likely to reach Kasmira and be contested. On ground the result was different; Advaita did not reach or overcome the influence of Kasmiri Shaivism in Northern India. With return of some Godmen from visits to Kasmira, with impressive knowledge of Kasmiri Shaivism, it was uncomfortable to accolades and Kasmiri Shaivism being also accepted and its influence on Sringeri and devotee's . Even today people in Kasmira are not aware of the contents of Adi Shankaracharya's biographies and conversely in Southern belt unaware of Scholars and religious philosophy in Kasmira. The sole aim of S'arada Temple Kasmira visit, debates etc was to project Kasmira as domain of Shankaracharya's.

Imaginary Visits of Adi Shankaracharya. Various places, scholars are mentioned where Adi Shankaracharya is supposed to have visited, his doctrine accepted and scholars defeated or humbled. Without going into details, I will mention the places, Scholars and let the readers make their own assessment. Bahlika (Bactria, modern Balkh), a group of Jaina's (in Bacteria, Jaina sect of Digambaras of Surasena (**Surasena** ancient Indian region present-day Braj region in Uttar Pradesh, with Mathura as capital. It was Established 700 BC Disestablished 300 BC).

'Triumphal propaganda tours through the lands of **Darada** (Drava-present day Gilgit Baltistan); **Bharata** (Exited during Vedic period (1700–600 BC), : **Kuru** (1200–900 BC) : **Panchala** (Panchala an ancient kingdom of northern India, did not exist after being annexed by Samudragupta son of the Gupta Emperor Chandragupta I (350-375 AD) and Avanti (Avanti was an ancient Indian Mahajanapada (Kingdom) roughly corresponded to the present day Malwa region. Needless to say, that the author of the biographies just picked up the names from various ancient scriptures of various places and fitted them in. One needs to plot these places on a map of erstwhile Bharatvarsh, to see these places and as to whether it was possible for Adi Shankaracharya to visit all of them. Even a layman will find lack of logic in naming the places, mostly of BC era or are far off places, which had long vanished even beyond the boundaries of India and would take years to travel.

Scholars Reportedly Humbled in Biographies

The list is long, one wonders as to how these names came into the biographies for debates, their defeat, when there was no possibility of such interactions and how their names were picked up. There are classes of Brahmins in the country who follow Vedic rituals and many keenly followed writings of such religious scholars. The fact is by 14th Century, the works, doctrines etc of the scholars were known throughout the religious institutions of Bharatvarsh. Briefly they are; **Prabhākara** (active latter half of the Sixth CenturyAD); **Bhatta Bana (Bāṇabhaṭṭa)** Seventh Century Sanskrit prose writer and poet in the court of King Harsha Vardhana (606-647 AD). **Mayura (Mayurbhatta),** a Seventh Century Sanskrit poet and scholar, who was *brother-in-law of Banabhatta*, the court poet of Harsha Vardhana, noted for having written Surya Satakam and **Daṇḍin** (active career took place around 680-720 AD). Udayana. **(Udayana, Udayanācārya) Udyan Acharya**, (Hindu logician of 10th Century) and **Khandanakara** (the famous dialectician, Harsha). They all as per the Biography: "abandoned their perverse" doctrines (All above places, scholars are mentioned in Verses 139-162, Canto, Chapter 15). Scholars who were either pre or post Adi Shankaracharya era, mostly unconnected with the vision or his religious philosophy.

Vakpati-in Biographies of Adi Shankaracharya. Another example is **Vakpati Bhatta**, whose crutches have been taken by these Biographers, to bolster Adi Shankaracharya's image. Vakpati Bhatta, a court poet of King of Kasmira (King is not named nor could they). In almost all the biographical accounts of post 14th Century till even today, mention him as author of a "Sankarendra Vilasa" by Vakpati Bhatta, a Kasmiri Scholar. Quote: "He (Adi Shankaracharya) defeated (in debate) the famous Vakpati Bhatta, a reputed scholar of the court of the King of Kashmir." It may give an impression that Adi Shankaracharya did visit Kasmira, as per accounts of a Kasmiri Scholar Vakpati Bhatta. Not factually so. Not much is known except is the only scholarly work mentioned in the name of Vakpati Bhatta; who has not been fully identified and not a scholar in the Court of Kasmira. Vakpati Bhatta was a great scholar of that time in ***tarkam*** (determining oscillation constituent in a mental process leading to inference is called

taraka or ***ūha***) but gets connected with Kasmira by his name **Bhatta,** a common prefix or suffix to Aryan Saraswat Brahmins of Kasmira in earlier centuries.

Here is one of the imaginative creations about Vakpati Bhatta in an Indian Chronicle: Aarsha Bharata Paramparyam: Part-2. It has created a new acronym for first millennium AD Aryan Saraswat Brahmins of Kasmira; **The Pandita Parishad**.

Quote: "**The Pandita Parishad**" or "Maha Vidya Peeth" was the most famous among the "Vidvan Sabhas" (assembly of intellectuals) during Abhinava Shankara's time (Adi Shankaracharya 8/9th Century). "Vakpati Bhatta", the "Sarva Shastra Pandit" (Pandit of all the sciences) was its Chief (Adyaksha). It is remembered that high scholars (Maha Panditas) belonging to the Chinese and "Trushka's (Muslims)" communities adored that Vijaya Peeth, themselves." (Islam had yet to take firm roots in the world):

"Reaching over there, the Acharya (Adi Shankaracharya) began His "Shastra Charcha" (discussion on science). The result of the Charcha, which prolonged for many days, was of the absolute victory ("Sampoorna Vijayam") of "Advaita Rakshanam" (protection of Advaita). All the great scholars (Maha Vidvans), including "Vakpati Bhatta", got up, adoring the Acharya, by giving the "Sarva Jnaana Petham" (the seat of the one who knew about everything-Apparently referring to Sharda Temple) and then attained the "Shishyatva" (studentship) of the Acharya. The Acharya was satisfied by giving His blessings to all of them by imparting "Advaita Vedanta Nishta Kriya Yoga" for the family men ("Grihasta Ashramees") and "Jnaana Yoga Marga" for the "Vairaagya Yukta Yaties". The Acharya did not prepare to continue over there at the "Sarvajnaana Peeth" (Referring again to S'arada Temple). Calling upon the disciples, who were with Him, the Acharya gave proper directions for the future activities and sent them to different Parts of India (Bharata)."

"The Guru-given Deeksha name of Abhinava Shankaracharya was "Shankarendra". A gifted Poet and disciple of Abhinava, namely, "waakpati Bhatta" (Vakpati Bhatta), had created a noble Poem, called, Shankarendra (Sankara) Vilasa, adoring the greatness of the Acharya on that name. From that Poem only, we could know, some of the history of the "Digvijaya" and the "jnaana Yoga Vaibhava" of "Abhinava Shankaracharya". (In the same write up it has been claimed that the poems– "ShankarendraVilasam" and the "Nirnaya Sangaram" are included in the "Kaavyamala Granthavali")

Authors Comment. This is blatant what is called "Intellectual Religious Cheating". Herewith I will explain How Vakpati Bhatta as well as The Pandita Parishad (Vidhvan Sabha) have been created for the debate during the reign of Lalitaditya. Lalitaditya after Victory over Yashovarman, being pleased over the efforts of his Foreign Minister (*samdhivigrahika*) bestowed upon him (Mitrasarman) the five (offices distinguished) by the term Great **Pancamahasabha**. From that time onwards (Reign of Lalitaditya) there have existed over the eighteen offices, which had been created before and he (Lalitaditya added five new one. These designations were 'office of high Chamberlain' (mahapratiharapida); Chief Minister of Foreign Affairs (mahasamidhivigraha); Chief Minister of Horse (*Mahavasala*); High Keeper of the Treasury (*mahabhandagra*) and the fifth Chief Executive Officer (*mahasadhanagara*). There were Sahi's (King) and other princes were the officers in the *Mahasabha*. (Rajatarangini Book IV 139-143). Cleverly all the contents of these verses have been manipulated to create a *Vidhvan Sabha of Pandits*, connect *Vakpati as Vakpati Bhatta of Ka'smira*, during the *reign of Lalitaditya*. What a pity!!!

Authors Intervention about Vakpati Bhatta. Now about the facts about Vakpati Batta. Kalhan in verse 144 Book IV *Rajtarangini* refers to one as Vakhpatiraja. Kalhan does refer to one Vakpatiraja, who is none other than Vakpati, but does not just not name him Bhatta, but apparently added raja, as an addendum. **Vakpati** was poet laureate or head poet at the court of Yashovarman, and enjoyed his favour. Yashovarman was King of Kannauj in the early Part of the Eighth Century and his reign was from 725 to 752 AD. *Sanskrit literature* Scholar K. Krishnamachari in his History of Sanskrit Literature has referred to "Shankarendra (Sankara) Vilasa by Vakpati Bhatt, a Kasmiri pandit, a biography of Dhir-Shankarendra Saraswati (Adi Shankaracharya). He has rightly commented that: "Sankarendra Vilasa, a poem in six Cantos (compare-Canto V. Verses 1-35) attributed to Sri Vakpati Bhatta of Kashmir, is an ugly trick and an unsuccessful attempt to **Fabricate**. This person (Adi Shankaracharya) was born in 788 AD, and thus Adi Shankaracharya could not have been **born during the time of Vakpati**."

Abhinav Gupta (933-1015 AD) and Others. Abhinav Gupta, noted Shaivite Scholar of Kasmira, was born and brought up, taught in Kasmira and finally entered a Cave in 1015 AD. He seems to be favourite for defeats etc of the Shankaracharya's of India. First Adi Shankaracharya (788-820 AD) defeats him in debate, then he is depicted as sorcerer and now 48th Acharya Advaitanandaboodha 1200 AD (1132-1200 AD) defeats him as per his achievements listed by Kanch Muth. Can the three eras of all three reconciled?

"Then he (Adi Shankaracharya) went to Kamarupa where he won victories over Navagupta, a leading thinker of the Sakta school and a commentator on the Vyasa Sutras from the point of view of that school. Navagupta now reflected in his mind thus: "He is like a sun to the lotus of the Vedas. Under his warmth, that lotus will bloom and our school will perish. In all the worlds, there is none equal to him in intelligence and learning. He must, therefore, be put down somehow. I shall do this through black magic." "Navagupta, the master of black magic, was, as stated before, planning, ever since his defeat at the hands of Sankara, to bring about his death by black magic.

By Abhichara (a form of black magic) this evil one produced in the body of the Acharya a rectal fistula of an incurable nature."

The Tribute. There is no denial about the very existence of Adi Shankaracharya on this earth. Bharatvarsh was blessed with his presence in this mortal world, at a time when we needed him most. What he achieved during his short life of 32 years is difficult even to imagine. He was a sage, a religious philosopher, never claimed to be God nor having supernatural powers. His life, short though, was a blessing to all those who believe in his "Brahma **Satyam. Jagan Mithya. Jivo Brahmaiva Na Aparah**." This translates roughly as: "God alone is real, the world is unreal, the individual is none other than God". Sad that many, most claiming themselves as Religious Philosophers and saintly persons, tried to create a differentiae life and teachings of Adi Shankaracharya. Abhor able is the way stories were created, which may have added to the influence and fame of writers, but definitely in long run, much they tried, finally truth is staring at our faces.

"Fallacies and not the correct explanations. But here follows a refutation of their reasonings independently of the texts. This is the difference. With regard to this the Sathkhyas"

–Adi Shankaracharya

8

Kishanganga Valley-Dard (Drava) Region and S'arada Civilisation

The person who is always involved in good deeds experiences incessant divine happiness. – Rig Veda

(The reference in this chapter as Kishanganga, Kishanganga/Neelam Valley and S'arada Shrine etc is on the current status of these places. Necessarily there are not all historically as they have been enumerated below. The factual history etc has been covered in Chapters 4 and 5)

Kishanganga-The Valley of Sharada

Kishanganga (Neelam) Valley. A peep into S'arada Valley (Kishanganga/Neelam Valley), where the S'arada shrine is located is blessed with a number of streams and of course Kishanganga River. From immemorial rivers in this Valley divided the area under different classifications to about 18th Century AD. Each segment dominated, as their fiefdom, by separate clans. Occasionally some of these areas came under nominal suzerainty of different neighbouring Kingdom's or countries. Collectively or individually, the clan heads, who actually where rulers of their own area/clan had to yield on to 'invasionŚ from outside. But at an opportune moment and times restore and exercise their freedom. These were states within a State and heads acting as rulers cum Warlords; in ancient times termed as Damras (War Lords).

This valley is a distinct piece of land divided by River Kishanganga. The river with this name is not mentioned in any of the verses of either Nilamata Purana or Kalhan's Rajatarangini. The ancient name, specifically mentioned at a point of confluence with Vitasta is **Krsna** (Nilamata Verse's 1278-79: confluence of the **Krsna** and the Vitasta; Verse 1446-47 and the sin-removing **Krsna**). During medieval period South of the River was part of one Chieftain's territory and area north of it under various other groups of Chieftains. Kishanganga River was considered the Northern Boundary of the Kasmira Kingdom, though on ground it acted as an independent strip across the Shamsabhari Range, with ethnic connection with the people tribes of Northern side: Dards. A clan of Chak's were also denizens of this Valley, but many migrated to Kasmira valley, where they ruled for few decades.

Kishanganga (Neelam) Valley of Neelam District of AJK, is more contiguous to Dard Country with affiliation and sympathy more towards Dardistan, than Kasmira. For brief years, in the first millennium and initial period of second millennium, joined Kasmira for a short period and drifted again. During dying Hindu rule and Muslim rule in Kasmira, the area was not under the rule of Kasmira or accessible to outsiders. It became a friendly heaven for any rebellious princes, nobles and warlords of Kasmira, not to talk of battle royal by King Jaisimha (1128-1149 AD), who had to fight to bring back fugitive nephew Bhoja. This battle brought the famous Sirhasila Castle of the Kishanganga Valley, castle of the Warlord, into lime light. With Kalhan being witness to the events, this expedition by Jaisimha against Bhoja and Warlord (Damra) of the area, Alamchakra, got reasonable mention in Rajatarangini. The castle and shrine also got mentioned: " He

(Bhoja) escaped from the Sirhasila Castle and took refuge in the area of Shrine".

During Kasmira King Jaisimha's rule, Yashodhara was the ruler of Dards and no friend of Kasmira Kingdom. On his death his Minister Ciddasiha placed Yashodhara's son, Viddasiha, as a puppet ruler. Attitude of Dardistan and Dards towards Kasmira is evident from this Rajatarangini verse: "Those who show the face of friend while they are ought to be feared". This reference is to then ruler of Darda and even Viddasiha; "Viddasiha became enraged against King of Kasmir (Jaisimha)". Finally, Damra Alamchakra took over as War Lord of the area and his Castle was Sirahasila. The hostilities continued and more so till Advent of Islam, while Kasmira Kings were fighting for their own survival. During Islamic rule also hostilities continued. Sultan's Shihabu'd-Din's (1359-1378 AD) and Zain-ul-Abdin (1420-1474 AD) rule, mounted separate expeditions, but had to return with high promises, continued hostility **and the Shrine from threat by Dards.**

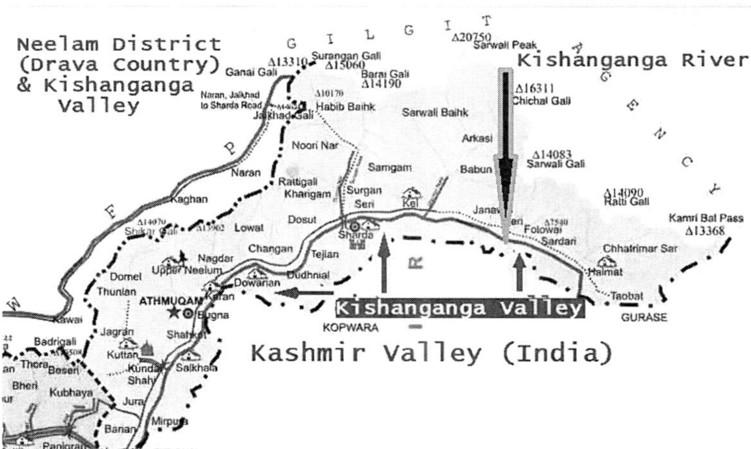

During Mugul as well as Pathan rule, the area of Karna and Drava (includes Kishanganga/Neelam Valley), were in the hands of petty Chiefs of Bomba Clan, independent of the rule of Kasmira Kingdom with nominal association with

Kishanganga Valley ruler. As a counter measure Durani (Afghan) Rulers established colonies of Afridi tribe of Afghanistan in the area, adding further to the dissenting forces, increased clashes with Dard's and Bomba's. Even as late as 20th Century Bomba's raided Kasmira as far as Srinagar. During this period Muslims from adjoining areas trickled in and settled in the valley, clearly changing demography of the area. Many Muslim families from Srinagar too migrated to the area due to persecution of their sect by Muslim rulers and clergy.

Except for short period during Jaisimha's rule, the area and its chieftain's maintained separate identity. It was only since the establishment of Dogra rule and suppression of Bomba tribesmen, that route from the valley could open to the Shrine/Temple, which was life line of Dogra presence in Gilgit-Baltistan and incidental to Kishanganga/Neelam Valley, but only after the Dogra Forces had established forts and posts in the area right up to Gilgit.

Fortified Watch Posts Constructed by Dogra Kings at the Back of the S'arada Shrine/Temple Nearly 150 Years ago for the Security of the Area

The purpose of bringing in the area and earlier inhabitants is relevant to focus on to the roots of the Dards in the area.

Dardistan-Dard (Drava) Country

Dardistan-Dard (Drava) Country. S'arada Shrine is located in Kishanganga Valley (Neelam Valley), after name of Kishanganga River. The current name of the valley, Neelam Valley, is after renaming of the Kishanganga River as Neelam River. Neelam, a town of the valley on the banks of the river, was more indicative of demographic change than sticking to pre-1947 name connected with Hinduism. The shrine is few Kilometres from Line Of Control (LOC), in Pakistan Occupied Kasmira (POK), next to a small village called Shardi. The complete area was known for millenniums as Drava Country (Transited to Dardistan).

Darada's (Dards). The main republic of the regrouped migration settlements including Aryans from Central Asia during Second millennium BC in North-Western India was named Kamboja Mahajanapada (Kingdom). Kamboja Kingdom extended from Eastern Afghanistan up to Rajapuri (Rajauri-Jammu and Kashmir) in South-West of Kasmira and shared borders with Gandhari's (Ancient residents of Gandhara (Afghanistan etc). Darada's were mostly various Tribes of the Bacteria, who moved in various groups, crossed Hindukush and settled on its Southern side Dards in Dardistan are of later vintage, as they had to veer somewhat North after crossing the Hindukush and had to settle for harsh terrain areas. The hardships of the area developed into Dardic aggressive traits.

Dardic Religion. The Dard religion was based on their earlier tribal religion, which developed later into Mixed Old Indic Religion. Majority adopted mixed rituals of Aryan Religion and own Tribal beliefs. Around 200 BC during the reign of Ashoka Buddhism spread as a whiff in North-Western India and continued till about 100 BC. As soon as Ashoka's reign was over, the religio-beliefs of the area slowly gave way back to their old beliefs. During rule of Scathanian's, Kushan's it was King Kanishka I, son of Kushan King Vimla Khadphis, who adopted a mix of two beliefs; ancestral Bactrian God Helio's and Buddhism, in the areas of Kamboja East (Dards). **It was not absolute Buddhism.**

Demographical Changes and Living Style. The demography of the area changed over the centuries, from original inhabitants Dards (Dravas), the warrior tribe of ancient history, to a mixed population. Some of the Eastern and Northern parts of the Kishanganga valley even now retain a fair percentage of Dards. The Dard area had restricted itself into a powerful bastion of warriors who for millenniums retained their aggressive stance. They saw the millenniums through, with their freedom and tribal clan living, fought against each other, to gain supremacy over other clans, refused to be part of any recognised single ruler or state. But at times, due to compulsions, inner rifts or strong rulers, had to accept the suzerainty of invaders, till they revolted again and back to their free state. They remained firm on their own identity, not only as a big chunk of mountainous territory but a group of smaller Kingdoms, which in present day be just equivalent to a cluster of few villages in the subcontinent. Each of these clan clusters retained their identity, different from each other, though common denominator now is Islam.

All said and done, in spite of push by Islamist Preachers from West Asia and then Persia, they continued with their old customs, faith etc, even till this day. Such denomination of clans, country, and religions were clubbed together and called Dards and the area Dardistan, notwithstanding present designations Gilgit, Baltistan etc. Thus, they emerged as a group of Indo-Aryan people found predominantly in Northern Pakistan,

North-West India, and Eastern Afghanistan, **Dards, speaking Dardic languages, of Indo-Aryan family**.

Dard Warriors (1850's)

Dards and Dardic People. The Darda's, Dards, whose territory does not seem to have changed since the time of Herodotus (Fourth century BC), north of Kasmira's Shamsabhari Mountain Range Barrier. In a well-known and story, Herodotus mentions these people war-like on the frontier of Indianames one of the groups in the area as Dadikai. The terms "Dardic" and "Dardistan" were coined by G.W. Leitner in the late 19th century, based on the Greek and Latin term Dardae for the people of the region (Darda's in Sanskrit). In recent decades **Asko Parpola,** a Finnish Indologist suggesting that the Dards are the linguistic descendants of the bearers of proto Rig Vedic culture 1700 BC, pointing to features in certain Dardic dialects that continue peculiarities of Rig Vedic Sanskrit.

Dard's Today. The largest populations of Dards is Gilgit–Baltistan and Khyber Pakhtunkhwa (Pakistan), Kishangnaga/Neelam Valley and in Kasmira, India. There are smaller Dard groups in Ladakh (India) and Eastern Afghanistan. The vast majority of Dardic people are Muslims, but many follow old sect beliefs. A minority in Chitral are polytheistic Kalash, exceptionally retained their ancestral Polytheistic Dardic religion till date and are officially protected by the Government of Pakistan. The people in the Karakoram and vicinity even today refer to themselves as Dards, their country as Dardistan and their language as Dardic.

Epigraphic references to Dard Kings. Three inscriptions on rocks along the Indus and Gilgit Rivers in the southern reaches of the Karakoram provide the earliest epigraphic references to Dard Kings. One is found on rocks where the present-day road between Gilgit and Skardu. The inscription is in poor Kharosthi, and Fussman read it as ***"daradaraya",*** meaning "**King of the Dards**". The second inscription found at Chilas Terrace, near to Chilas village along the Indus River, deciphered more recently by Hinuber (1989) is in **Brahmi script;** transliteration: ***srirdaranmaharajavaisrava***, which he interprets as *Daran-maharaja "great king of the Dards*". A third inscription is immediately below the Thalpan bridge, over the Indus River on the Thalpan side of the bridge is also in ***Brahmi script***. This is to bring in a point that Dardistan was not fully covered into Buddhism, when it was its peak and slowly gave way to their own old religious beliefs. Neither it had connection with Goddess Saraswati nor Goddess S'arada or S'arada Script or language. The last being of much later vintage.

No Buddhist rock edits, or inscriptions or sketches of Kushan's have been found in the Kishanganga Valley, as have been traced on Gilgit Highway. This is ample to discount that Kishanganga Valley was a nerve centre of Buddhism or Hinduism or part of Kushan Empire nor was it centre of teaching religions (Buddhism-Hinduism) in any organised way or institutions, big or small.

Under Kings of Kasmira. From ancient times, Drava was historically, ethically different from Kasmira and its people. The area maintained its separate entity all throughout, though as a group of various clans and tribes. Even as late as early 20th Century Dard Tribes of Kishanganga Valley used to come and raid Kasmira villages and towns. The clans were ruled by War Lords and even though they came under different rulers at times, they acted more as independent War Lords or Clan Chieftain's. There is no account of any of the Kings or Rulers of Kasmira having Kishanganga Valley as effective permanent part of their Kingdom. The area was heaven for rebels, princes etc.

During Muslim Rule-14th Century AD Onwards. Darda's and Dardistan continued to have belligerent stance during the second millennium also. It was only during the Chak rule, Kasmira ruled by a Chak Clan, there was some understanding, more between the two warring clans, even then the warring clans kept up clan court intrigues. During Dogra rule though the complete area up to Gilgit-Baltistan was conquered, yet the Dogra rulers had to position their soldiers to safeguard lines of communication, maintain law and order. In fact, it is ridiculous to claim that all along this portion of Drava Country was part of Kasmira Kingdom. The visits of Kings like Zaina-ul-Abdin etc is fiction. The accounts by Al Biruni written from Kurukshetra and by Abul Fazal, have been dealt with in detail in Chapter V. Both to a great extent certainly reveal some of the most important new facts concerning S'arada shrine (s), though none of them physically visited the area(s).

Spread of Buddhism–North-West India–Kasmira

Pattern of Initial spread of Buddhism. Claim of Buddhist roots in Kishanganga Valley invariably takes you to analyse spread of Buddhism in this area and neighbouring areas. We are aware that Buddhism made significant inroads during 300 BC to 200 AD; Ashoka to Kushan's. Kasmira too became a big landmark of Buddhism spread. To a common man it may mean that places from Kasmira Northwards were the hubs of spread of Buddhism, and so also Drava country and Kishanganga Valley. It was not so. Spread of Buddhismduring the life time of Buddha was restricted so also creation of Buddhist Religion Monuments. Even in the heartland nascent Buddhism had to compete with then existing religions: Vedic Hinduism, Jainism and Ajivka.

Buddha's message was well understood, his following increased, Buddhist Monks ordained, but spread of Buddhism was restricted around Magada Kingdom only. Ordained Buddhist monks composed initial doctrines, reduced them into scriptures and taught them at few selected places; Nalanda being one. Two Buddhist Councils were organised during Buddha's lifetime and Monks were sent to few selected places to spread Buddhism. During Ashoka's reign four ***Thedas*** (Chief Preachers) were selected and sent in different directions: **Madhyntika** (Mid Third century BC) North, to Gandhara (Afghanistan via Taxasila (Taxila) and **to Kasmira, *not directly, but on way to Gandhara*.**) Most of them were able to create a local band of followers, were given some sort of patronage by few rulers and even dwellings made for them called Viharas. It is interesting to know the routes taken by these *Thedas* and Monks. From Maghada to Mathura-Multan-Taxasila-Peshawar-Kabul and famous Bamian-***Oddiyana*** (***Uddayana*** (North of Peshawar) along the Swat River; furthest part of northern ancient India. These became the initial visit centres of Buddhist Monks, were given some sort of recognition, place to live and preach: known as **Vihara's** (Vihara (Sanskrit: vihāra) generally refers to a monastery for Buddhist Monks). As a concept it meant arrangement of space and facilities but in architectural concept it refers to living quarters for monks, term also found in Ajivika, Hindu and Jain religions. Inspite of it all, degree of influence of Buddhism spread during Buddha's life time was restricted.

A museum Sculpture of Theda Madhyntiika

It is gross misunderstanding that Buddhism spread all over, as we are given to understand. Pilgrims from other countries or visitors or traders too used these limited routes, saw the spread of Buddhism in these hubs and the routes and spread word of Buddhism spread back home. They never ventured away from these beaten tracks, as their own sustenance was dependant on the local hospitality along the trade routes.

Ashoka and Spread of Buddhism in North-Western India. Ashoka gave impetus to spread of Buddhism in India and further North towards North-Western India and Gandhara.

After Ashoka the state of Buddhism wanned till Central Asian Tribes and Indo Greeks took on the spread. As part of spread of Buddhism, various monuments, structures were created; **Stupa.** In Kasmira we have remains of a Stupa at Uskura (By Kushan King Huvishka (Post Kanishka). There are **no Buddhist monuments beyond this area**, towards North or immediate West. ***Chaitya*** a shrine, sanctuary, temple or prayer hall in *South Asian* religions. By first half of the Seventh Century, the role of the Chaitya Hall was being replaced by the Vihara.***Mahavihara*** (Mahāvihāra) is the Sanskrit and Pali term for a great Vihara (Buddhist monastery) and is used to describe a monastic complex of Viharas.

Stupa, in Swat founded Third Century AD lasted until 10th or 11th Century AD

We have many such remains of such monuments in North-Western India, but none of the remnants or ruins of any such Stupa, Chaitya or Vihara have been found in the Kishanganga Valley or areas to its West. The explanation of extreme weather conditions etc in the area does not hold, as in the similar conditions, just North of the area, in Gilgit and

Baltistan, such remains have been found.

Stupa-Probably Mauryan Era, Third Century BC

Buddhist Centres of Buddhism Learning. Nalanda, Odantapura (in the Eighth Century AD), Vikramashila (Established by King Dharamapala (783 to 820 AD) and Taxasila (Ancient Taxila or Takshashila, in ancient Gandhara, was an early *Hindu and Buddhist* centre of learning). They are erroneously termed as University's. There is one **Mahavihara (Takht-I Bahi)** in Gandhara, which is generally called so because of multiple Vihara's around it.This mention was necessary to claim of ancient **Buddhist University or even Centre of Buddhist learning** at Sharada, Kishanganga Valley, Part of S'arada Civilisation. This contention cum assertion is not backed up by Archaeological finds; in style, architecture, material, ruins of vintage monument (s) fitting in any of the categories of Stupa, Vihara, Mahavihara and Centres of Buddhism Learning (University).

Routes Buddhist Preachers to Kasmira. A small group of Preachers under **Madhyntiika were diverted from Taxasila to Pravarpura (Srinagar-Kashmir).**The route taken by Preachers (Theda's) to Kasmira was ***not*** over the mountains or from North or East, but from West from the direction of Taxasila (Near Rawalpindi) along the course of Jhelum (Vitasta), which was common for all the visitors or preachers or invaders to Kasmira. They then diverted in suitable directions, mostly towards South Kasmira or East. In all cases routes to Gilgit Baltistan and of course Kishanganga Valley from Kasmira was not used, as the route was inhospitable, rugged and treacherous. The pattern of routes taken was typical; along known ancient routes, avoiding harsh terrain and mountains, from one urban area to another along the route, which became halting places and selected hubs for Buddhism. Naturally the influence on such hubs was at limited scale, with local spread including ordaining of locals.

Buddhism in Kasmira. In Kasmira the spread of Buddhism had same pattern and certain tell tales where left. It was within the Mountainous barriers of Pir Panchal, Jhelum Basin, Kafir Khan Range along Shamsabhari up to Himalayan Range. It spread along the Western and Eastern arcs of Jhelum (Vitasta) River. The areas deep in East remained free from such spread as these areas were under War Lords (Damra's) and local Tribes. Buddhist Monuments have been found only on the Western side of Vitasta or it towards South Kasmira and East like Harvan, Lower Sindh. Ancient Buddhist sites in Kasmira, few as they are; Stupa's (3) (Excavated Remains); one Chaitya and Monastery (Parihaspora and Harvan) and few Rock cut sculptures, which indicates restricted extent and area of influence of Buddhism to certain pockets in the valley.

In erstwhile part of Kasmira, across LOC (AJK), just two sites of relevance have been mentioned by Pakistan ASI, amongst a list of 29 of ancient monuments, and attributed to

Buddhism. **One so called S'arada Buddhist and Archaeological Site (Sharada)** (S'arada Temple (S'arada Fort Ruins). None of finds have been dated to be of the period of Fourth Century BC to **Third Century AD (Ashoka to Kushan's).**

Spread towards North-Western India. Although Buddha did not visit this area, during his lifetime, Buddhist traditions localized several **Jataka**'s (In Pali and Sanskrit: means "Birth") i.e., stories of former lives of the Buddha. Mauryan Emperor Asoka (268-232 BC), got inscribed edicts constructed in northern Pakistan and eastern Afghanistan. Menander, an Indo-Greek ruler in Second Century BC was also a major patron of Buddhism. Later it spread beyond North-Western India to Central Asia and China during Kushan period (First – Third centuries AD), definitely not via lower Dardistan or Kishanganga/Neelam Valley.

Later Centuries. For many centuries thereafter, routes through the North-West linked older Buddhist centres in India with emerging Buddhist communities. For example, Buddhist monasteries in Gilgit in northern Pakistan maintained close ties with monasteries in Bamiyan in central Afghanistan and with Khotan in the Tarim Basin. Accounts of Chinese pilgrims, who travelled to India, show that these parts of the Buddhist world were closely interconnected during the first millennium AD but gradually declined with diminishing Royal support and growing prevalence of Hinduism and Islam.

Routes of Travel-Chinese Pilgrims/Monks. Some famous Chinese pilgrims/monks are known to have visited Udyan (Swat) through Gilgit. Faxian, Xuanzang, and Yijing were among hundreds of Chinese monks who made pilgrimages to India during the first millennium CE. The detailed accounts of their journeys provide meticulous accounts of the nature of Buddhist doctrines, rituals, and monastic institutions in the area. If S'arada was a Buddhist Centre of repute for spread of Buddhism, they or at least few of would have visited the area and mentioned in their travelogue. It is clear that they did not go anywhere near Neelam Valley.

Statute Faxian

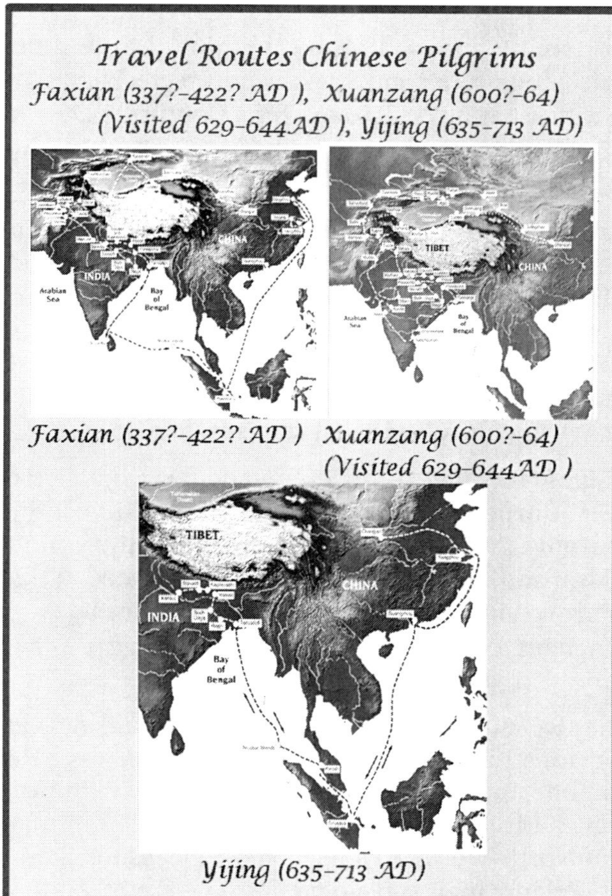

Travel Routes Chinese Pilgrims

Fa Hien (Faxian (337? –422?) pilgrimage to India (395–414)) started his journey on 400 AD and through Gilgit. Monk Fo Young took the same route, Wu Kong followed the route to Yasin and Gilgit. In the later Part of the Eighth Century the pilgrim envoy Wu Kong followed the route to Yasin and Gilgit to reach Indus. The Gilgit route was an important link between Sub-continent and China, along which Buddhism spread from Gandhara to West China. Large number of Buddhist monasteries and Stupas were erected along with rock the carvings, dating back to the First Century AD.

Yijing (635–713) and Xuanzang (600? –64 (visit 629–644)) were two other prominent monks to travel in India. Xuanzang (Hsuan-tsang) reports that there were over a hundred Buddhist monasteries at Kapisa and 6, 000 monks and it was also the place where Hsuan-tsang for the first time in his life met Jains and Hindu. **Kapisa** Province (Afghanistan) is situated in Central-Eastern Afghanistan and was the summer capital of Kanishka and present-day India, Bangladesh and Pakistan was controlled by Kushans from Kapisa.

Chinese travellers have left behind fairly detailed records of their journeys. Travelogue of these Chinese pilgrims are the only available writings describing the condition of Buddhism and the Buddhist sites as they existed at that time, which proved invaluable in locating their ruins by Alexander Cunningham together with other archaeologists in Nineteen Century.

They went to remotest places wherever relics of Buddha or Buddhist Institutions were located. If S'arada was a Buddhist Monument and also a Buddhist University, hundreds of Buddhists Monks, who extensively travelled in almost all areas of North-Western India would have visited S'arada and mentioned it in their travelogue.

Rock Inscriptions and Religious Attributions. Rock inscriptions found in Sogdian (Sogdiana–present day Uzbekistan, Tajikistan, Kazakhstan and Kyrgyzstan) were in Kharosthi and Brahmi script. The sites represent hundreds of inscriptions in Brahmi etc; nearly 80 percent of the writings are in Brahmi. According the Scholar Hauptmann, the historic period of early Buddhism started from this area because of findings of old Indian style Kharosthi language or Sanskrit. The venerations of Buddha and names of different kings show the climax of Buddhism in this area.

Brahmi inscription-MartavyamSmartavyam (Always) remember that (one day) you must die)

The names of emperor of Kushan Empire appear in these inscriptions, as well as names of emperor's Kanishka and Huvishka. There is also a school of thought that after Buddhism, the area of Gilgit and surrounding came under Zoroastrian's rulers during mediaeval period. As far as Islam is concerned, Islam came to this region at the end of Thirteen or beginning of the fourteen Century from Kasmira and Central Asia.

Caprine (Goat Like) Depiction Rock Carving Discovered in Chilas (Harald Hauptmann)

Mysterious "Giant Figures" (Harald Hauptmann)

Buddhism in Kishanganga/Neelam Valley? The spread of Buddhism in North-Western India was manifold and Buddhist inclined rulers etc, ensured that the marks of the spread of Buddhism, earlier or during their rule were left in the area; right from Ashoka to Kushan's. The routes taken by monks followers for the spread of the movement was all along the alignment of Uttarpatha, which avoided treacherous routes, high mountains and turbulent rivers. The movements of Buddhist preachers to Tibet via Ladakh (Little Tibet), was not through Kasmira but in from the direction from Gilgit and then to Ladakh. If one looks at the map of the spread, there is a prominent area of the belt of erstwhile Kasmira, across the Shamsabhari Range, which remained untouched by the spread of Buddhism; which includes Kishanganga/Neelam Valley.

It is preposterous to think that a Buddhist monument or teaching institute would be established in an area, where Buddhism had no roots, even with no indication that area had Buddhist influence, ever at all. The area even today remains isolated, termed in remote category and extreme weather and snow. Literally isolated area bound by massive mountain barriers from South (Shamsabhari Range), East (Greater Himalayan Range) and in North (Nanga Parvat, K2

Range). Life even today in the area is of difficult conditions of an isolated area, extreme limited resources, difficult access and extreme weather. Imagine these 2000 years back and a learning institute with hundreds of students from various far-off countries. This must also be viewed that when spread of Buddhism was in nascent stage, not spread beyond North-Western India, how could one think of a university, when attention is towards spread of Buddhism!!

S'arada Civilisation

Term Civilisation. Civilisation term means an advanced state of human society, in which a high level of culture, science, industry, and governance has been reached. People or their way of living has a state, with a particular type of culture, society, at a specific place as a group and time; like Indus Valley Civilisation, Aryan Civilisation, Greek Civilisation. Historically, civilisation is a larger and 'more advanced' culture, in contrast to smaller, ***supposedly*** primitive cultures and contrasts with non-centralized tribal societies, including the cultures of nomadic pastoralists, Neolithic societies or hunter-gatherers and contrasts with the cultures found within Civilisations. These have organized settlements, divided into hierarchical social classes, with a ruling elite, subordinate urban and rural populations, which engages in intensive agriculture, mining, small-scale manufacture and trade.

We all are conversant with worlds earliest Civilisations like Indus Valley Civilisation. Latter civilisation encompassed multi geographical areas, with varied individual culture and people, but all emanated from one Base: Indus Valley (Erstwhile North-Western India, present day Pakistan and parts of Southern Afghanistan). This civilisation was distinct and left its traces even till today, dating back to that era. Excavations in Indus Valley revealed that these developed, even before other parts of Northern Indian Subcontinent. There were many more sub groups of this Civilisation like Hakkra, Mythical Sarasvati River, Harappa, Mohenjo-daro etc. There is no need to dwell further on ancient civilisations and sites of the Indian Sub-Continent.

S'arada Civilisation. It is intriguing that **S'arada** name, a Hindu Deity, is being specifically used to give designation 'S'arada Civilisation' and that too restricted to belt around Kishanganga/Neelam Valley and adjoining areas. **S'arada** Civilisation designation comes from Sharada, a sub form of Hindu Goddess Saraswati, apparently a Hindu religion connotation. Never heard of this specific civilisation named after a Hindu Goddess, and that too where Islam is the religion of the people. Surprisingly the contours of this civilisation remain vacillating between S'arada Language domination of the area, S'arada Shrine of Goddess Sharada, which brought a separate Civilisation: Kishanganga/Neelam Valley Neolithic Civilisation and Neelam Tahzeeb (Civilisation-Culture).

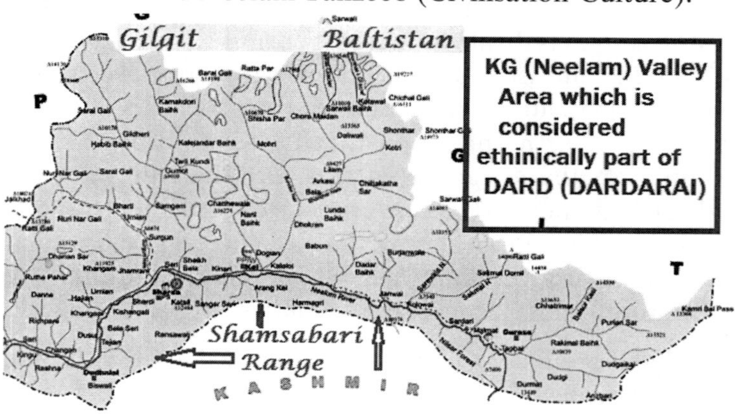

Kishanganga (Neelam) Valley (Neelam District)

The present demography of the claimed civilisation is purely Muslims and Islam. One of the reasons is that even in present S'arada name and places connected are revered by the present people, as a matter of faith. The effort is to create a separate non-existent civilisation, use S'arada name to exploit it politically, religiously and regionally. On the other hand, proponents in the Valley, miniscule though, try to apportion the acronym exclusive to the Valley, but sans the proper S'arada location.

Sirhasila with Sirhasila Castle in Ruins Jutting out over River Kishanganga. Right-Rock below the Castle which resembles Elephant Rock Head

[Sirhasila Rock has resemblance to Lord Ganesha's head /Elephant Head. Sirhasila; *Sirah* – head; *sila* (shila)-rock]

This is an effort is to put across that there was a separate civilisation in the area, unconnected with Kasmira Kingdom, but with a mix of Buddhist and Hinduism culture. At present it is being touted as with a miniscule part of erstwhile Jammu and Kasmira State: Kishanganga Valley-Neelam Valley, some parts adjacent to this valley in the West and North. In folk lore Kishanganga River is personified with name of Parvati-Ganga, many saner elements of this valley differentiate this from nearby areas, terming it Parvati-Ganga-Neelam Tahzeeb (Culture) and not S'arada Tahzeeb (Culture or Civilisation).

S'arada Script. S'arada Goddess has lent its name to a new language and script in then North-Western India. It was during first millennium AD, language and script S'arada developed, **which spread in the** North-Western India, an abugida (neosyllabary or pseudo-alphabet), writing system of the Brahmic family of scripts. Its usage was widespread between the 8th and 12th centuries in the North-Western Parts of Indian Subcontinent, and Kasmira, but later restricted to Kasmira, and it is now extinct. S'arada script was used in Punjab (West and East Punjab), Partly Himachal Pradesh and Kasmira. From the 10th Century onwards, regional differences of languages and scripts started and S'arada proper was eventually restricted to very limited ceremonial use in Kasmira, as it grew increasingly unsuitable for writing the Kasmirai (Kashmiri) language. If this civilisation foundation is based on S'arada Language/Script Sharada, S'arada Civilisation, then complete area of North-Western India where this language or its dialects were in vogue qualify to be grouped with this Civilisation. S'arada Script or language cannot be, therefore, termed as a ground for a **SharadaAncient Civilisation**. One wonders if the name **S**'arada Shrine is attributable to S'arada Language or script.

Gilgit Manuscripts Connection with S'arada Shrine. With find of Gilgit Buddhist Manuscripts unearthed in 1931 AD at Naupur (Next to Gilgit Cantonment), it has been subject of discussion all over by Scholars for various purposes and quoted in support of Buddhism in Kishanganga Valley and areas north of it. Generally dated Fourth/Fifth Century AD, they are not connected to spread of Buddhism in the area, including Kishanganga Valley and does not support to the theory that S'arada Shrine/Tirath/Temple as a Buddhist monument and that a Buddhist University existed. Detailed analyses of Gilgit Manuscript and connection, claims of Buddhist association with the S'arada Shrine/Temple has been dealt in a separate chapter of the Book.

In the sky, there is no distinction of east and west;
people create distinctions out of their own minds and then
believe them to be true
–Gautama Buddha

9

Gilgit Manuscripts

"Oh Bhavani! bestow on me your slave, (your) look endowed with compassion"
–Verse 22 Saundarya Lahari

Gilgit Manuscripts Connection with S'arada Shrine. With find of Gilgit Buddhist Manuscripts unearthed in 1931 AD at Naupur (Next to Gilgit Cantonment), it has been subject of discussion all over by Scholars for various purposes and also quoted in support of Buddhism in Kishanganga Valley and areas north of it. Generally dated Fourth/Fifth Century AD, they are not connected to spread of Buddhism in the area including Kishanganga Valley and the manuscripts are quoted to bolster the claim to the theorythat S'arada Shrine/ Tirath/Temple Kishanganga Valley as a Buddhist monument and that a Buddhist University existed. Coverage of Gilgit Manuscripts, separately and in detail, became necessary mainly for this reason. The spread of Buddhism across the present Line of Control (LoC) was mainly in Gilgit-Baltistan area, directed towards further North (Central Asia), China (Khotan) and across Karakorum Range to China and hopefully Tibet. The archaeological finds in Gilgit area are mainly on the known and well chronicled Silk Route, which does not pass through the Southern Part of Gilgit or touches Kishanganga/Neelam Valley.

These manuscripts and the Vihara found in Naupur and many places in Gilgit are given example of similar set up in Sharada/Kishanganga valley, which got destroyed over the centuries due to vagaries of weather. Gilgit Manuscripts were found in an area which has much harsher vagaries of weather, terrain, logistics than Kishanganga/Neelam valley and Southern portion of Gilgit. The way they these were preserved at Naupur, surely, they would have been preserved in similar way at S'arada also. No recognisable and known Buddhist structures: Stupa's etc. around S'arada Shrine Complex and nearby areas. The Buddhist architectural structures are distinct and radically different from the S'arada complex.

Naupur (Gilgit) was like a staging camp, where these manuscripts were stocked to make these available as Buddhism manuscripts, enumerating Buddhist doctrines for translators for onward transmission to China/Tibet. This was part of strategy during Kushan and subsequent rule for spread of Buddhism beyond the frontiers of erstwhile India into Central Asia and East (China/Tibet). As Buddhism had started waning in the heartland, the thrust was on need to spread it in untouched areas. There is no doubt that Pakistan, which was earlier part of North-Western India, Afghanistan are treasure trove of Buddhist monument (mostly in Ruins), which came up during Third Century BC under Ashoka. Mainly connected with spread of Buddhism, these were restricted in one direction of Northern fringes of Afghanistan. During the later period this methodology continued during the rule of Central Asian tribes including Kushan's. Extensive archaeological survey has been undertaken by Pakistan's official agencies, archaeologists and scholars from all over the world to find Ancient and Buddhist monuments. It included the erstwhile area of Jammu and Kasmira, now occupied by Pakistan; Pakistan Occupied Kasmira (POK), which includes Kishanganga/Neelam Valley.

Buddhism Edicts in North-Western India. The history of Buddhism in erstwhile Bharatvarsh spans from the Sixth Century BC, when it arose in the Eastern part of Ancient India, in and around the ancient Kingdom of Magadha (now in Bihar, India). It spread slowly in India until the time of the reign of the Mauryan Emperor Ashoka (273–232 BC). The period of Ashoka and thereafter marks the first known spread of Buddhism beyond frontiers of erstwhile India. As part of this thrust to spread Buddhism, Ashoka took lead by installation of Plates and Pillars known as left Edicts of Ashoka. According to the edicts of Ashoka, emissaries were sent to various countries various parts of the Indian Sub-Continent especially in North-Western India and countries close by. However, no such edicts have been found of Ashoka era in the complete Drava country, including Kishanganga Valley.

Buddhism in North-Western India after Maurya's. After Ashoka, reasonable tempo for Buddhism was kept by various rulers, like Indo-Greek's, Scythian's, Sasanian's till Kushan's came to power. Kushan's (mid-First–Third Century AD) came to control the Silk Road trade through Central and South Asia, which brought them to interact with ancient Buddhist monasteries and societies involved in trade in these regions. These links had been established during Mauryan reign and later, to certain extent, by Indo-Greeks. Kushan's patronized Buddhist institutions, Kanishka I (128–151 AD) particularly known for his support of Buddhism, built stupas and monasteries in the Gandharan (Gandhara) city of Peshawar (Sanskrit: *Purusapura*), which he used as a capital. Kushan royal support and the opening of trade routes allowed Gandharan Buddhism to spread along the Silk Road to Central Asia, the Tarim Basin and thus to China. This is confirmed by finds of some of the earliest written documents/manuscripts of the Buddhism, called Gandharan Buddhist texts, dating from about the 1st Century BC to Third Century AD.

Scripts Used. The oldest extant Buddhist manuscripts are attributed to the Dharmaguptaka Sect and are also the oldest Indian manuscripts written in Gandhari (Ghandari) (**Gandhari** is the modern name, coined by scholar Harold Walter Bailey (in 1946), for a Prakrit language described generally as Middle Indo-Aryan language, Kharosthi, that deviates from Sanskrit).These texts, dated between the Fourth Century BC and Fourth Century AD in the North-Western region of Gandhara (Afghanistan and parts of present day Pakistan). Some of the Buddhist texts were written in the Kharosthi script, a script that was predominantly used in the Greco-Bactrian and Indo-Greek kingdoms of Northern India and that played a prominent role in the coinage and inscriptions of their kings. Kharosthi script was used in Central Asia as well as in Bactria, Kushan Empire, Sogdiana, and along the Silk Road. During the First Century AD, under the Kushan's, Buddhist texts were produced in the local languages, such as Khotanese (a Middle Iranian language), Sogdian (also Iranian), Uighur (Turkish), Tangut, Tibetan, and Chinese.

Buddhist Literature to Central Asia and China. After the fall of the Kushan's, small kingdoms ruled the Gandharan region, and later the Hephthalite White Huns conquered the area (440–670 AD). Under the Hephthalites, Gandharan Buddhism continued to thrive in cities like Balkh (Bactria), as remarked by Xuanzang (Hsuan tsong) who visited the region in the Seventh Century AD. The Kingdom of Khotan was one of the earliest Buddhist kingdoms in the area and helped transmit Buddhism from India to China. The first translators of **Buddhists scriptures into Chinese were Iranians**, including the Parthians and Yuezhi Zhi Qian and Kang Sengkai (from Samarkand). Thirty-seven early translators of Buddhist texts are known, and the majority of them have been identified as hailing from the Iranian cultural sphere.

Buddhism also flourished in the eastern part of Central Asia (Chinese Turkestan, Tarim Basin). The region has revealed extremely rich Buddhist works of art, Buddhist texts such as those found in Dunhuang **(Dunhuang** city in North-Western Gansu Province-Western China). During the mid-seventh Century, Arab conquest of the Iranian Plateau followed by the Muslim conquests of Afghanistan and the later establishment of the Ghaznavid kingdom in Central Asia (977–1186 AD) led to the decline and eventual disappearance of Buddhism from most of these regions.

Origin of Tibetan Buddhism. It is believed that Buddhism spread to Tibet directly from India in the Fifth Century AD. Local tradition says that first Buddhist scriptures reached Tibet in a basket **but they were written in Sanskrit**. The scriptures were finally translated almost a Century later thanks to a Chinese Buddhist princess who was married to a Tibetan king. Although many Buddhist missionaries have come to Tibet from China, their impact was never as strong as the one coming from India. Another princess from China married a Tibetan king and she allowed fleeing Buddhist monks from Khotan to settle in Tibet.

Unearthing of Gilgit Manuscripts. Gilgit Manuscripts, unearthed in 1931 AD at Naupur (Next to Gilgit Cantonment), have been subject of discussion all over by Scholars for various purposes. Location of Naupur, Nau (Nav) means **New** and Pur means a **Hamlet,** where they have been found. Naupur is a clean open area and away from hustle bustle of Subsidiary Silk Route Trade Centres through Gilgit/Baltistan-Gilgit. There can be no doubt that the name of the place is not in local language but more than that sourced from Late Brahmi script. This is the first indication that establishment of Naupur is not on localised basis.

Oldest Manuscript Collection in Pakistan and India

Generally they are Given Dates of 4-6th Century AD

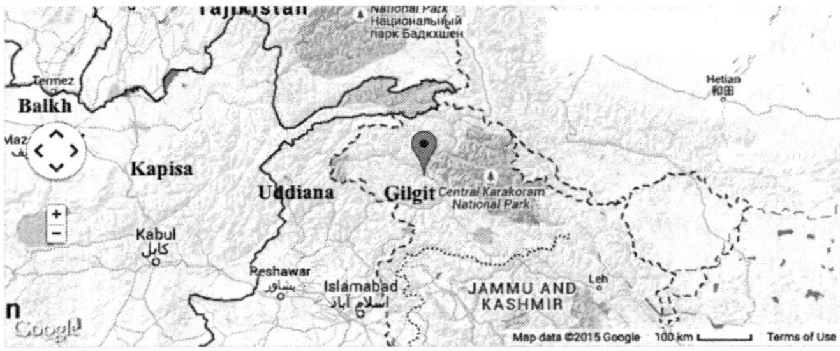

Discovered in a wooden box in a circular chamber inside a Buddhist stupa by cattle grazers in 1931, the Gilgit manuscripts may be the earliest surviving Buddhist documents. They were named after the city of Gilgit, now part of Pakistan, in which they were discovered. Gilgit was an important city on the Silk Road, along which Buddhism was spread from South Asia to the rest of Asia.

A wild euphoria was created with initial analysis of the manuscripts but later decades effort was mostly to decipher them and each scholar trying to give antiquity as well as isolated analysis. The contents of the Manuscripts still baffle the world over, except few odd converted into two Books. Even these books have been used selectively to bolster a particular view; Buddhism flourished in the area from BC era, Kanishka I was the ruler when these were written, etc. However, there is no clarity, till date, of its roots, purpose, circumstances, time line they were written and time they were capsuled. The contents of the manuscripts, deciphered only in bits and pieces, do not give any clue indicating their origin or if they were transported to this location. The language and script in vogue then in the general area of Gilgit was either Gandhari or Kharosthi. There is no indication of either script having been used in the manuscripts. Manuscript contents, somewhat deciphered till now, could not give any details of their contents and historic connection either with Theravada (Hinayana) or Mahayana Buddhism. Absence of these indicators gives one important clue that they were prepared bereft of the doctrines of these two sects, which got prevalence post Buddha.

Analysis of the manuscripts, their condition and contents were done by various scholars, linguists over the decades, including translations of various pages of manuscripts by Dr Nilankash Dutt, Prof Lokesh Chandra etc. Except Dr Dutt, who has religiously given the details of the texts and direct inferences, all others have been more concerned to prove its antiquity. Wild guesses of the period when they have been written, overlooking the script used, ignoring known contents, the sect or ideology of Buddhism they possibly pertain to and type and spread of Buddhism in various areas around during the period. From all available details it was evident that these manuscripts are no way connected with Ashoka's spread of Buddhism and also Kanishka I and his successors.

Known Facts. These facts can be confirmed or cross-checked with traces, monuments or references to this area during BC era. Chandragupta Maurya, Bimbisara's religious inclination, Ajivika, is well known in the area under their domain in North-Western Area of erstwhile India or when Ashoka governed.The archaeological city of Taxila, located in south and Abbottabad lies very near to the east of the area Ashoka governed as a prince.

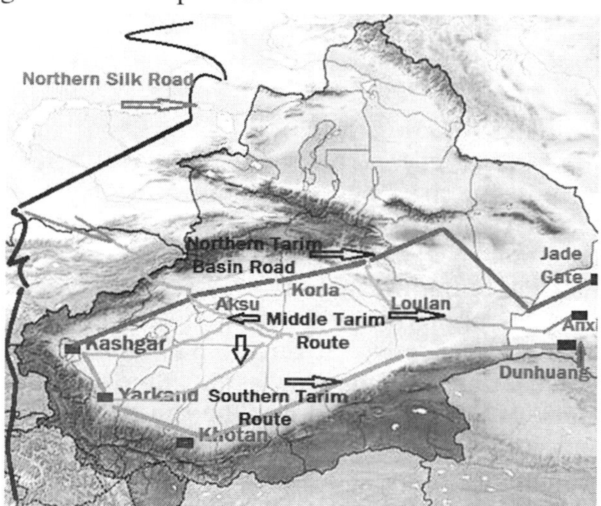

Silk Route(s) Map

Location Map Mansehra and Hunza

Ashoka's Buddhist Edicts. There are fourteen edicts of Ashoka, inscribed on rocks. for spread of what is called Dharma in the area. One of them in the North-Western India, **with reference to closeness to Gilgit and is the last and Northernmost Ashoka edict and on the Silk route: Mansehra** (Khyber Pakhtunkhwa (Pakistan). These edicts are closest **to Gilgit or Naupur.** Ashoka governed this area first as a prince and later he ascended to the throne in 272 BC. This Silk Road was called Uttarpatha, during Mauryan time and subsequently got name of Silk Road and was the route taken by traders, pilgrims, forces to reach China (Mainly Khotan). Subsequently when some more routes were found and use this route was called Northern Silk Route. There were no Ashoka edicts in and around Gilgit-Baltistan or Lower Drava Country which included Kishanganga Valley.

Mansehra Rock Edicts are cut into three boulders and date back to 3rd Century BC and they are written in the ancient Indic script of Gandhara culture: Kharosthi. The edicts mention aspects of Ashoka's *dharma* (Religious beliefs). Located near to the Karakoram Highway on ancient Silk Route, they represent some of the earliest evidence of writing, middle of the third Century BC, in South Asia and are in the Kharosthi script.

Buddhist Relics Monuments in Pakistan Gilgit-Baltistan. First in Pakistan, which includes Pakistan Occupied Kasmira (POK, Called Azad Jammu Kasmira in Pakistan (AJK). A study of the relics/monuments/carvings and scripts used is generally **Kharsothi** script, which was indigenous to the North-Western India and does not match with the script of the Gilgit Manuscripts.

Edicts of Ashoka, the Mansehra Rock Edicts lie in the extreme North-West of the Mauryan Empire

Sacred Rock of Hunza. Sacred Rock of Hunza is carved rock as well as a cultural heritage site in Gilgit-Baltistan, two kilometres from Ganesh village on the Karakorum Highway (KKH) in between Ganesh village and Attabad Lake (See Map above). The rock is on a top of a hill which lies in east of Hunza River and carvings on the rock have been dated to First Millennium AD. The site has nothing to do with any religion or Kingdom. The background of these rock etchings is being analysed separately.

Hunza Sacred Rock

Other Rock Edicts. There are many more Rock Edicts located in North-Western India (Afghanistan and Pakistan), apart from Mansehra and Hunza Rocks. These are: Minor Rock Edicts Ashoka, a set of 14 Major Rock Edicts with Greek Inscriptions on portions of few rocks. 12 and 13 Edicts in Greek and Bilingual Rock Inscriptioncalled bilingual Greek-Aramaic Rocks; Set of 7 Major Pillar Edicts (Kandahar- Afghanistan). In present day Pakistan rock edicts at: Shahbazgarhi (in Kharoshti Script) and Fragments of Seven Pillar Edicts Ranigat, (Khyber Pakhtunkhwa Province). (Only Hunza Sacred Rocks and Mansehra Rock edicts are relevant to Gilgit Manuscripts)

Buddhist Sites in Gilgit-Baltistan. In Gilgit 24 Ancient sites connected with Buddhism have been identified. Most of them are of Fourth and Fifth Century vintage. Gilgit Buddhist complex with images of Buddha and stupas attributed Fourth or Fifth Century AD. This is generally the area of Naupur (Gilgit) and where the Gilgit Manuscripts were found. Rock carvings at Thalpan, Thor and Ziarat (near Taplin). One of the major one is **Kargah Buddha** a carved image of a large standing Buddha located about six miles (9.7 km) outside of Gilgit, in the cliff-face in Karghah Nala; probably dates to the Seventh Century AD.

Kargah Buddha image

Manthal Buddha Rock is a large granite rock located in Manthal village, which has engraved picture of Buddha, attributed to Eighth and Nine Century AD.

Henzal Stupa and Thaplan Selective Rock Etchings. While Henzal Stupa is attributed to Eighth/Ninth Century AD, irrespective of anything else, Thaplan and nearby etchings are attributed to earlier era, by locals, travellers etc and none of them have any religious inclination or inference.

Henzal Stupa and Thaplan Selective Rock Etchings.

Rock with Buddhist inscription on the step; path to the trace of Shigar with Buddhist ruins and petrogluyphs, may be marking the acces to the holy precinct. Br inscriptions, carvings of stupas, (later) animal carvins. (Photo The Walt)

Buddhist Inscriptions Rock Shigar (Gilgit)

Rock with Buddhist Inscriptions Shigar (Gilgit). It was written on behalf of the lord of a district, most likely identical with Shigar, and testifies him as a pious Buddhist. (Maybe his son had lived under the tutorial of the monks, and the inscription reminds the solemn return to the father). Palaeography indicates an earliest date: Seventh or even Sixth Century AD.

Kanishka I Rule Inscriptions. Named inscriptions dating from year 64 to 98 AD and Kanishka era (Roughly 2nd Century AD) (There were three Kanishka's with Great Kanishka being first. The other two were also called by other local names as in Kasmira). He was the last great Kushan emperor, and the end of his rule coincides with the invasion of the Sasanians as far as North-Western India, and the establishment of the Indo-Sasanians or *Kushanshahs,* in what is nowadays Afghanistan, Pakistan and North-Western India. Archaeological evidence of a Kushan rule of long duration is present in an area stretching from Surkh Kotal, Bagaramand Kapisa the summer capital of the Kushan's under Kanishka I. **Gilgit Baltistan or Dard Country was out of his domain.**

Rabatak Inscription. The recently discovered Rabatak inscription, is an inscription written on a rock in the Bactrian language and the Greek script, which was found in 1993 AD at the site of Rabatak (near Surkh Kotal-Afghanistan) and hence the name. The inscription relates to the rule of the Kushan emperor Kanishka, and gives remarkable clues on the genealogy of the Kushan dynasty and dates it to the Second Century AD. A statement follows regarding the writing of the inscription itself, indicating that the language used by Kanishka in his inscription was self-described as the Aryan language". "It was he who laid out (i.e. discontinued the use of) the Ionian ("ιωνα, Yona, Greek) speech and then placed the Arya ("αρια, Aryan) speech." The inscriptions are dated to early Kanishka era (incept probably 127AD), indicating that in the early Second Century AD Kushan dominion expanded into the heartland of Northern India. Kushan's under Kanishka made various forays into the Tarim Basin, seemingly the original ground of their ancestors the Yuezhi, where they had various contacts with the Chinese. Both archaeological findings and literary evidence suggest Kushan rule, in Kashgar, Yarkand **and** Khotan. (The facsimile of this inscription can hardly be of any use to a reader and hence has not been shown here).

From all above it is apparent that while Ashoka's Buddhism went Northwards. say up to Manshera only, Kushan's went further North (left of Gilgit Baltistan). Their aim was threefold: Conquer areas up to their ancestral domain, continue to spread and adhere to three religions of Kushan's (Zorashtrianism, Hinduism, Buddhism) and lastly go further North and East toward the China lands of Khotan. **Kanishka's expansion into the Tarim Basin** probably initiated the transmission of Buddhism to China.

Tian Shan with the ancient silk road

A study of the routes adopted by Kushan's will give enough indications that Buddhism entered Han (China) via the Silk Road, beginning in the First or Second Century AD. After Kushan's, Hephthalites dominated the area until they were defeated in 565 AD by an alliance between the Gokturk's (nomadic confederation of Turkic peoples in medieval Inner Asia), Sassanids (**Empire of Iranians**) and some Indo-Sassanid authority was re-established.

The Kanishka Casket. The 'Kanishka casket' or 'Kanishka reliquary', is dated to the first year of Kanishka's reign in 127 AD, which was discovered during the archaeological excavations in 1908–1909 in Shah-Ji-Ki-Dheri, just outside the old city of Peshawar. in a deposit chamber under Kanishka stupa. The casket has dedication inscription in Kharosthi. The attribution of the casket to Kanishka has been recently disputed, essentially on stylistic ground (for example, the ruler shown on the casket is not bearded, to the contrary of

Kanishka). Instead, the casket is often attributed to Kanishka's **successor Huvishka.**

Inscribed Kanishka casket found at the site of the Kanishka Stupa containing relics of the Buddha (Peshawar Museum, Pakistan)

Buddhist Documented Doctrines and China.

Buddhist Translated Manuscripts. The first documented translation efforts by Buddhist monks in China (all foreigners) were in the Second Century AD under the influence of the expansion of the Kushan Empire into the Chinese territory via Tarim Basin and brought Gandharan Buddhist culture into territories adjacent to China proper. Direct contact between Central Asian and Chinese Buddhism continued throughout the 3rd to Seventh Century, well into the Tang period. From the 4th Century onward, with Faxian's pilgrimage to India (395–414 AD), and later Xuanzang (629–644 AD), Chinese pilgrims started to travel by themselves to Northern India, their source of Buddhism, in order to get improved access to original scriptures. Much of the land route connecting Northern India (mainly Gandhara) with China at that time was ruled by the Kushan Empire, and later the Hephthalite Empire.

Huns -The White Huns tribes from Central Asia, conquered Kabul Valley, Indus Valley and Northern Areas in the early Sixth Century AD. Huns were non-Buddhist and hence the official patronage of Buddhism stopped during their reign. As the Hun power declined, the local rajas got independent and the area was ruled from 612 AD to 750 AD by Patola Shahi dynasty. The Patola Shahi's were Buddhist and had close ties with Chinese empire. The Kushano-Hephthalites or Turk-shahis were replaced by the Shahi in the mid Eighth Century. The Indian form of Buddhist tantra (Vajrayana) reached China in the Seventh Century AD. Tibetan Buddhism was likewise established as a branch of Vajrayana, in the Eighth Century. But from about this time, the Silk Road transmission of Buddhism began to decline with the Muslim conquests.

Gilgit Manuscripts

Details. In 1931, Aurel Stein, a renowned archaeologist of the region, in his third and largest expedition to Central Asia, passed through Darel and Tangir and reported some "boys watching flocks above Naupur village, about two miles west of Gilgit cantonment, who are said to have cleared a piece of timber out on the top of a small stone-covered mound. Further digging laid bare a circular chamber within the ruins of a Buddhist stupa, filled with hundreds of small votive stupas and relief plaques common in Central Asia and Tibet". After further excavations, a great mass of ancient manuscripts was found packed in a locked wooden box. The site appeared to be an ancient ruin which may have been the residence of Buddhist monks. There were five wooden boxes, the fifth containing the other four, which kept all the manuscripts discovered in Gilgit, hence Gilgit manuscripts. According to Sir Aurel Stein's report in The Statesman of 24th July, 1931, Gilgit Manuscripts found at Naupur situated in the foothills of southern rocky heights of Gilgit (now the capital of Gilgit-Baltistan, Pakistan), where centuries old Buddha stupa of Yachini Kargah Buddha is also located about six miles (9.7 kilometres) outside of Gilgit.

Strategic Location of Gilgit in Ancient Times. Gilgit was at that time, early first millennium AD, at the cross roads where South Asia, Central Asia and Eastern Asia met and it was an important stop on the Karakorum Subsidiary Silk Road. Many monks from India carried the message of the Buddha from here to Tibet, China, Korea and even as far as Japan. Earlier the routes for any forays or expeditions were from the flanks of Gilgit Baltistan. It was along this subsidiary Silk Road that Buddhism spread eastwards towards the rest of Asia. Gilgit hence played an important part in the spread of Buddhism to this end. This spread of Buddhism was not connected at all with Ashoka or later Indo Greeks or Kushan's. Kushan's for their expedition followed by spread Mahayana Buddhism propounded during Kanishka I's period Second Century travelled what is called Northern Silk Route now and was the one which was used by monk pilgrims. (See Maps above)

Deciphered and Recovered Manuscript Pages. Portion of Gilgit Manuscripts deciphered thus far cover a wide range of subjects such as religion, religious rituals, philosophy, iconometry, monastic discipline, folk tales, medicine and culinary art. These manuscripts were written on the birch bark, experts opine Palm leaf, and similar to those discovered by Aurel Stein (Khotan) in Central Asia. The pages of the manuscript were approximately 23″ long and 5″ wide, with almost ten lines per page. They are also called Naupur Manuscripts, after the village where they were found.

In August 1938, seven years after the discovery of the texts, the archaeologist Madhusudan Kaul Shastri discovered another larger chamber at the base of the structure and was able to discover three to four more manuscripts, along **with votive objects and probably Buddhist cult bronzes.** Roughly 60 manuscripts and 17 Avadnas (type of Buddhist Literature correlating past lives' virtuous deeds to subsequent live's events) emerging from Naupur are of unmatched significance in Buddhist studies. Scholars agree that local Buddhist devotees compiled, not wrote, these texts between the Fifth and Sixth Century AD. With the exception of only a few scripts, all the manuscripts were written on birch bark in Buddhist hybrid Sanskrit language in the Gupta Brahmi and post-Gupta Brahmi script. Gupta script (Late Brahmi script) The Gupta script (sometimes referred to as Gupta Brahmi Script or Late Brahmi Script) was used for writing Sanskrit and is associated with the Gupta Empire of India which was a period of material prosperity and great religious and scientific developments.

In 1956, Professor Giuseppe Tucci, a well-known Italian scholar, secured another small group of manuscripts from a street vendor in Rawalpindi. These were later presented to the Karachi Museum. These manuscripts were written on the birch bark and similar to those discovered by Aurel Stein (Khotan) in Central Asia. The pages of the manuscript were also similar in size and writings that were found at Naupur.

The Buddha (See Below) is one of the three earliest datable sculptures associated with the kingdom of Gilgit in Northern Pakistan. All were commissioned by Queen

Mangalahamsika, known from Gilgit manuscripts to have been the senior queen to King Vajraditayanandi (reigned 600 AD). ...Mangalahamsika and her king were members of the Patola Shahi dynasty. The Sanskrit donor inscription engraved on the front cartouche states: "Om. This is a pious gift. This pious gift was ordered to be made by the Shri Paramadevi (Highest Queen)." According to renowned scholar Karl Jettmar, inscriptions on these bronzes "reveal that they were produced and dedicated due to the generosity and the religious zeal of a Patola Shahi". The Patola Shahis, also known as Palola Shahis, were the rulers of Gilgit and Baltistan from the late sixth to the early eighth centuries AD. **The Palola Shahi Dynasty (Sixth–Eighth Century AD)** "In the Sixth–Eighth C. AD, the Patola (Palola) Shahis ruled the country of Bolor, in what today is Northern Pakistan. There are a number of Buddhist artworks and texts that can be attributed through inscriptions to this royal family. Although the dynasty's visual record is clearly Buddhist, no comprehensive art historical scholarship has been conducted on it."

Enthroned Buddha Granting Boon – Patola Shahi Period-Inscription 600 AD

After the Patola Shahi dynasty, most of the area came under the control of the Turks–deposed from their Central Asian home by the Arab conquest. From the Third Century to the Eleenth Century, Gilgit was a Buddhist centre. Locals described as 'Dards' in the rock inscriptions ruled the Northern Kishanganga valley. This is the only instance of the people of the area using the term 'Dards' for themselves.

Contents Gilgit Manuscripts. The Gilgit Manuscript contains the texts on Vinay Vastu, the treatise on monastic discipline. There are texts on Ayurvedic medicines like Anna Panna Vidhi and Bhaisajya Guru Sutra. There are references to icon-meter, folk tales, philosophy and culinary skills. It also has a chronological list of the various Buddhist Shahi kings of Gilgit.

From the different Chinese translations referred above, it is evident that the original sutra was in existence before the Second Century AD, but in view of the fact that the earlier translations were of a shorter text. Herewith I am quoting general contents of some parts of the translated Manuscripts.

Vinay Vastu (Treatise on monastic discipline)

"Translation of these stanzas are absent. Evidently, these were compositions of a date later than the Ninth Century AD, when the Tibetan translation was made. Author)"

Part Contents Chapter XVI of Gilgit Manuscripts. In this chapter (XVI) Buddha recounted the experiences of one of his past existences when he was born as the son of Matiraja. The second part of the chapter deals with the prediction about the deterioration of the morals of the Buddhist monks. Buddha said that there would be in future monks, who, though donning on yellow robes, would abuse the privileges of a monk, adhere to the notion of the existence of self, and avoid out of fear listening to the doctrine of sunyata, but still they would be respected by the people. Candraprabha (Queen?) was warned not to place faith in them. This is distinctly a fling cast at the Hinayanist's and particularly at those monks who would be morally degraded and not observant of the disciplinary rules. The ancient manuscripts have proven to given world renowned historians a run for their money, as no one has been able to fully decipher them yet. The manuscripts published in Devanagari script were brought out in four volumes from 1939 to 1959 AD.

Baltistan. Baltistan is now together with Gilgit called as Gilgit-Baltistan: GB for short. Baltistan was controlled by the Tibetan King Songtsen Gampo during the Seventh Century AD. Culturally influenced by Tibet, the Bon and animist Balti's began to adopt Tibetan Buddhism. Religious artifacts such as *gompas* and *stupas* were built, and lamas played an important role in Balti life.

Authors Evaluation of Gilgit Manuscripts and Its Connect

Based on the deep analysis and research of these Manuscripts, certain combined conclusions can be made, as under:

1. Buddhism spread in areas around Magadh and Mauryan Empire around Fifth Century BC: progress was slow and restricted. Mauryan Kings Chandragupta, Bhimbisara though were in control of North-Western India, did not spread Buddhism in these area as both followed Ajvika.

2. Ashoka gave impetus to new Dharama (Buddhism) which was Thervada (Hinayana) and also propagated it right up to the borders of erstwhile Gandhara (Afghanistan) touching Pamirs. Ashoka erected Edicts write up to Northern tip of his empire, around Mansehra. But none in the erstwhile Drava Country (Gilgit-Baltistan), which includes lower valleys of Gilgit and the strip across Kishanganga River right up to its confluence with Jhelum (Vitasta). His thrust was basically North-Western India and beyond. The movement of his missionaries was not through Kasmira at all, but took off generally from Taxila (Western Punjab Region) onto Afghanistan and beyond. His or his successors never ventured into the areas of Kishanganga (Neelam Valley). Connecting S'arada with Ashoka's or his successors is just a red herring.

3. Simultaneously where Buddhism spread and took roots, monasteries were created, which also became Buddhist monks stay and logistics, task of distributing Buddhist literatures, mostly on Palm leaf, which were delivered to these places, from various centres of Buddhism, mainly Taxila. Later on, Kandahar (Afghanistan) became another staging centre for such Buddhist literature. Monks moving into these areas were one of the modes of spreading the Buddhism with Buddhist literature; carried, copied, re-written and passed on. The contents of these Buddhist literature, mostly doctrines, were based on the original tenets of Buddhism; Thervada (Hinayana).

4. After Ashoka there was lull till Indo Greeks and Kushan came into picture. Indo Greeks did not do much for spread of Buddhism but adopted Buddhism in the area under their control.

5. Kushan's after capturing areas around Tarim Basin turned south into heartland of India adopted Buddhism

and now took it beyond Mansehra/Pamirs, right to their native land. However, the Buddhist doctrines with emergence of Mahayana Buddhism had bifurcated.

6. Though Kushan's developed Mahayana Buddhism, the spread of Buddhist doctrines in these areas was a mix. The Buddhist literature used were manuscripts mainly of doctrines of Buddha era. The Mahayana Buddhism literature had yet been not been composed. This was the stage when Chinese monks started coming to India and copying or taking Buddhist manuscripts back home. Subsequently these were translated by translators, into various scripts. Thirty-seven early translators of Buddhist texts are known, apparently, they were assisted by monks who knew the script of the literature to be translated.

7. Buddhism was in a slow phase during the rule of Guptas and Huns in North-Western India.

8. In Sixth Century, with arrival of Kabul Shahi's, new route to China was explored for trade vide Baltistan/Gilgit. Patola Shahis were of Buddhist inclination though the people they ruled were from different tribes and beliefs, who then adopted double beliefs; mix of their own ancient beliefs and selected ones from neo-Buddhism.

9. With development of subsidiary Silk route; Buddhist preachers, monks, traders and travellers moved from North-Western India to Gilgit and through Baltistan to China and Tibet.

10. With patronage of Shahi's, Monks selected places on this route which had three roles; Halt point for establishment of Monasteries to provide religic support for monks, for travellers to spread Buddhism to China and facilities for monks from Tibet/China to understand the tenets of Buddhism, doctrines, translate and carry it back to their respective monasteries in Tibet and China.

11. Tibet at this stage was not keen on Hinayana or Mahayana Buddhism but had a modified Buddhist code. With move of Padmasambhava Rimpoche from Udyan to Tibet, a modified version of Buddhism took shape in Tibet. The monks took back the translated versions and side by side compiled their own Buddhist literature based on the doctrine propounded by Padmasambhava.

12. With terrain constraints the Buddhism messengers moved along known routes, erected Monasteries etc and spread Buddhism along and in the vicinity of the route they had taken. Few places in Gilgit were thus selected as Halt cum monastery points, patronised by Patola Shahi rulers Monks stationed here started spread of Buddhism.

13. Buddhism never spread even beyond 40 percent in Gilgit and less than 15 percent in Baltistan and that too North of Indus. Belt around Kishanganga River/Neelam Valley remained untouched from the spread of Buddhism during Ashoka's reign and thereafter during Kushano period. Even Buddhist beliefs of Patola Shahi's, remained restricted North of Indus River.

14. Naupur a place was a place next to Gilgit, a trade Centre, close to seat of Kings, lords, where a series of Stupas and Monasteries were erected. **Monks stayed there, enrolled new monks, prepared texts manuscripts with the help of translators from manuscripts, which were brought from India**.

15. Contents of manuscripts are indicative of pre-Ashoka period composition. With a new area of Gilgit Baltistan under Buddhist rulers' patronage, they were sent for further transmission to China. The Northern area of Tarim Bhasin had come under various invaders, Arabs, Turks etc and there was no place for spread of Buddhism there from Seventh Century onwards; in fact, right after retreat of Kushan's in Fourth Century to their native places.

16. If these manuscripts are claimed to have been written during Kushan or early period they had to be in Gandhari/Kharosthi script. These are in typical Brahmi and its variants. This enough to prove that they were not written/composed at Naupur. Manuscripts are on Palm leaf, which is not found in Gilgit. Some translated parts of Manuscripts primarily are of the events in Buddhas life and the message of early Buddhism.

17. The number of pages of Gilgit manuscripts being enormous would have taken at least a Century to write at the site with hundreds of Monk writers. The primary source has to be Nalanada, Bodh Gaya, may be Taxila, from where these texts were sent to Naupur and with the end of Patola Shahi rule and non-Buddhist invaders seem to have been buried in Ninth Century under a stupa for preservation, with a hope that Buddhism may stage a comeback.

18. In Ninth Century Tibetans came to Baltistan and China Ming Dynasty intervened. It was blow to the Patola Shahi's as well Buddhist Monks in Gilgit or elsewhere. It is at this stage they buried these manuscripts under a Stupa. Another clue is that they were found in Wooden boxes, locked and there were artefacts of bronze attributed to Shahi's.

19. Overall, these seem to have been centrally made and sent, kept at the monastery at Naupur for distribution to monks who were being assigned task to spread Buddhism. It is also indicative that these were held as a Library for Monks from China, to stay here, translate them on the spot with the help of Monks, who were conversant with the script or trained visiting monk's translators to decipher the contents.

It is a fallacy that either similar manuscripts were prepared or stored at S'arada Monument for spread of Buddhism in the area. In fact, Gilgit manuscripts have no connection whatsoever with claimed Buddhist S'arada Monument. (In this Chapter lot of other information, photographs, ancient contents of manuscripts etc have not been included).

To attain knowledge, add things everyday.
To attain wisdom, remove things every day."
–Lao Tse

10

Epilogue

"The truth can't be told loudly.
It can't be told in normal voice also.
It has to be told in a whisper as soft as silence."

–Shunya

Initial Focus. I was euphoric when I got the Colour Photograph of S'arada Shrine/Tirath/Temple Kishanganga Valley in 2003 AD, for the first time in colour and after nearly seven decades. Sharing in various media's in the country, developed into quest to know more about this shrine. I generally knew, little bit about the Goddess Saraswati. Frankly idea about S'arada Goddess was abysmal. The accolades turned into some studies and an article: **Goddess S'arada of Kaśmira (Kashmir),** which was uploaded on internet and published in few magazines/periodicals, was well received. It had main coverage on the S'arada Kishanganga Valley, Adi Shankaracharya and whether a University, teaching religious doctrines etc, ever existed there. The former coverage was purely on then established view but I somehow was not convinced, even then, on other two. Over nearly two decades the subject never left my mind, till a stage came few years back, I wanted to know more and more.

Periodical studies revealed how ill-informed I was, about the Shrine and had just depended upon few references. What finally stared at me were host of connected issues, mainly: The Sa'rada Shrine of Kishanganga Valley and Life and Events of Adi Shankaracharya. Each of them got connected with something or the other. It required my keenness to be turned into a book, over a period of few years. Crunch objectives were evolved as enumerated in Chapter I and a stage finally came for the effort to see the light of the day in the form of this book. Happy that results have been outstanding with new revelations. I don't want to create a lengthy epilogue briefly enumerate what has been achieved.

S'arada of Kishanganga Valley. No longer one can be vague about this Shrine, mostly called Forgotten Monument. It may be in news, but facts and its history remained obscure and over a period created myths overshadowed the history of the Shrine. A Buddhist Monument with a University, Millenniums old Shrine with an Institution of Learning as part of it. It was part of Kasmira Kingdom King's from Ashoka, Kanishka, Lalitaditya so on, forgetting that the area was fiefdom of a belligerent War Lord and Dards of the area were inimical to Kasmira. The Shrine, located inside a defensive like quadrangle, seems to be incidental and not coincidental. Possibility of local War Lord, de facto ruler having constructed it has all along been discounted and not even considered.

Adi Shankaracharya. Initially got just mentioned as having connection with Kasmira by his visit and occupying the seat of omniscience at Sharada. His life events got somehow connected with this shrine as a result of created fictional accounts of his life. He was not even spared from an account of his entering a dead body of a non-existent King Amaru of Kasmira to gather knowledge on sexology by staying in his harem.

Anyway, there have been some take aways and revelations, which I consider a reward for diligent study and drawing possibly correct inferences.

- Roles of Goddess S'arada as Shakti Goddess of Knowledge so different from Sharadaamba as Mahavidya.
- The sanctity of Kund's for veneration and the mystery of actual S'arada Kund at Shardi Kishanganga Valley.
- As to how indicators from Nilamata Purana, mentions by Al Biruni, in Rajatarangini and Abu Fazl were wrongly, may be inadvertent or even intentional, interpreted to focus only on S'arada of Kishanganga Valley. Had above inferences been correctly assessed actual River Madhumati would have been in focus and away from the Shrine.
- Sanctity and antiquity of oldest Shrine of S'arada at Kaloosa (Kalash) on the banks of Madhumati (Bandipur) was revealed by this effort.
- The genesis of Kishanganga River name from ancient name Krsna came about.
- The solved mystery of Sandalwood idol of Sharadaamba installed at Kudali shifted to Sringeri or legend of this idol taken by Adi Shankaracharya from S'arada Shrine Kishanganga Valley.
- As to how a redacted recent Mahatmaya, lifting names and contents of Nilamata Purana to create a parallel Shrine, more so in competition than faith.

There is much more what has been achieved. To me the most valuable achievement has been that my mind is clear about Goddesses Sharada, Sardaamba and the Life and Events of Adi Shankaracharya. Biggest achievement, in my own way, is **Reverence and Restoration of the factual legacy of Adi Shankaracharya, the great Saint Philosopher of Bharatvarsh (India). And the book is not a whisper.**

This takes me to **Rig Veda** Verse which extolled me:

"There is no religion greater than truth and a truthful person knows no fear"

Bibliography

Chronicles of Kasmira (Rajatarangini)

1. Kalhana's Rajatarangini-Chronicle of The Kings of Kashmir (1148-50 AD) (Codex Archetypus by Rajanaka Ratanakantha (1648-9 AD or 1685-86 AD) -Sir Auriel Stein (1900 AD).
2. The Kings of Kashmir – 2nd Series Rajatarangini of Jonaraja-Jogesh Chander Dutt (tr.) Delhi, 1986.

Ancient Scriptures

1. Nilamata Purana of Kasmira (500-600 BC) -Translations, Commentary and Explanatory notes by Dr Ved Kumari Ghai.

Reports by Foreign Travellers in Kasmira

1. Professor Johann Georg Bühler : -Detailed report of a tour in Kashmir (1877); Kharosthi alphabets (1895); Vikramankacharita with an introduction (1875).
2. Major General Sir Alexander Cunningham KCIE CSI-Archaeological Survey of India Vol. 1-4 (1871); Corpus Inscriptionum Indicarum (Volume 1. (1877); Ancient Geography of Kashmir; Temples of India and Kashmir; Temple Architecture of Kashmir First Edition, 2021 (Shubhi Publications).

3. Walter R. Lawrence-The Valley of Kashmir-Archaeology; Races and Tribes (Main); Illustrating Ancient Geography of Kashmir.

Travelogues of Chinese Pilgrims

1. Monks: Faxian, 337?-422?, Xuanzang, 600-664 and Yijing Yijing, 635-695 (Ancient Buddhist Texts).
2. The Travel Records of Chinese Pilgrims Faxian, Xuanzang, and Yizing by Tansen Sen.
3. Travelogue of the Grand Old Buddhist Monk:-International Journal of Scientific Research and Reviews.
4. Chinese State and Buddhist Historical Sources on Xuanzang: Historicity and the Daci'ensisanzangfashizhuan by Jeffrey Kotyk.
5. James Legge's; *A Record of Buddhistic Kingdoms: Account by the Chinese Monk Fa-Hien of his Travels in India and Ceylon* (399–414 A.D.)
6. A Popular Narrative of Xuanzang's pilgrimage to India-Sally Hovey.
7. Xuanzang's travels biography; Huili and Yancong.
8. Li Rongxi's -A Biography of the Tripitaka Master of the Great Tang Dynasty (Numata Centre for Buddhist Translation and Research, 1995).
9. "Kasmīr, Tang China, and MuktãpaḍaLalitā-Ditya's Ascendancy over the southern Hindukush Region. Tansen Sen. Journal of Asian History, Vol. 38, No. 2 (2004), pp. 150-151.

Veda's

1. All the four Veda's; Rig, Atharv, Sam and Yajur. Translations, explanations, commentary and analysis

by various saints and scholars. (Ralph T.H. Griffith, translator 1889 Sam Veda 1885).

2. Ancient Indian Religion-Richard K. Hines.
3. Antiquity of Vedas-Thosophist October 1879.
4. Antiquity and Continuity of Indian History (Part 1-Part 2).
5. How We Got the Vedas-Swami Sunirmalananda.
6. Rig Veda Analysis by Arthur Macdonell (1854-1930)-1917.

Biographies and Works of Adi Shankaracharya

1. (Sankaradigvijaya by Mādhava (17th c.) and Sankaravijaya by Anandagiri are the most cited).
2. Madhavīya Shankaravijayam (of Madhava, c. 14th Century).
3. Anandagirīya Shankaravijayam (of Anandagiri, not extant).
4. Cidvilāsīya Shankaravijayam (of Chidvilasa, c. between 15th Century and 17th Century).
5. Keralīya Shankaravijayam (extant in Kerala, 17th Century AD).
6. Anantanadagiri Shankaravijayam (extant from 15th Century AD, but controversial in nature).
7. Citsukhṛcṛrya and his Brahat Sankara -Vijaya - Narayana Sastry.
8. Swami Tapasyananda, The Sankara-dig-vijaya of Madhava-Vidyaranya, Ramakrishna Mission, Madras,
9. The Age of Sankara-TS Narayana Sastry BA BL Edited by TN Kumaraswamy BA.
10. Date of Sri Sankara, His Life, Philosophy and Relevance

to Man in Modern Times, -S. Sankaranarayanan, Adyar Library and Research Centre, 1995 AD.

11. Sankaracharya Philosopher and Mystic-Kenneth Tryambak Telạng.
12. Sankara: His Life and Times-S. K. Belvalkar, Poona: (Evidence in support of 788-820 AD).
13. Sri Madhvacharya by Sri Narayana Panditacharya.
14. A Note on the Date of Sankara-S. Srikantha Sastri, (Quarterly Journal of the Mythic Society, Bangalore, Vol. 20, 1930).
15. Date of Life of Sankara-S. Radhakrishnan, Sringeri Souvenir, Madras, 1965.

Works of doubtful authenticity of Adi Shankaracharaya

1. Commentaries on Nrisimha-Purvatatapaniya and Shveshvatara Upanishads.
2. Author of Vivekacūḍāmaṇ (S Madhavananda (Translator), Advaita Ashrama (1921).
3. Aparokshanubhuti and Atma bodha are also attributed to Shankara, as his original philosophical treatises.
4. Lalita-shasranama, Suta-samhita and Sandhya-bhasya.
5. The commentary on the Tantric work Lalita-trisati-bhasya attributed to Shankara.

Miscellaneous Connected With Adi Shankaracharya

1. The Acharyas of The Shri Kanchi Kamakoti Peetham
2. Kanchi Kamakoti Math -A Myth. – V Raj Gopal Sharma.
3. The Dates of Mandana Misra -Allen Wright Thrasher, Wiener Zeitschrift, Vol. 23.

4. The Advaita Vedânta Home Page -Biographies of Sankara and Sankara's Life.
5. Sri Madhva Vijaya Sri Sumadhva Vijaya ("The story of the victory of Madhva").
6. Sri Vidyaranya Dakshinamnaya Sri S'arada Peetham, Sringeri.
7. Sri Sundar's Observation on Sarada at Kudali (Shakti Sadhana).
8. Sri Kamakoti Mandali Ubhaya Bharati.
9. Mandana Misra (Encyclopedia Britannicas).
10. Soundarya Lahari.
11. The advaita home page by Adi -Sankaracharya, Translated by P.R. Ramachander-Part I -Ananda Lahari (The waves of happiness) -Part II - Soundarya Lahari (The waves of beauty).

Miscellaneous

1. Times of Gautam Buddha, Mahavira and Adi Shankara (BC). Commentary and explanatory notes.
2. Times and events of Kings; Ashoka and Kushan King Kanishka and his successors. Commentary and explanatory notes.
3. Biographical accounts of Kalhan, Abhinav Gupta and Bilhana.
4. Kashmiri Shaivism. Translations, commentary and explanatory notes.
5. Monuments of Kashmir by R.C. Kak.
6. Muslim Rule in Kashmir R.K. Parmu, (Dr),
7. Panchastavi. Translations, commentary and explanatory notes.

8. Languages and Lipi's of Bharatvarasha.
9. Amaru Shataka-Wikipedia.
10. Erotic Love Poems from India- Amaru shataka, translated by Andrew Schelling.
11. Amaru Shataka by Kavi Amaru By C. R. Devdhar, M.A (Published Motilal Banarsidas).
12. Mankha – 12th Century Kashmiri Poet by Abhilash Rajendran period of Jayasimha (1127-1149 AD) .
13. A Story for a Verse-Mankha-Shatavadhani Dr. R. Ganesh (The original article is from the anthology *Kavitegondu Kathe).*
14. Mankha and Sri Kanthacaritam Mankha and "Sri Kanthacaritam" by Dr. Kaushalya Wali.
15. Tarikh-i-Hind by Al-Biruni (Written in 1031AD- English Edition 1888 AD.
16. Ain-I-Akbari by Abu-al-Fazal (1551-1602); Blochmann, H. (Henry), 1838-1878, Vol. I and II.
17. The Valley of Kashmir (1895) by Sir W.R. Lawrence (1857–1940).

Gilgit Manuscripts

1. The Gilgit Manuscripts, the Oldest Manuscript Collection Surviving in Pakistan and India (Encyclopedia of buddhism.org/wiki/Gilgit_manuscripts).
2. Saddharma Puṇḍarīka Sūtra-English translations.
3. Lotus Sutra.
4. Jatakamala manuscript 8th-9th Century AD.
5. Gilgit Manuscript UNESCO.

6. Gilgit Manuscripts: A National Heritage at Large-Syed Mujahid Ali Shah.

7. Gilgit Manuscript (5th C. AD) -Okar Research.

8. The Patola Shahi Dynasty (6–8th C. AD) -Okar Research.

9. The Gilgit Manuscripts Prashant Mathawan-July 21, 2018.

10. The Mystery of Gilgit manuscripts, Daily Times, Lahore (Pakistan) 11th Jan., 2019.

11. Tracing the roots of Buddhism in Gilgit Baltistan - Masud Ahmad Khan, November 7, 2018, (Daily Times, Lahore, January 20, 2019).

12. What is the Lotus Sutra-Nicherin Shu.

Index